Nathaniel Hawthorne

A BIOGRAPHY

BY
RANDALL STEWART

16172

ARCHON BOOKS
1970

ISBN: 0-208-00829-2
Library of Congress Catalog Card Number: 74-114425
Printed in the United States of America

To
STANLEY T. WILLIAMS

ACKNOWLEDGMENTS

In addition to the several particular acknowledgments made in footnotes, I can only mention here, with gratitude, my indebtedness to the following:

To the Pierpont Morgan Library, the Henry E. Huntington Library, the Duyckinck and Berg Collections of the New York Public Library, the Houghton Library of Harvard University, the Yale Collection of American Literature, the Essex Institute, the Boston Public Library, and the Massachusetts Historical Society, for assistance in the use of letters and journals by Hawthorne and his wife, and to Herbert C. Schulz of the Huntington Library and Mark D. Brewer of the Morgan Library, who helped me in the restoration of inked-out passages in the letters and journals.

To Manning Hawthorne, Norman Holmes Pearson, and Stanley T. Williams, who have collaborated with me in collecting the materials for a complete edition of Hawthorne's correspondence.

To Eva Margareta Israel, who typed the manuscript, and to Louise Barr MacKenzie, Theodore Hornberger, Richmond Croom Beatty, Norman Holmes Pearson, John B. Harcourt, Roberta Yerkes, and Eugene Davidson, who read the manuscript and suggested many improvements.

To the Guggenheim Foundation, whose award of a Fellowship in 1943-44 furnished a welcome opportunity for necessary research.

And to my wife, Cleone Odell Stewart, who has given both encouragement and assistance in the preparation of this biography.

R. S.

Brown University

CONTENTS

Acknowledgments   v

  I. *Ancestry and Boyhood*   1

  II. *College, 1821–1825*   13

  III. *The "Solitary Years," 1825–1837*   27

  IV. *Courtship, Marriage, and the Old Manse,
1838–1845*   45

  V. *Salem and* The Scarlet Letter, *1846–1850* 75

  VI. *With Melville in the Berkshires, 1850–1851* 101

  VII. *West Newton and the Wayside, 1851–1853*   122

  VIII. *England, 1853–1857*   148

  IX. *Italy, 1858–1859*   183

  X. *The Wayside Once More, 1860–1864*   214

  XI. *The Collected Works*   242

Chief Biographical Sources   266

Index   269

NATHANIEL HAWTHORNE

CHAPTER I

ANCESTRY AND BOYHOOD

NATHANIEL HAWTHORNE'S earliest American ancestor, William Hathorne,* came from England to Massachusetts in 1630, the year of John Winthrop's migration, and settled first at Dorchester and later at Salem. He became an important man in the young colony, rising to the office of speaker in the House of Delegates and to the rank of major in the Salem militia. Hawthorne wrote of him in "The Custom House":

The figure of that first ancestor, invested by family tradition with a dim and dusky grandeur, was present to my boyish imagination as far back as I can remember. It still haunts me, and induces a sort of home feeling with the past. . . . I seem to have a stronger claim to residence here [in Salem] on account of this grave, bearded, sable-cloaked and steeple-crowned progenitor—who came so early, with his Bible and his sword, and trode the unworn street with such a stately port, and made so large a figure, as a man of war and peace— a stronger claim than for myself. . . . He was a soldier, legislator, judge; he was a ruler in the Church; he had all the Puritanic traits, both good and evil. He was likewise a bitter persecutor, as witness the Quakers, who have remembered him in their histories, and relate an incident of his hard severity towards a woman of their sect, which will last longer, it is to be feared, than any record of his better deeds, although these were many.

Hawthorne liked to remember particularly his ancestor's bold defiance of an edict of Charles II ordering Hathorne and the governor of Massachusetts to come to England and explain, if they could, the colony's persistent insubordination to royal authority. One of his most prized possessions was a document which he endorsed as follows: "Copy of a letter supposed to have been written

* Nathaniel Hawthorne added the "w" in his spelling of the name not long after his graduation from college.

by Major William Hathorne of Massachusetts defending that Colony against the accusations of the Commissioners of Charles II, and excusing the General Court for declining to send over Governor Bellingham and himself in compliance with the King's order." An ancestor who had defied a king was obviously one to be proud of, whatever his faults may have been.

William's son, John, is famous and infamous in history as one of the three judges in the Salem witchcraft trials of 1692—the other two being William Stoughton and Samuel Sewall—though, unlike Sewall, he is not known to have repented of his error. "He made himself so conspicuous in the martyrdom of the witches," Hawthorne wrote in "The Custom House," "that their blood may fairly be said to have left a stain upon him." There was a tradition in the family that one of the witches had pronounced a curse upon Judge Hathorne and all his posterity. Hawthorne seems to have had a superstitious respect for this curse, for—more than half seriously, perhaps—he attributed the subsequent decline of the Hathornes to its influence.

The intervening Hathorne ancestors were relatively obscure. The judge's son, Joseph, was a farmer in the Salem township. Joseph's son, Daniel, went to sea and commanded a privateer during the Revolutionary War. Daniel's son, Nathaniel, born in 1775, also followed the sea. In 1801 he married Elizabeth Clarke Manning and their children were Elizabeth Manning, born in 1802, Nathaniel, the subject of this biography, born July 4, 1804, and Maria Louisa, born in 1808. While on a long voyage in 1808, Captain Nathaniel Hathorne died in Dutch Guiana.

Hawthorne could have seen but little of his father, who was much absent on voyages to distant parts of the earth. The Salem *Gazette* on October 19, 1804, for example, announced the arrival of the "ship Mary and Eliza, Capt. Nathaniel Hathorne, in 118 days from Batavia." After greeting his family and saluting his three months' old son, the captain gave a brief account to the press of the commerce of the Dutch East Indies, reporting that all the crop of coffee had been exhausted and no more was to be had for the season, and that no less than forty-five neutral ships, principally American, had loaded there from September to June. The captain's son was later to cherish a logbook kept by his father during one of his voyages to the Far East; Hawthorne inscribed his name in it several times and copied in the margins and between the lines many nautical phrases taken from the text of the log—"moderate breeze, hazy weather and variable," "heavy head swell" and the like. Though he was never to spend much time on the sea, the sea was congenial to him and stimulated his imagination. He preferred a seaside residence to any other, and he relished accounts of sea adventures.

Less is known of Hawthorne's ancestry on his mother's side. The Mannings migrated from England in 1679 and for a century and a half in Massachusetts they showed a talent for business. Hawthorne's uncle, Robert Manning, for many years operated a stagecoach line. The Salem *Gazette* advertised in 1818, for example, "Manning's Daily Stages" to Marblehead, Newburyport, and Boston. Between Salem and Boston there were four stage-coaches daily each way. The stage line was an important and profitable business. Robert Manning also cultivated and experimented with fruit trees; by the time of his death in 1842 he had acquired considerable fame as a pomologist. It was Uncle Robert who looked after the business affairs of the widow Hathorne and made financially possible the education of her son.

The determination of ancestral influences is always conjectural. But it would seem that Hawthorne inherited through his father a sternness (Captain Daniel Hathorne was said to be "the sternest man that ever walked a deck"), a moodiness (Captain Nathaniel had a reputation for melancholy), and a tendency to solitude. "He had his mother's gray eyes," writes Manning Hawthorne, "and her gentle manners, her reserve and thoughtfulness as well; but he was all Hathorne otherwise—in appearance, in thought, in feeling, and in imagination. The Mannings had very little effect upon him." The Manning influence, however, should not be too much discounted. From his mother's side came a practicality in business affairs which is rarely found conjoined with "genius," and from the Mannings also, it would appear, was derived a trait even more important than practicality, namely, a sense of humor. A letter by Robert Manning to his eleven-year-old niece Elizabeth jests goodnaturedly about her astronomical studies: "A learned little lady," he bantered, "studying the stars, my dear when will the next Eclipse take place, can you tell, how many stars is there, what is the moon made of, all these things you must learn before you will be a female Newton." Hawthorne's early letters have a similar vein of humor.

After the death of Captain Hathorne the widow returned with her three children to the Manning house. It was a large and hospitable household, including four uncles and four aunts, all unmarried. Nathaniel was "particularly petted," his sister Elizabeth recalled many years later, "the more because his health was then delicate and he had frequent illnesses." He was said to have been a very handsome boy and a great favorite not only with the members of his family but with the drivers of the Manning stages. At the age of nine he injured his foot while playing ball at school, and suffered a lameness which persisted for a long while. The prescribed therapy consisted of pouring showers of cold water from a window in the second story upon the lame foot, extended from the window below. At the time of his injury Hawthorne was attending the school taught by J. E. Worcester, and throughout the period of his lameness the great lexicographer came to the house to hear the boy's lessons. His earliest extant letter dated December 9, 1813, reports that he had been absent from school for four weeks, had been carried to the doorstep and to the stage office, and once had "hopped out into the street." Later he was able to walk with the aid of crutches. Not until after some three years, when he was twelve, was the lameness completely overcome.

A natural love of books, encouraged by the leisure thus enforced, led to his acquiring early the habit of reading. Spenser's *Fairie Queene*, Thomson's *Castle of Indolence*, Bunyan's *Pilgrim's*

Progress, and Shakespeare were boyhood favorites. Elizabeth remembered that he used to lie upon the carpet while reading, or that he would sit in a large chair in the corner of the room, near a window, and read half the afternoon without speaking. He liked to quote with mock heroic effect a line from *Richard III*, "My Lord, stand back, and let the coffin pass." Cats also amused him, and the Manning household was well supplied with felines bearing such Bunyanesque names as "Apollyon" and "Beelzebub."

In the summer of 1816, when Hawthorne was twelve years old, his mother moved to Raymond, Maine, where the Manning brothers, Robert and Richard, owned a tract of land. Here she had a home of her own, for Robert allowed her the use of his house, which was located near Richard's. She must have welcomed also the outdoor life for her children. Raymond was a village situated on Sebago Lake and surrounded by forests. Hawthorne spent the better part of three years in this delightful region. According to the recollections of Elizabeth, "he became a good shot and an excellent fisherman, and grew tall and strong. His imagination was stimulated, too, by the scenery and by the strangeness of the people; and by the absolute freedom he enjoyed." In the winter there were sleighing and skating, and in the summer sailing and fishing. In one letter to his uncle Robert, Hawthorne reported having shot a partridge and a henhawk and caught eighteen large trout. He often took long walks with Elizabeth across the lake in winter and along its margin in summer. His diary records friendly associations with the boys of the village. The entry "Swapped pocket-knives with Robinson Cook yesterday" is evidence of normal behavior. Hawthorne was later to regard the Raymond years as the happiest of his life; he often told his family and friends of this glorious epoch when, as he expressed it, he "lived like a bird of the air."

But the Maine idyl could not go on forever. It was necessary that the boy, his health now fully restored, settle down to systematic study, for his schooling had been somewhat irregular.

Reluctant to leave Raymond, he wrote a humorous protest to his Uncle Robert in May, 1819: "I am sorry you intend to send me to school again. Mother says she can hardly spare me." But his mother, who was both tolerant and competent in her management of domestic affairs (it was not until the illness of her old age that she became a recluse), sent her son back to Salem, where he began study on July 5, 1819, the day after his fifteenth birthday.

He first attended Mr. Archer's school on Marlbro Street, which had only recently been established, for the following advertisement appeared in the Salem *Gazette* on January 12, 1819:

NEW SCHOOL

SAMUEL H. ARCHER

Has taken the School Room formerly occupied by Mr. George Titcomb, near the Rev. Mr. Bolles' meeting house, where he intends opening a School on the first Monday in February, for the instruction of Young Masters in the following branches: Reading, Writing, English Grammar, Geography and Astronomy, Book-keeping, Rhetoric and Composition, Chemistry, Natural and Moral Philosophy, the common branches of the Mathematics, and the Latin and Greek Languages. Terms of Tuition—5 & 6 dolls. per quarter.

On July 26 Hawthorne wrote to his Uncle Robert in Raymond: "I have begun to go to school and can find no fault with it except it's not being dear enough only 5 dollars a quarter and not near enough for it is up by the Baptist Meeting House." In September he wrote to his sister Louisa in a similar jesting vein, adding a literary flourish: "I now go to a 5 dollar school, I, that have been to a 10 dollar one. 'O lucifer, son of the morning, how art thou fallen!' " *

In March, 1820, he left Mr. Archer's institution and began more seriously to prepare for college under the direction of

---

* It is not clear whether the 10 dollar school was Mr. Worcester's or the school at Stroudwater, Maine, which he attended for a short time.

Benjamin L. Oliver, a Salem lawyer. He studied his lessons at home and recited daily to Mr. Oliver at seven in the morning. His tutor thought he might be able to enter college the following autumn, but Uncle Robert wisely objected to such an accelerated program. By the summer of 1821 there seemed to be no doubt in the teacher's mind as to the adequacy of his pupil's preparation. "Mr. Oliver says I will get into College," he wrote his mother; "therefore Uncle Robert need be under no apprehensions."

Study did not occupy all of the boy's time during this period. "I am a man of many occupations," he told his mother in September, 1820. One of these was keeping books, afternoons, for the stage company. The salary of a dollar a week, he said, was "quite convenient for many purposes," though the work, he objected later, hindered his literary pursuits. "No man," he declared, "can be a Poet and a Bookkeeper at the same time." Recreational activities were not lacking. There are references in his letters to swimming and fishing. He and his sister Louisa attended Mr. Turner's dancing school, and Elizabeth Hawthorne testified that her brother was a "good dancer." Louisa took the dancing school more seriously than Nathaniel, who made fun of her for putting on stately airs and making curtsies, but he was present nevertheless at the particularly brilliant ball which marked Mr. Turner's retirement from his profession in October, 1820. Uncle Robert complained of the extravagant preparations: "Nathaniel & Louisa are preparing for the Ball on Thursday next —much time & money lost to no good purpose I fear." The *Gazette* described the company assembled on this occasion as "comprising the fashion and grace of the town." Louisa reported a "beautiful time," which lasted until after one o'clock.

Other public occasions mentioned about this time in Nathaniel's letters include a concert, the theater, and church services. The concert was an oratorio performed by the Handel Society of Salem. Hawthorne may not have enjoyed it very much for he always professed an inability to appreciate music. He seems still less to have enjoyed religious services, at which he was in "constant" attendance, he affirmed, in 1821; their effect, he confessed to his mother, was sleep producing. But he found the theater more interesting, though he was never to become a devotee. On May 3, 1820, he saw Mrs. Inchbald's *Lovers' Vows* and a farce entitled *The Weathercock or What Next* performed in Washington Hall at Salem by a company of actors from Boston. In March, 1821, he went to Boston to see Edmund Kean in *King Lear*, and was moved, but not too much moved: "It was enough to have drawn tears from millstones," he wrote to his mother with a suggestion of humorous control; "I almost forgot that I did not live in the age of Lear." In May, he again attended the theater, probably to see Kean in a return engagement.

During these precollege years he was also doing a good deal of reading and a little writing. A letter to Louisa in 1819 mentions his having read *Waverly*, *The Mysteries of Udolpho*, *The Adventures of Ferdinand Count Fathom*, *Roderick Random*, and the *Arabian Nights*. In 1820 he wrote her enthusiastically about reading Scott and Godwin:

I have bought the Lord of the Isles and intend either to send or to bring it to you. I like it as well as any of Scott's other Poems. I have read Hogg's Tales, Caleb Williams, St. Leon & Mandeville. I admire Godwin's Novels, and intend to read them all. I shall read The Abbot by the Author of Waverly as soon as I can hire it. I have read all Scott's Novels except that. I wish I had not that I might have the pleasure of reading them again. Next to them I like Caleb Williams.

Later in the same year he made a list of books read: *Melmoth*, *Tom Jones*, *Amelia*, Rousseau's *Héloïse* ("which is admirable"), Edgeworth's *Memoirs*, *The Abbot*, and Lewis' *Romantic Tales*. Apparently the purchase of a book was unusual. Most of the fiction was obtained from a rental library.

Hawthorne was beginning to enjoy also the pleasures of composition. The most interesting of his juvenilia is *The Spectator*, which was neatly printed by pen on small sheets and purported to be a weekly newspaper. The first number appeared on August

21, 1820, and the last on September 18 of that year. Its circulation was probably limited to members of the immediate family. The work was modeled partly on the *Spectator* papers of Addison and Steele and partly on the local newspaper. The treatment was humorously satirical. There are essays entitled "On Wealth," "On Benevolence," and the like. The tone of these is sufficiently suggested by the opening sentences of the essay "On Industry": "It has somewhere been remarked that an Author does not write the worse for knowing little or nothing of his subject. We hope the truth of this saying will be manifest in the present article. With the benefits of Industry we are not personally acquainted." The department of "Domestic Intelligence" satirizes the personal columns of the newspapers in items like this: "The lady of Dr. Winthrop Brown, a son and Heir. Mrs. Hathorne's cat, Seven Kittens. We hear that both of the above ladies are in a state of convalescence." The following advertisement may not have been especially pleasing to his Aunt Mary: "Wanted—A Husband not above seventy years of age. None need apply unless they can produce good recommendations, or are possessed of at least ten thousand dollars. The applicant is young, being under fifty years of age, and of great beauty. —Mary Manning, Spinstress." Interspersed through the *Spectator* are poetical compositions which it would be a mistake to regard too solemnly. This for example, from the fourth number:

> Days of my youth, ye fleet away,
> As fades the bright sun's cheering ray,
> And scarce my infant hours are gone,
> Ere manhood's troubled step comes on.
> My infant hours return no more
> And all their happiness is o'er;
> The stormy sea of life appears,
> A scene of tumult and of tears.

The young poet was obviously writing with his tongue in his cheek. Concerning similar verses included in a letter to Louisa, he remarked: "Though those are my rhymes, yet they are not exactly my thoughts. I am full of scraps of poetry. . . . I could vomit up a dozen pages more if I was a mind to." He was half imitating, half parodying, the sentimental verse which was then the fashion in newspapers and gift books.

Although there is no reason for regarding the stanza just quoted as a bit of poignant self-revelation, Hawthorne's life at this time, despite his "many occupations," was not entirely to his liking. His grandmother and aunt, he said, scolded him constantly. Grandmother was stingy, besides: she kept the guava jelly "against somebody is sick," and she insisted on eating the bad oranges first and holding back the good ones till they became bad. He longed to be with his mother and sisters in Raymond. But throughout his discomfiture his sense of humor never deserted him. One compensation for the faultfinding, he saw, was that it "gave employment in retaliating," and thus had a stimulating effect which kept up his spirits. There is a Mark Twain touch in his statement to his sister Elizabeth that his spirits were fortified also by the vigorous chewing of tobacco. On another occasion he wrote to his mother and sisters at Raymond: "I dreamed the other night that I was walking by Sebago, and when I awoke was so angry at finding it all a delusion that I gave Uncle Robert (who sleeps with me) a most horrible kick." The author of these reports, culled from his letters, was not likely to succumb long to melancholy or self-pity.

There seemed to be no difficulty in choosing a college. Bowdoin at Brunswick, Maine, was the inevitable choice because of its proximity to Raymond. The boy's thoughts at this time traveled Maineward. While at Bowdoin he would be able to spend the vacations at his beloved Sebago. About this time his aunt tried to persuade Mrs. Hathorne to return to Salem. Nathaniel urged her to remain at Raymond, pointing out that she was now mistress of her own house but in Salem she would be under the authority of Miss Manning. He did not neglect to point out also the convenience of the Raymond residence during Bowdoin vacations, and the greater cost of travel between Brunswick and Salem. For one reason he was reluctant to go to college. He could not bear the thought, he said, of living upon Uncle Robert for four years longer. But as the time for going approached, a new seriousness overcame this reluctance. He felt that he must prepare himself for a profession—preferably the profession of letters. Beneath the surface humor in the following letter to his mother, written in the spring of 1821, he was seriously considering the question of his future:

I have not yet concluded what profession I shall have. The being a Minister is of course out of the Question. I should not think that even you could desire me to choose so dull a way of life. . . . As to Lawyers there are so many of them already that one half of them (upon a moderate calculation) are in a state of actual starvation. A Physician seems to be Hobson's choice, but yet I should not like to live by the diseases and infirmities of my fellow creatures. And it would weigh very heavily on my conscience if in the course of my practice, I should chance to send any unlucky patient "ad inferum," which being interpreted, is "to the realms below." . . . What do you think of my becoming an author, and relying for support upon my pen? . . . Indeed I think the illegibility of my handwriting is very authorlike. How proud you would feel to see my work praised by the reviewers as equal to the proudest productions of the Scribbling Sons of John Bull. But authors are always poor devils and therefore Satan may take them.

By the time he was seventeen, then, Hawthorne was seeing with growing clearness what he was to be and do. He was beginning to feel, too, the force which was animating American writers everywhere at the time—the desire to produce an American literature which would match the great literature of England.

All told, Hawthorne's boyhood was not as abnormal as has sometimes been supposed. Although it is true that, except while at Raymond, he may not have played with other boys as much as would have been good for him, and that his activities were too much centered in his immediate family, his life was by no means physically inactive or socially impoverished. After his recovery from the lameness which handicapped him between the ages of nine and twelve, he became healthy and strong. Especially in Maine, where he spent a good deal of time between the ages of twelve and seventeen, he enjoyed a variety of outdoor sports—swimming, skating, fishing, hunting. A large family of uncles and aunts, sisters and cousins, stimulated his inclination to study the varieties of human nature. His relations with his mother and sisters were affectionate; his sister Louisa was especially congenial to him because of her fun-loving disposition. He did considerable reading—though not an excessive amount for a person who likes books—and began, in a juvenile way, to write. His was not a precocious development, but slow rather, and substantial.

CHAPTER II

COLLEGE, 1821–1825 *

SEVERAL reasons doubtless prompted the choice of Bowdoin. Besides its proximity to Raymond, there was its comparative cheapness—a factor which had weight both with Robert Manning, who assumed financial responsibility for his nephew's education, and with Hawthorne himself, who was sensible of his position as a dependent. Three terms made up the academic year. One of Hawthorne's term bills, dated May 21, 1824, was as follows: tuition, $8.00; chamber rent, $6.65; damages, $0.33; sweeping and bedmaking, $1.00; library, $0.50; monitor $0.06; bell, $0.12; reciting room, $0.25; chemical lectures, $0.25; fines, $2.36—total $19.62. Meals were obtained in private homes at $2.00 a week, and wood, of which a considerable quantity was burned during a Maine winter, cost $1.00 a cord. Expenses at Harvard, perhaps the only alternate choice, would have been a good deal more. A third reason for choosing Bowdoin may have been its social and political liberality. One historian describes it as "a thoroughly democratic seat of learning" and "a less Federalistic institution" than Dartmouth—a contrast which would be even more pronounced if made with Harvard. Young men of Democratic, as opposed to Federalist, sympathies would be drawn to Bowdoin.

Accompanied by his Uncle Robert and provided with a letter from Mr. Oliver, his Salem tutor, Hawthorne arrived in Brunswick for matriculation in early October, 1821. As becomes an entering freshman, he was fearful of failing the entrance examination, which was given orally by the faculty. The catalogue of 1822 specified the following requirements for entrance: "Candidates for admission into the Freshman Class are required to write

* In the present chapter, I am greatly indebted to Norman Holmes Pearson's unpublished monograph, listed in the biographical sources, p. 267.

Latin grammatically, and to be well versed in Geography, in Walsh's Arithmetic, Cicero's Select Orations, the Bucolics, Georgics, and the Aeneid of Virgil, Sallust, the Greek Testament, and the Collectanea Graeca Minora. They must present certificates of their good moral character." These were the standard requirements of the time. After an hour's questioning in the president's office, Hawthorne was admitted. He later reported that he had done as well as most of the candidates. Various college arrangements had then to be attended to. A room and a roommate (the son of the Honorable Mr. Mason of Portsmouth) were assigned to him. Furnishings were purchased, since the students had to furnish their own rooms. The process of getting settled involved dickering with tradespeople, which Hawthorne apparently enjoyed. And finally, arrangements were made for his board at the house of Professor Newman, where three other students also took their meals. Robert Manning was well pleased with what he saw: "Brunswick," he wrote to the boy's mother, "is a pleasant place, the Inhabitants respectable & attentive to Strangers, & the Institution flourishing."

Founded in 1794, Bowdoin in the fall of 1821 had a total of 114 students, who were classified as follows: senior sophisters, 24; junior sophisters, 36; sophomores, 19; freshmen, 35. They came from five states: 84 from Maine, 19 from New Hampshire, 9 from Massachusetts, 1 from Vermont, and 1 from Connecticut. Hawthorne's description of the undergraduates in his college novel *Fanshawe* was doubtless written with Bowdoin in mind:

From the exterior of the collegians, an accurate observer might pretty safely judge how long they had been inmates of these classic walls. The brown cheeks and the rustic dress of some would inform him that they had but recently left the plough to labor in a not less toilsome field; the grave look, and the intermingling of garments of a more classic cut, would distinguish those who had begun to acquire the polish of their new residence; and the air of superiority, the paler cheek, the less robust form, the spectacles of green, and the dress, in general of threadbare black, would designate the highest class, who were understood to have acquired nearly all the science their Alma Mater could bestow, and to be on the point of assuming their stations in the world. There were, it is true, exceptions to this general description. A few young men had found their way hither from distant seaports; and these were the models of fashion to their rustic companions, over whom they asserted a superiority in exterior accomplishment which the fresh though unpolished intellect of the sons of the forest denied them in their literary competitions.

Although Hawthorne was among those who came from a distant seaport, his residence being listed in the catalogue as Salem, his affectionate connection with Raymond must have given him a sympathy with the sons of the forest.

The 1821 catalogue lists eight faculty members: Rev. William Allen, D.D., President; Parker Cleaveland, A.M., Professor of Mathematics, Natural Philosophy, Chemistry, and Mineralogy; Samuel P. Newman, A.M., Professor of Languages; Nathan Smith, M.D., Lecturer on the Theory and Practice of Physic and Surgery; John D. Wells, M.D., Professor of Anatomy and Physiology; John Abbot, A.M., Librarian; Alpheus S. Packard, A.M., Tutor in Languages and Mathematics; and Benjamin Hale, A.M., Tutor in Geometry and Natural Philosophy. Professors apparently had a better general education then than now and were more versatile. President Allen, a pious and rather precise Congregational minister, though not very popular, was respected as the author of the *American Biographical and Historical Dictionary*, published in 1809, which Hawthorne himself was to draw upon in *Grandfather's Chair*. Cleaveland, author of *An Elementary Treatise on Mineralogy and Geology*, published in 1816, was the most distinguished and also the most popular member of the faculty. Newman, courteous and scholarly, is said to have admired Hawthorne's English compositions and to have read them to the members of his family. Wells' lectures on anatomy and physiology were sufficiently interesting to attract Hawthorne's voluntary attendance during his senior year. The Bowdoin faculty was an unusually able one for a small, new college.

The course of study was entirely prescribed. The curriculum in force in 1822 was described as follows in the catalogue:

FRESHMAN YEAR

First term: Xenophon in Graeca Majora; Livy; Arithmetic in Webber.

Second term: Graeca Majora; Livy; Arithmetic.

Third term: Graeca Majora; Livy (5 books); Murray's English Grammar; Blair's Rhetoric; review of the studies of the year.

During the whole year: Weekly translations into Latin and Greek; private declamations; recitations from the Bible every Sunday evening.

SOPHOMORE YEAR

First term: Graeca Majora (extracts from Plato and Homer); Excerpta Latina (Tacitus); Algebra and Geometry in Webber; Playfield's Euclid, 2 books; Hedge's Logic.

Second term: Graeca Majora; Excerpta Latina; Mensuration of Superficies; Solids, Heights, and Distances in Webber; Surveying in Webber; Euclid finished.

Third term: Navigation in Webber; Review of Studies; English composition.

During the whole year: Weekly translations in Latin and Greek alternately; private and public declamations; recitations from the Bible every Sunday evening.

JUNIOR YEAR

First term: Graeca Majora; Horace; Conic Sections in Webber; Enfield's Natural Philosophy; Locke's Essay; Paley's Evidences.

Second term: Graeca Majora; Horace; Enfield's Natural Philosophy; Paley's Evidences; Locke's Essay, concluded; Lectures on Chemistry.

Third term: Priestley's Lectures on History; Henry's Chemistry; Paley finished; review of studies; forensic disputation; lectures on Experimental Philosophy.

During the whole year: Translations into Latin and Greek alternately every fortnight; private and public declamations; English composition every fortnight; recitations from the Bible every Sunday evening.

SENIOR YEAR

First term: Henry's Chemistry; Paley's Natural Theology; Stewart's Philosophy of the Mind (Vol. I); Paley's Evidences.

Second term: Astronomy in Enfield; Dialling, Spherical Geometry and Trigonometry in Webber; Stewart's Philosophy of the Mind (Vol. II); Burlemaqui on Natural Law; Butler's Analogy.

Third term: Natural History; Cleaveland's Mineralogy; Butler's Analogy.

Exercises during the year: Private declamations and public declamations; compositions in English; forensic disputations; recitations in the Bible every Sunday evening.

It is evident that the emphasis was upon Greek, Latin, mathematics (including astronomy, surveying, and navigation), and philosophy (including Christian apologetics). Considerable attention was being given, though, to the natural sciences, with courses in chemistry and mineralogy. The chief weakness of the curriculum from the modern point of view was the neglect of history, the modern languages, and modern literature. Aside from the Greek and Roman classics, apparently the only literature studied was the Bible. There was a course in rhetoric, however, with frequent essays, and many students no doubt made up for the deficiency in literary instruction by independent reading. The extracurricular study of French was provided for under the instruction of a Frenchman residing in Brunswick, and Hawthorne appears to have taken that up in his senior year, for there is a French grammar bearing his autograph over the date 1825. His reading in French literature after graduation shows that he had attained some proficiency while in college.* All told, Hawthorne's course of study does not seem as defective today as it did during the long era (now apparently closed) when free election was rampant.

Hawthorne did not make a brilliant record as a student. Like many young men of literary inclination he did well in the things he enjoyed and less well in the others. He confessed later that he

---

* He did not undertake the study of German until about 1840, and making little progress, he soon gave it up.

had been "an idle student," choosing rather, he said, "to nurse my own fancies than to dig into Greek roots and be numbered among the learned Thebans." He excelled in Latin and English. None of his English themes are extant, but a Latin composition, which has survived, is competently done. Though not Tully's every word, it is undoubtedly better than the average undergraduate performance.

Hawthorne's rank at graduation was eighteenth in a class of thirty-eight. His position would have been higher if he had not neglected the declamations which were required at frequent intervals throughout the four years. He had a strong aversion to public speaking but he was not absolutely incapable of it. Although he was fined several times for "neglect of declamation," it is not reasonable to suppose that he omitted it altogether, for in that case he could hardly have graduated at all. One of his letters home refers, with characteristic humor, to "a very splendid appearance in the chapel last Friday evening, before a crowded audience." But given the aversion, these splendid appearances required a greater effort than he was willing to make as often as the rules required, and as a consequence he was not only fined but denied a part on the commencement program. President Allen called him to his study in July, 1825—Hawthorne wrote his sister Elizabeth—and informed him that though his rank in the class entitled him to a speaking part, it was contrary to the laws of the college to give him one because of his neglect of declamation. "I am perfectly satisfied with this arrangement," Hawthorne added, "as it is a sufficient testimonial of my scholarship, while it saves me the mortification of making my appearance in public at commencement." Years later in England, when he could not escape public speaking so easily, he acquitted himself well; but he had to be "so screwed up to the point"—as he put it in his journal—that he "did not care what happened next."

Extracurricular activities have always occupied a good deal of an American collegian's time. With Hawthorne the chief of these was very properly miscellaneous reading. He said later that while at college he was "always reading desultorily right and left." There is unfortunately no specific account of this reading. His letters home make no mention of it except to say that as a member of the Athenean Society he had access to the Society's library of 800 volumes and (tongue in cheek) that this collection contained "Rees' Cyclopedia and many other valuable works." A manuscript catalogue of the library of the Athenean Society, dated 1829, shows a good representation of English poetry and fiction and a sprinkling of works by Irving, Paulding, Cooper, and other American writers less well known. The library depended for accessions upon gifts by members and Hawthorne was a generous contributor. Jointly with one other member, he gave Percy's *Reliques of Ancient Poetry* and Las Cases' *Journal* in 3 volumes; with three other members, Beattie's *Works* in 10 volumes; with four others, Johnson's *Works* in 12 volumes; and with five others, Swift's *Works* in 24 volumes. If Hawthorne exercised a guiding hand in these selections—a supposition which seems likely enough—the substantial editions of Swift and Johnson show an early appreciation of the great English Augustans. Despite the romantic reaction against these authors, they were favorites of his throughout his life.

Literary societies played an important part in the college life of the early nineteenth century and they probably conferred greater educational benefits than the fraternities which supplanted them. In addition to building up good general libraries, they conducted weekly programs consisting of declamations, orations, debates, and other literary exercises. Both within the society and between rival societies, there was a wholesome spirit of emulation. Since Hawthorne maintained his good standing, he must have delivered the required declamations and orations. Membership in a literary society provided both intellectual stimulus and an unusual opportunity for the formation of friendships. Hawthorne's closest friends in college—Horatio Bridge, Franklin Pierce, and Jonathan Cilley—were fellow Atheneans. These early friendships proved to be enduring. Bridge and Pierce were lifelong friends of Hawthorne, and staunch loyalty was repeatedly manifested on both sides. When Cilley, then a member of Congress, was killed in a duel in 1838, Hawthorne wrote a sketch of his friend which is Cilley's best memorial.

There was a significant differentiation—social, economic, and political—between the two literary societies at Bowdoin in the 1820's. The Peucinian and Athenean societies "typified respectively"—as Hawthorne later described them—"the respectable conservative and the progressive or democratic parties." The Peucinians were likely to be Whigs; the Atheneans, Democrats. In the presidential election of 1824 the Peucinians inclined to John Quincy Adams; the Atheneans to Andrew Jackson. Elizabeth Hawthorne later described her brother as a "partizan" of General Jackson, whose victory over the British at New Orleans had doubtless appealed particularly to the boy's imagination and patriotism. Hawthorne's lifelong connection with the Democratic party was owing partly to principle and partly to the influence of his friends and associates in the Athenean literary society. Henry W. Longfellow was a Peucinian, and for that reason chiefly the two classmates were not well acquainted in college.

A biographer of Longfellow has said that the Peucinians were "the best students" and the Atheneans were "jolly good fellows." Even though this distinction may be a little overdrawn, Hawthorne's college life appears to have been sociable enough. In a reminiscent volume Bridge recalled that during their Bowdoin days Hawthorne

was a slender lad, having a massive head, with dark, brilliant, and most expressive eyes, heavy eyebrows, and a profusion of dark hair. . . . His figure was somewhat singular, owing to his carrying his head a little on one side; but his walk was square and firm, and his manner self-respecting and reserved. . . . Though quiet and most amiable, he had great pluck and determination. . . . He was neither morose nor sentimental; and, though taciturn, was invariably cheerful with his chosen friends; and there was much more of fun and frolic in his disposition than his published writings indicate.

The fun and frolic sometimes went counter to the strict laws of the college. About midway in his freshman year, Hawthorne was fined fifty cents for playing cards for money, and President Allen addressed a letter to Mrs. Hathorne in which he requested her cooperation in the attempt to induce her son "faithfully to observe the laws of the institution." "Perhaps he might not have gamed," Allen added extenuatingly, "were it not for the influence of a student whom we have dismissed from college." Hawthorne's letter to his mother concerning the incident shows an admirable candor and a confidence in her tolerant understanding:

I have nothing in particular to inform you of except that all the Card Players in College have been found out, and my unfortunate self among the number. One has been dismissed from College, two suspended, and the rest with myself have been fined 50 cts. each. . . . When the President asked what we played for, I thought proper to inform him it was 50 cts. although it happened to be a Quart of Wine, but if I had told him of that he would probably have fined me for having a blow. There was no untruth in the case, as the wine cost 50 cts. I have not played at all this term.

I have not drank any kind of spirits or wine this term, and shall not until the last week.

The casuistry of Hawthorne's reply to the president suggests a certain amount of social experience as well as political judgment. The young man's independent spirit was a little offended by Allen's charitable suggestion that he had been led astray by an unprincipled companion. "I was full as willing to play as the person he suspects of having enticed me," he wrote to Elizabeth, "and would have been influenced by no one. I have a great mind to commence playing again, merely to show him that I scorn to be seduced by another into anything wrong." But for reasons of expediency he wisely restrained this quixotic impulse: "The reason of my good conduct," he later confided to an unidentified correspondent, "is that I am very much afraid of being suspended if I continue any longer in my old courses."

The incident just related was Hawthorne's most serious re-

corded breach of college decorum. Whether he refrained from
"gaming" thereafter or became more expert in avoiding detection
it is impossible to say, but he continued to accumulate fines.
Indeed his list of fines in the faculty records and term bills makes
his college career seem wayward as compared with that, say, of
Longfellow, whose conduct was always exemplary. "Henry's bill
was perfectly free from fines," Mrs. Longfellow reported to her
husband in one of her letters, "and his part at the exhibition was
very handsomely performed." Most boys lack the gift of such
exemplariness. Hawthorne's offenses included neglect of declamation, neglect of theme, absence from recitation, absence
from religious services (especially Sunday evening prayers),
attendance at the tavern on Saturday night (a major offense—fine
$1.00—since the Puritan Sabbath, which began at sundown
Saturday, was still observed in Brunswick), and other misde-
meanors. So strict were the rules of Bowdoin and so efficient was
their enforcement that only a paragon of propriety could have
avoided fines altogether. On one occasion Franklin Pierce was
fined fifty cents for "sitting in an improper posture in Chapel." On
another Hawthorne and three companions were fined twenty-five
cents each "for walking unnecessarily on the Sabbath."

But Hawthorne and his friends enjoyed themselves despite the
fines. Ward's Tavern, situated at the edge of the campus, was a
favorite rendezvous. Small sub-rosa clubs facilitated the good
times. Hawthorne belonged to three of these, the most famous of
which was the "Pot-8-o Club." The following names are inscribed
in the autograph of each member on the "Constitution" preserved
in manuscript at the Essex Institute: Jonathan Cilley, Alfred
Mason, Jeremiah Dummer, George W. Pierce, David Shipley, and
Nathaniel Hathorne. The list shows that Hawthorne's social
connections were not confined to one or two close friends. The
constitution of the Pot-8-o Club specified that at each weekly
meeting an original dissertation or poem should be read and re-
freshments provided "consisting of roasted Potatoes, Butter, Salt,
and Cider or some other mild drink." The italicized prohibition,

"*Ardent spirits shall never be introduced,*" gives color to the suspicion that the organization was more convivial than literary.

But it would be easy to exaggerate the clandestine incidents of the college years. Horatio Bridge recalled a number of activities which even President Allen did not disapprove of, on weekdays: hunting and fishing, "rough-and-tumble games," in which Hawthorne took a part "occasionally," and walking. In true New England fashion, Hawthorne always preferred walking to any other form of outdoor exercise, and the banks of the Androscoggin, which flowed near by, and the pine forest which stood back of the college afforded pleasant places for it. Bridge was his most frequent companion on these walks. Hawthorne owed much to his friend then and was to owe even more to him later. In the famous preface to *The Snow Image and Other Twice-Told Tales,* which Hawthorne dedicated to Bridge, he recalled, a little romantically perhaps, their college association and the special kind of encouragement which he received from his sympathetic and perceptive friend at that time: "If anybody is responsible for my being at this day an author, it is yourself," Hawthorne wrote, more than twenty-five years after the events referred to:

I know not whence your faith came; but, while we were lads together at a country college—gathering blueberries in study-hours under those tall academic pines; or watching the great logs as they tumbled along the current of the Androscoggin; or shooting pigeons and gray squirrels in the woods; or bat-fowling in the summer twilight; or catching trout in that shadowy little stream which, I suppose, is still wandering river-ward through the forest . . . two idle lads, in short (as we need not fear to acknowledge now), doing a hundred things that the Faculty never heard of, or else it had been the worse for us —still it was your prognostic of your friend's destiny, that he was to be a writer of fiction.

How much or exactly what, Hawthorne wrote while at Bowdoin is not known, but it must have been enough to furnish a basis for Bridge's "prognostic." He probably began *Fanshawe* there, for Elizabeth Hawthorne remembered a letter from Bowdoin in which he spoke of "progress on a novel." He may also have started "Seven Tales of My Native Land," for Elizabeth, in one account, said that she saw the tales in the summer of 1825, though in another she said he wrote them soon after he left college. But whether *Fanshawe* or the "Seven Tales" or something else, Hawthorne was almost certainly absorbed in writing stories and making literary plans during 1824–25, his senior year.

This literary absorption would easily account for a growing dissatisfaction with college routine, and particularly with the frequently required and heartily disliked "declamations." The senior year had begun with a little flourish of campus ritual. "Since my arrival," he wrote to Elizabeth October 1, 1824, "I have put on my gold watch-chain and purchased a cane; so that, with the aid of my new white gloves, I flatter myself that I make a most splendid appearance in the eyes of the pestilent little freshmen." He confessed in the same letter, however, to being "very low-spirited": "I am tired of college," he said, "and all its amusements and occupations." He then proceeded to "the serious part" of his letter, in which he told of his arrears with the college treasurer: like all college students, he was constantly in need of money. But the low spiritedness was not owing to financial difficulties (Uncle Robert, though sometimes tardy, could still be depended upon). It was partly a temperamental affliction from which, like most sensitive persons, he was to suffer at intervals throughout his life. And in this particular instance the depression of spirits probably came from the conflict between his creative desires and the requirements of the college. Just as a few years earlier he had found it difficult to versify and at the same time keep books for his uncle, so now he found the preparation of lessons an annoying obstacle to the writing of fiction.

Commencement was the occasion for outbursts of youthful oratory. The large proportion of contemporary topics discussed by the graduates on September 7, 1825, shows that the class had not confined its attention entirely to the problems of classical antiquity. Such subjects as "The Effects of the Late Struggles in

Greece and South America on Literature and Liberty," "The Probable Result of Efforts for the Emancipation of Slaves," "The Writings of Byron, Scott, and Irving," and "Our Native Writers" bore the stamp of modernity. Hawthorne was content to listen. The last-named topic, "Our Native Writers," must have interested him especially, and he must have found himself in emphatic agreement when the speaker, young Longfellow, declared enthusiastically and justly:

Yes!—Palms are to be won by our native writers!—by those that have been nursed and brought up with us in the civil and religious freedom of our country. Already has a voice been lifted up in this land,—already a spirit and a love of literature are springing up in the shadows of our free political institutions. . . . Of the many causes which have hitherto retarded the growth of polite literature in our country . . . the greatest which now exists is doubtless the want of that exclusive attention which eminence in any profession so imperiously demands.

Four years earlier, the reader will recall, Hawthorne had said to his mother, "How proud you would feel to see my works praised by the reviewers as equal to the proudest productions of the scribbling sons of John Bull." A new movement was in the air. America would soon have a noble race of professional writers instead of mere dilettantes—writers who would give to literature the exclusive attention necessary for distinguished work.

Hawthorne had got a good education at Bowdoin not only in the classics but in English composition, Christian philosophy, and the natural sciences. He had enjoyed a healthy participation in the social and intellectual life of the college community both in the meetings of the Athenean Society and the more convivial gatherings of the Pot-8-o Club at Ward's Tavern. In the give-and-take of the college world, he had held his own, won a general respect, and formed several friendships which were to last through a lifetime. Before graduation his literary bent had become so evident that Hawthorne himself and at least one other were aware that the writing of fiction was to be his "destiny." There is no record of a special dedicatory moment; the awareness developed gradually. But his later life was to demonstrate a dedication felt as intensely as Milton's when Phoebus touched his trembling ears.

CHAPTER III

THE "SOLITARY YEARS," 1825–1837

As it turned out, Hawthorne was unable to spend many college vacations at Raymond, for his mother and sisters returned to Salem to live in the summer of 1822, and it was to his mother's Salem residence that he came after graduating from Bowdoin in 1825. The period from 1825 until 1837, when he published the *Twice-Told Tales*, has often been called the "solitary years." Doubtless they were solitary to an unusual degree, but not in the sense of a hermit's deliberate withdrawal from the world. Hawthorne was actively interested in the world about him and maintained a reasonable amount of contact with it. But his chief object was to master the writer's difficult art—something which cannot be done in the hubbub of social activity. Probably his life at Bowdoin had been more social than was compatible with a severe literary discipline. The degree of compositional skill which Hawthorne achieved during the post-college years can be appreciated in some measure if it is recalled that the almost flawless writing of his notebooks was done rapidly, with scarcely an erasure or emendation.

After graduation Hawthorne settled down to a serious literary career. He did a great deal of reading and writing. Although he destroyed much that he wrote, he had published by 1838 a novel of indifferent merit and at least forty-four tales and sketches, many of which were of high excellence.

Hawthorne felt the need of a solid foundation in reading. Works of fiction were obtained from a circulating library; non-fictional works from the library of the Salem Athenaeum. No list of rentals from the circulating library is in existence, but his sister Elizabeth has testified that he "read a great many novels" and "made an artistic study of them." The charge books of the Salem Athenaeum, preserved in the Essex Institute, show between 1826 and 1837 no less than 1,200 withdrawals by Mary Manning and Nathaniel Hawthorne. * It is hardly reasonable to suppose that Hawthorne read all of the works listed in the charge books. Elizabeth Hawthorne, who attended to the borrowing of the books ("It was one of my brother's peculiarities," she said, "that he never would visit the Athenaeum himself, nor look over the Catalogue to select a book"), was a great reader, too; and other members of the family no doubt read some of the books which Elizabeth brought home. But Hawthorne was the person for whom the 1,200 items were chiefly selected. Elizabeth recalled his special interest in the *Gentleman's Magazine*, Howell's *State Trials*, and books related to the early history of New England. The following charges, made during the last two months of 1826, can be safely taken as indicating the scope and variety of Hawthorne's reading, exclusive of fiction, at this time: George Crabbe's *The Borough*, Jeremy Taylor's *Discourses on Various Subjects*, Clarendon's *History of the Rebellion and Civil Wars in England*, the *Edinburgh Review*, Francis Bacon's *Works*, Paolo Sarpi's *History of the Council of Trent*, the *Collections* of the Massachusetts Historical Society, Sarah Kemble Knight's *Journals*, Montaigne's *Essais*, C. F. X. Millot's *Élémens de l'Histoire de France*, Thomas Coryate's *Coryate's Crudities*, *Blackwood's Edinburgh Magazine*, Thomas Hutchinson's *Collection of Original Papers Relative to the History of the Colony of Massachusetts Bay*, Thomas Hutchinson's *History of Massachusetts*, and Alden Bradford's *History of Massachusetts*.

Hawthorne's reading, though wide and varied, was subordinate to his writing and occupied less of his time. Elizabeth Hawthorne recalled that the evenings were devoted to reading, while "it was his custom to write in the forenoon, and usually in the afternoon unless the weather was especially fine, when he took a long walk." His first publication was *Fanshawe*, a novel based in part upon his life at Bowdoin. It was published anonymously in 1828 at the

---

* Miss Manning's "share" in this subscription library was transferred to Hawthorne in 1828.

author's expense. Shortly afterward Hawthorne became so dissatisfied with this work that he did everything in his power to suppress it. His attempt was so successful that *Fanshawe* is now one of the rarest and most expensive titles in American literature. His closest friend, Horatio Bridge, destroyed his copy at Hawthorne's urgent request, and *Fanshawe* was never again mentioned between them. Hawthorne concealed this first heir of his invention even from his wife who, when a copy of the book turned up after her husband's death, at first stoutly denied his authorship. If *Fanshawe* was a false start, Hawthorne was not long in correcting his error, for before its publication, and perhaps concurrently with its writing, he was discovering the kind of short tale which was to be a distinctive expression of his genius.

In his early literary career Hawthorne undertook several projects * which proved abortive, though most of his work and perhaps the best was published in magazines and eventually collected. Soon after leaving college he completed a group of stories which he called "Seven Tales of My Native Land." Elizabeth read them in manuscript and found them "very striking, particularly one or two Witch Stories." After offering these compositions to a number of publishers and booksellers without success, Hawthorne in a fit of impatience and despair threw some of the manuscripts into the fire. This rash act is related in a sketch entitled "The Devil in Manuscript," in which the following account is perhaps not greatly exaggerated:

Of all the seventeen booksellers, only one has vouchsafed even to read my tales; and he—a literary dabbler himself, I should judge—has the impertinence to criticise them, proposing what he calls vast improvements, and concluding, after a general sentence of condemnation, with the definitive assurance that he will not be concerned on any terms. . . . One honest man among these seventeen . . . tells me fairly that no American publisher will meddle with an American work—seldom if by a known writer and never if by a new one—unless at the writer's

* In my account of Hawthorne's early literary plans I am greatly indebted to N. F. Adkins' monograph, listed in the biographical sources, p. 266.

risk. . . . These people have put me so out of conceit with the tales that I loathe the very thought of them, and actually experience a physical sickness of the stomach whenever I glance at them on the table. I tell you there is a demon in them! I anticipate a wild enjoyment in seeing them in the blaze; such as I should feel in taking vengeance on an enemy or destroying something noxious.

The passage reflects Hawthorne's passionate nature, usually so well controlled. It also tells something of the state of letters in America in the 1820's and '30's.

Two tales, which (as the author put it) "chanced to be in kinder custody at the time," escaped destruction. One of these was identified by Elizabeth as "Alice Doane's Appeal," which was published in 1835 in the *Token*, a Boston annual in which some twenty-two of Hawthorne's stories were eventually to appear. The other surviving story has not been positively identified, but the most likely conjecture is "The Hollow of the Three Hills," published in the Salem *Gazette* in 1830.

Hawthorne's despair was short lived, for he soon undertook a second group. As early as 1829 he was in correspondence with Samuel G. Goodrich, Boston publisher and editor of the *Token*, about a proposed volume to be called "Provincial Tales." Goodrich gave no encouragement, possibly because he believed such a publication would be unprofitable and certainly because he wanted the compositions for his annual. "As a practical evidence of my opinion of the uncommon merit of these tales," he wrote to Hawthorne in January, 1830, "I offer you $35 for the privilege of inserting 'The Gentle Boy' in the 'Token,' and you shall be at liberty to publish it with your collection provided it does not appear before the publication of the 'Token.'" Finding no publisher for "Provincial Tales," Hawthorne permitted the inclusion of "The Gentle Boy" and three other tales ("The Wives of the Dead," "Roger Malvin's Burial," and "My Kinsman, Major Molineux") in the 1832 number of the *Token*, which appeared—as was customary with that publication, since it enjoyed great favor as a Christmas gift—in the preceding autumn.

All of these stories—and indeed all of Hawthorne's work prior to 1837—appeared anonymously or pseudonymously. Most of his stories bore no indication of authorship. In several, such identifications as "by the author of the Gentle Boy" or "by the author of the Gray Champion" were employed. Pseudonyms were used in a few. "The Devil in Manuscript," for example, was by "Ashley A. Royce." It was not until the publication of the *Twice-Told Tales* that Nathaniel Hawthorne's name appeared over his works. Goodrich preferred the anonymity because he was using a large number of Hawthorne's stories in the *Token* (one in 1831, four in 1832, two in 1833, three in 1835, three in 1836, and nine in 1837) and he did not want it to be known that he was drawing so much of his material from one author. The editors of the *New England Magazine*—the other periodical in which a considerable amount of Hawthorne's early work appeared—doubtless had the same attitude; in 1835 this magazine contained no less than eight of his pieces. He had undoubtedly been shy about acknowledging his work in the beginning, as the anonymous appearance of *Fanshawe* testified. But the persistence of anonymity in the 1830's, when he was developing skill and confidence, seems owing in large part to the peculiarly restricting circumstances of publication.* Such enforced anonymity must have towered higher and higher in his mind's eye as an obstacle to recognition.

Hawthorne was finding periodical publication easy, if not highly remunerative, but his attempts to bring out a volume of tales continued to be unsuccessful. A third projected collection—abortive like the two already mentioned—was to be called "The Story Teller." A raconteur was to be represented as wandering over New England and regaling village audiences with his stories. Accounts of the storyteller's travels would provide homely, dramatic settings for the stories themselves. It was an admirable plan, for it would have united in one work Hawthorne's imagina-

---

* Hawthorne's exclusive attention to the short piece in these years also seems to have been dictated by the requirements of magazine publication.

tive and reportorial faculties as none of his published writings quite do. The failure of the project to materialize can be attributed to the ineptitude of the publishers and editors.

In 1834 Hawthorne submitted two manuscript volumes to Goodrich, who passed them on to the editors of the *New England Magazine*. Serial publication was soon begun in that magazine, but the procedure was altered the following year when Park Benjamin took over the editorship. Benjamin continued to print the individual stories but dropped out most of the connecting material, "Mr. Higginbotham's Catastrophe" being the only story which appeared in its original setting. "The Gray Champion," "The Ambitious Guest," and "Young Goodman Brown" (all published in the *New England Magazine* in 1835) were among the stories designed to fill out a New England panorama. Hawthorne later spoke severely of Benjamin for "cutting up" "The Story Teller"; the stories, he said, had a richer significance in their original setting. Benjamin and Goodrich do not appear either generous or wise in the history of Hawthorne's literary career.

Hawthorne kept on writing despite his failure to bring out a volume of tales and despite the poor pay. Goodrich, as we have seen, paid only $35 for "The Gentle Boy," which runs to about 12,000 words; the amount paid for nine pieces in the 1837 *Token* was $108. The remuneration from Benjamin was probably even paltrier. Hawthorne told Bridge in 1836, when his pen had for some time been very productive, that $300 a year was as much as he could hope to make by writing fiction for the magazines and annuals. Although, being still a member of his mother's household, his living expenses were small, it became necessary to supplement such a meager income by hackwork. From March through August, 1836, he edited the *American Magazine of Useful and Entertaining Knowledge*, published in Boston. The contents, which consisted largely of excerpts and digests, were supplied jointly by Hawthorne and his sister Elizabeth. As the salary was $500 a year, he must have received $250 for his six months' labor, though he had difficulty in collecting the sum due him. He had obtained the editorship through the aid of Goodrich, who was connected with the publishers of the magazine and acted as their literary agent. After a month's work in Boston, Hawthorne wrote to his sister Louisa in Salem:

I came here trusting to Goodrich's positive promise to pay me 45 dollars as soon as I arrived; and he has kept promising from one day to another; till I do not see that he means to pay me at all. I have now broke off all intercourse with him, and never think of going near him. . . . This world is as full of rogues as Beelzebub [the cat at home] is of fleas. I don't want but two or three dollars. Till I receive some of my own, I shall continue to live as I have done. . . . My present stock is precisely 34 cts. . . . All that I have spent in Boston, except for absolute necessaries, has been 9 cents on the first day I came—6 for a glass of wine and three for a cigar.

"It is well that I have enough to do," he added, "or I should have had the blues most damnably." Despite his low opinion of Goodrich, however, Hawthorne did another hack job for him while editing the magazine: again assisted by Elizabeth, he sent to Goodrich in September, 1836, the copy for *Peter Parley's Universal History*. The publisher, though not the authors, found this popular compendium very profitable.

Better success, however, was soon in prospect. Thanks to the generous friendship of Horatio Bridge a volume of tales was actually in press by the end of 1836; Bridge in October of that year put the matter squarely up to Goodrich and took the very practical step of giving him $250 in cash as a guarantee against loss. Hawthorne did not know, at the time, of Bridge's friendly act, and attributing the turn of events solely to Goodrich's initiative, was with difficulty dissuaded by Bridge from dedicating the *Twice-Told Tales* to Goodrich. The volume, with the author's name on the title page, appeared in March, 1837; it contained eighteen of the thirty-six tales and sketches which had been published up to that time.

The publication of the *Twice-Told Tales*, to use the author's

own phrase, "opened an intercourse with the world." Owing
largely to anonymity, Hawthorne had been very slow in acquiring a reputation. With a good deal of justice he was later to
describe himself during these early years as "the obscurest man
of letters in America." Before the autumn of 1835, when the
Token for 1836 appeared, his tales had been completely ignored
by the press. Sometime in 1836 Hawthorne wrote in his notebook, "In this dismal chamber Fame was won." The grounds for
this declaration were modest enough; they consisted of two
notices, one by Park Benjamin in the *New England Magazine*
and another by Henry Chorley in the London *Athenaeum.**
Benjamin regarded "the author of the 'Gentle Boy' . . . as the
most pleasing writer of fanciful prose, except Irving, in the
country." Chorley commended "The Wedding Knell" and "The
Minister's Black Veil" for their "singularity" and printed generous excerpts from "The Maypole of Merry Mount." It was the
English recognition, we may be sure, which especially delighted
Hawthorne, for it was a beginning, however small, toward the
realization of his early ambition to rival "the scribbling sons of
John Bull." "My worshipful self," he wrote (with some exaggeration) to Elizabeth, "is a very famous man in London."

Divulging in part the secret of Hawthorne's authorship in
the *American Monthly Magazine* for October, 1836, Park Benjamin declared: "If Mr. Hawthorne would but collect his various
tales and essays into one volume, we can assure him that their
success would be brilliant." The immediate success of the *Twice-
Told Tales* was scarcely brilliant but it was substantial enough
to afford encouragement to the author and to ensure the continuation of his literary career. The Salem *Gazette* and other
newspapers praised the volume, and the *North American Review*
for July, 1837, published a laudatory article by Longfellow.

* Here, and in subsequent accounts of the reception of Hawthorne's writings,
I am greatly indebted to Bertha Faust's monograph, listed in the biographical
sources, p. 266.

Although these Bowdoin classmates had not seen each other since graduation, Hawthorne had ventured to send Longfellow a complimentary copy of his book, and Longfellow responded generously. Written with lush sentimentality, the article showed more friendship than critical acumen: "Beautiful sketches [Longfellow said] are interspersed among the stories like green leaves among flowers. . . . To this little work we would say, 'Live ever, sweet book.' . . . Like children, we say, 'Tell us more.'" But the magazine and the reviewer enjoyed great prestige; Hawthorne could hope for nothing more propitious on this side of the water. His publisher informed him that the book was "spoken of in the highest terms by discriminating gentlemen" in Boston and Cambridge. Goodrich was able to refund to Bridge the $250 which had been deposited as a guarantee, and within a year after publication the edition of 1,000 copies was almost exhausted.

Hawthorne fully appreciated the practical worth of Longfellow's review and he was equally appreciative of the friendly spirit which prompted the reviewer. "I have read with huge delight," he wrote to Longfellow,

your review of "Hawthorne's Twice-Told Tales." I frankly own that I was not without hopes that you would do this kind office for the book; though I could not have anticipated how very kindly it would be done. Whether or no the public will agree to the praise which you bestow on me, there are at least five persons who think you the most sagacious critic on earth—viz. my mother and two sisters, my old maiden aunt, and finally, the sturdiest believer of the whole five, my own self.

The incident was the beginning of a warm friendship.

The "solitary" years have often been described somewhat sentimentally. In a famous letter addressed to his fiancée, Miss Sophia Peabody, October 4, 1840, Hawthorne himself gave encouragement to a sentimental view of his apprentice years:

Here sits thy husband * in his old accustomed chamber [he wrote], where he used to sit in years gone by, before his soul became acquainted with thine. Here I have written many tales—many that have been burned to ashes—many that doubtless deserved the same fate. This deserves to be called a haunted chamber; for thousands upon thousands of visions have appeared to me in it; and some few of them have become visible to the world. If ever I should have a biographer, he ought to make great mention of this chamber in my memoirs, because so much of my lonely youth was wasted here, and here my mind and character were formed; and here I have been glad and hopeful, and here I have been despondent; and here I sat a long, long time, waiting patiently for the world to know me, and sometimes wondering why it did not know me sooner, or whether it would ever know me at all—at least, till I were in my grave. And sometimes (for I had no wife then to keep my heart warm) it seemed as if I were already in the grave, with only life enough to be chilled and benumbed. But oftener I was happy—at least, as happy as I then knew how to be, or was aware of the possibility of being. By and bye, the world found me out in my lonely chamber, and called me forth—not, indeed, with a loud roar of acclamation, but rather with a still, small voice; and forth I went, but found nothing in the world that I thought preferable to my old solitude, till at length a certain Dove was revealed to me, in the shadow of a seclusion as deep as my own had been. And I drew nearer and nearer to the Dove, and opened my bosom to her, and she flitted into it, and closed her wings there—and there she nestles now and forever, keeping my heart warm, and renewing my life with her own. So now I begin to understand why I was imprisoned so many years in this lonely chamber, and why I could never break through the viewless bolts and bars; for if I had sooner made my escape into the world, I should have grown hard and rough, and been covered with earthly dust, and my heart would have become callous by rude encounters with the multitude; so that I should have been all unfit to shelter a heavenly Dove in my arms. But living in solitude till the fulness of time was come, I still kept the dew of my youth and the freshness of my heart, and had these to offer to my Dove.

* In the letters written during their engagement, Hawthorne often referred to himself as "husband" and to Sophia as "wife."

The phrases "lonely youth" and "lonely chamber" recur with affecting iteration; his life was one of "solitude" and "seclusion"; he was "chilled and benumbed." It is not necessary to question the writer's sincerity or the core of truth in the description. For a young man of Hawthorne's sensibilities and literary aspirations, the Muse was an exacting mistress. He spent many lonely and despondent hours in the chamber where fame was won. The life of a serious writer is likely to be in large part lonely. But the pathos which pervades the letter just quoted must be discounted somewhat in the light of the circumstances of composition. When writing a love letter, a man may be tempted to darken his former years so as to brighten by contrast his present felicity. In a more sober and responsible mood, Hawthorne later described these same years as "tranquil and not unhappy."

Although closely occupied with literary tasks, Hawthorne found time for diversion and recreation. His life was not without social contacts. There were uncles, aunts, and cousins at hand, and there were associations outside the family. For a time after college he enjoyed a game of cards at frequent intervals with three others —his sister Louisa, Horace Conolly, an Episcopal clergyman, and David Roberts, a Salem lawyer. The members of this foursome went by impressive nicknames: Hawthorne was "Emperor," Louisa "Empress," Conolly "Cardinal," and Roberts "Chancellor." Hawthorne was apparently on friendly terms with the uncles, aunts, and cousins. "I often go in to see your father and mother," he wrote to his cousin, John S. Dike, in Steubenville, Ohio, "and find them quite contented and comfortable." Indeed, the letters written to Dike in 1830–31 are full of friendliness and social gossip. There is news not only of the family but of local events both great and small: the White murder, the doings of the ministers (one after drinking too much wine overturned his chaise and broke several bones), the theater, the Lyceum, a Washington's Birthday Ball, illnesses, deaths, births, marriages, engagements, and other Salem matters that would be of interest to a young man far from home. Hawthorne wrote goodnaturedly of Dike's engagement: "I advise you to get married before cold weather comes on; and I should expect to be groomsman if I were within any reasonable distance of you." These lively letters are not the compositions of a man who was divorced from the society around him or who viewed it with an indifferent or unfriendly eye.

"My brother went out when there was a fire," Elizabeth Hawthorne said, "and if there was any gathering of people in the town he always went out; he liked a crowd." Elizabeth recalled that when President Jackson visited Salem in 1833 her brother walked out to the boundaries of the town "to welcome the General with a good cheer." "When there were visitors in the family," she testified further, "he was always social." ———

During the years after college Hawthorne kept up his friendship with two fellow Atheneans, Franklin Pierce and Horatio Bridge. Pierce he saw infrequently, meeting him in Boston or at Fresh Pond, where on one recorded occasion there was "good cheer." Although, as Hawthorne put it later, their "modes of life had been as different as could be imagined," they always met "on the old ground of friendly confidence." Hawthorne watched with interest and admiration his friend's rapid advancement in public life. Upon Pierce's election as speaker of the New Hampshire Legislature in 1832, he wrote a friendly, congratulatory letter which proved to be more prophetic than either man could have known at the time:

I sincerely congratulate you on all your public honors, in possession or in prospect. If they continue to accumulate so rapidly, you will be at the summit of political eminence by that time of life when men are usually just beginning to make a figure. I suppose there is hardly a limit to your expectations at this moment; and I really cannot see why there should be any. If I were in your place, I should like to proceed by the following steps,—after a few years in Congress, to be chosen governor, say at thirty years old; next a senator in Congress; then minister to England; then to be put at the head of one of the departments (that of War would suit you I should think), and lastly,—but it will be time enough to think of the next step some years hence. You cannot imagine how proud I feel when I recollect that I myself was once in office with you on the standing committee of the Athenean Society. . . . I wish you would send me some of the newspapers containing articles laudatory or abusive of you. I shall read them with great interest, be they what they may. It is a pity that I am not in a situation to use my pen in your behalf, though you seem not to need the assistance of newspaper scribblers.

Such a use of his powers, Hawthorne must have thought, would be no derogation from the high office of literature, for the pens of the Augustans had been active in the service of political leaders.

Except in the last five years of his life, Hawthorne was closer to Bridge than to Pierce. During the twelve years after graduation he and Bridge occasionally enjoyed convivial meetings in Boston and elsewhere, and they corresponded frequently. Although their letters prior to 1836 have not survived, Bridge's letters in that year reveal an intimate friendship of long standing. "I take advice from you kindly," Bridge wrote; "It seems divested of the presumption and intermeddling spirit with which advice is usually tinctured." There was a fine reciprocity between them, for Bridge bestowed good advice with a liberal hand. He urged Hawthorne to stop his anonymous writing for the magazines. "I hope to God," he declared, "that you will put your name upon the title-page of your book, and come before the world at once and on your own responsibility. . . . I thought of writing a notice of the 'Token' and naming you as the author of several articles, with some candid remarks upon your merits as a writer." With the undiscriminating judgment of a businessman, Bridge congratulated Hawthorne upon his editorship of the *American Magazine of Useful and Entertaining Knowledge.* He wanted him to be engaged in "active and responsible business" and thought this position, though not too impressive in itself, "the introduction to other and better employment." "Besides," he added jovially, "it is no small point gained to get you out of Salem. . . . There is a peculiar dullness about Salem." When Hawthorne was despondent, Bridge conveyed rough electric shocks of optimism and courage: "I have been trying to think what you are so miserable for. Although you have not much property, you have good health and powers of writing, which have made and can still make you independent. . . . I wish to God that I could impart to you a little of my own brass." Although Bridge lacked a sensitive appreciation of the artist's standpoint—the only standpoint which Hawthorne was capable of taking in his serious writing—Hawthorne enjoyed and profited from the bluff, hearty tone of Bridge's letters.

The dullness of Salem, to which Bridge objected and which Hawthorne himself often found oppressive, was frequently relieved during these years by walks and excursions to points both near and far. Walking to Hawthorne, as to Thoreau, was always an important means of recreation, and in the earliest published journal there are many accounts of walking excursions. Sample entries in 1835–36 began with "A walk down to the Juniper," "A walk in North Salem in the decline of yesterday afternoon," "A walk yesterday down to the shore, near the hospital," "A walk yesterday through Dark Lane, and home through the village of Danvers," "Walking along the track of the railroad"; and the editor of this now missing notebook, Mrs. Hawthorne, who selected only parts of it for publication, said that there were "a great many more walks in this little book." If Hawthorne spent much of his time sitting in the solitary chamber, he also devoted many hours to walking. He possessed an abundance of physical energy and he walked with something of Thoreau's vigor. In the same early journal there are many references also to drives to more distant points: for example, "I rode to Boston in the afternoon with Mr. Procter," "A drive to Nahant yesterday afternoon," "A drive to Ipswich with Bridge." A morbid solitariness is hardly compatible with such mobility.

More important than these brief journeys on foot or by chaise were the excursions made in the summer or fall when, as Hawthorne later said, he "enjoyed as much of life as other people do in the whole year's round." Although the records are incomplete, it is reasonably certain that he took a trip of some length every summer, and several passages in his letters reflect a keen delight in these experiences. The Manning stage lines had perhaps long stimulated his interest in travel.

Hawthorne visited Raymond once or twice after graduation from college, but the charm of that place had fled with the passing of his youth and the return of his mother to Salem. In October, 1828, he was in New Haven, Connecticut, with Samuel Manning, his uncle, who traveled all over New England, partly for amusement and partly to obtain horses for the stagecoaches. Horace Conolly, then a student at Yale, reported many years later his conversations with Hawthorne at this time, their visit to the graves of the regicide judges, in whom Hawthorne was particularly interested, and Hawthorne's disappointment in the Judges' Cave, which he went out to West Rock to see at a cost of $3.50 for hack hire. He called the cave, Conolly said, "the damndest humbug in America," adding that "there was not even a hole in the ground deep enough to bury a dead cat." But Hawthorne enjoyed New Haven and the journey, for in August, 1829, he expressed "much pleasure" in the prospect of joining Samuel Manning there again. In August, 1831, he traveled in New Hampshire, again in the company of Uncle Samuel, and was amused especially by the antics of the Shakers at Canterbury. "I was most tickled," he wrote to Louisa, "to see a man in a common frock coat and pantaloons between two little boys, and a very fat old lady in a black silk gown, rolling along in a stream of sweat between two young girls, and making ten thousand mistakes in the ceremonies." A jolly old Shaker gave him a tumblerfull of their "superb cider," and Hawthorne averred that it was "as much as a common head could carry." He teased his sister with ostensibly serious talk about joining the Shaker community. At the Canterbury inn he enjoyed the conversation of the villagers. "I make innumerable acquaintances," he wrote Louisa, "and sit down in the doorstep in the midst of squires, judges, generals, and all the potentates of the land, discoursing about the Salem murder, the cowskinning of Isaac Hull, the price of hay, and the value of horseflesh."

He was again in New Hampshire in September of the following year. He spent two nights at Crawford's Inn, situated in the Notch of the White Mountains (the Notch was later used as the scene of "The Ambitious Guest"), and climbed Mount Washington. From Burlington, Vermont, he sent his mother a spirited and humorously exaggerated account of his adventurous journey to and up the mountain:

I mounted what the people called a "plaguey high-lifed crittur" [he wrote], and rode with four gentlemen and a guide six miles to the foot of Mt. Washington. It was but four o'clock A.M. when we started, and a showery morning, and we had to ride through the very worst road that ever was seen, mud and mire, and several rivers to be forded, and trees to be jumped over (fallen trees, I mean) through all which I galloped and trotted and tript and stumbled, and arrived without breaking my neck at last. The other particulars, how I climbed three miles into the air, and how it snowed all the way, and how, when I got up the mountain on one side, the wind carried me a great distance off my feet and almost blew me down the other, and how the thermometer stood at twelve degrees below the freezing point, I shall have time enough to tell you when I return.

The journey which he had planned at this time extended to Albany, Niagara, Montreal, and Quebec, but the outbreak of cholera in Canada compelled him to confine his travels, apparently, to New Hampshire and Vermont.

There were other journeys, but it is impossible to date them exactly. He probably visited Niagara and Detroit in 1833 or 1834, for apparently firsthand sketches describing a journey to those points appeared in the *New England Magazine* in 1835. He spent a month at Martha's Vineyard sometime before 1836 and wrote an article about the island for the *American Magazine of Useful and Entertaining Knowledge*. Young Hawthorne was obviously fond of travel. Because longer journeys were too arduous and expensive, and perhaps also because the New England scene was more relevant to his literary work, he did not travel much outside New England. But his interest extended farther. He enjoyed Dike's account of his journey to Ohio and said that he would like to take the same route. Although in later years he was to go to England, France, and Italy, he never traveled in his own country farther west than Detroit or farther south than the lower bank of the Potomac.

In his journeys about New England, which he knew in its entirety better than any other of the great New England authors, his attention was not confined to the beauties of nature and the humors of Shakers and villagers. Hawthorne always had an appreciative eye for female beauty, and there is reason to believe that he was interested in several girls. The evidence, though fire may not be clearly visible, provides a good deal of smoke. Elizabeth Hawthorne recalled her brother's captivation by a girl in Swampscott, the daughter of a fisherman and the keeper of a little shop. This village maiden had, Hawthorne said, a great deal of what the French call *espièglerie*. Their affair was apparently only a summer flirtation. The young man brought home as a memento a pink sugar heart, which he kept a long while before eating it. "I should have feared that he was really in love with her," Elizabeth remarked, "if he had not talked so much about her." Elizabeth doubted if her brother was quite serious, furthermore, because there had been others—for example, "a girl in the interior of Massachusetts as captivating in a different style."

A more serious romance apparently occurred in Edgartown on Martha's Vineyard. An unpublished reminiscence by a resident of Edgartown tells of Hawthorne's proposal of marriage to Miss Eliza Gibbs, "a tall, darkeyed queenly maiden." * The date is unknown, but Bridge's letters in the spring of 1837 suggest that Hawthorne was contemplating marriage: "Are you seriously thinking of getting married," he asked; and again, "What has become of your matrimonial ideas? Are you in a good way to bring this about?" In a letter to Longfellow in June, 1837, Hawthorne spoke of soon

* I am indebted to Benjamin C. Clough for this information.

having a "sharp spur to exertion" which he had previously lacked. But whether Miss Gibbs or another was the lady in question, it is impossible to say.

Hawthorne appears, at any rate, to have enjoyed friendly relations with women during the "solitary" years. On several occasions he was actively interested, and his experiences seem to have ranged from ephemeral flirtations to more serious entanglements. But he had not yet, apparently, been deeply in love.

The years from 1825 to 1837 were active, busy, productive ones. Hawthorne was doing just what a young author ambitious of enduring fame should and must do. He was reading much and writing much. Severely critical of his own work, he was mastering the writer's craft. By his travels over New England, he was re-creating his mind, enlarging his knowledge of human nature, and gathering impressions which could be used in his writings (was making himself indeed the chief literary authority in New England life and manners). Recognition was slow, but the appearance of the *Twice-Told Tales* in 1837 was the beginning of an enduring reputation, for the volume contained some of the finest productions of his pen.

CHAPTER IV

COURTSHIP, MARRIAGE, AND THE OLD MANSE, *1838–1845*

IT was altogether appropriate that Hawthorne should have visited Bridge at Augusta, Maine, in the summer of 1837. They could contemplate with objectivity the success of the *Twice-Told Tales*, whose publication Bridge had made possible and whose merits their classmate Longfellow had just advertised to the world. Hawthorne stayed a month, and wrote in his journal (the earliest manuscript journal now extant) a detailed account of his visit. Bridge was leading a bachelor life in his paternal mansion and had as a regular inmate of his household Monsieur Schaeffer, "a queer little Frenchman." Hawthorne described Bridge as a man "of excellent temper and warm heart, and well acquainted with the world." Schaeffer had "the vivacity and gaiety of his nation"; he was "a philosopher and infidel," with "very just notions on ethics though damnably perverted as to religion." Thus there were gathered together, Hawthorne observed, "three characters, each with something out of the common way."

It was a very happy visit. Hawthorne enjoyed the lively conversation of Bridge and Schaeffer, the food and drink (mutton, ham, smoked beef, boiled eggs, claret, and brown sherry), the excursions with Bridge to fish for trout, salmon, and perch or to visit the shanties of the Irish and Canadians who were building a dam across the Kennebec River. Everywhere he went Hawthorne saw "remarkable items" and "hints for characters." The detail of his journal is realistic and homely:

With Mr. Schaeffer yesterday to pick raspberries. He fell through an old log bridge, thrown over a hollow; looking back, only his head and shoulders appeared through the rotten logs, and among the bushes.

Shower coming on, the rapid running of a little barefooted boy, coming up unheard, and dashing swiftly past us, and showing the soles of his naked feet, as he ran adown the path before us, and up the opposite rise.

On the return journey from Augusta Hawthorne stopped at a boardinghouse in Thomaston, where he "talked with everybody —to Mrs. Trott, good sense—to Mary, good sense with a mixture of fun—to Mrs. Gleason, sentiment, romance, and nonsense." He felt an attraction, he confessed, to the "frank, free, mirthful daughter of the landlady, about twenty-four years old, . . . between whom and myself there immediately sprang up a flirtation, which made us both feel rather solemncholy when we parted on Tuesday morning. She is capable, I know, of strong feelings; and her features expressed something of the kind, when we held out our hands for a parting grasp." The excursion of 1837 was doubtless similar to the excursions which he had been making for at least ten summers here and there in New England. The purpose in view was both recreational and literary. Entering into the life around him he seldom escaped a passing infatuation with some village maiden. But he was able to maintain a professional equilibrium, seeing things with clear objectivity. The journal account of Cilley, whom he saw in Thomaston, was too severe for friendship; in the memorial sketch written after Cilley's death a short while later, the asperities were removed and objective truth was sacrificed somewhat to the claims of the heart. Hawthorne was to recognize the conflict more than once in his literary career. Possibly it was the artist's aloofness which kept him unmarried for so long.

The publication of the *Twice-Told Tales* was not made an occasion for the relaxation of literary effort. Hawthorne kept on writing assiduously and publishing as before. In the autumn of 1837 the *Token* (for 1838) contained four pieces by him. About the same time he began to publish in the *Democratic Review*. J. L. O'Sullivan, the editor of this newly established magazine, had invited Hawthorne's contributions in a letter which promised both fame and riches: "This magazine," O'Sullivan had announced, "is designed to be of the highest rank. . . . The compensation to good writers will be on so liberal a scale as to command the best and most polished exertions of their minds. It is therefore intended that nothing but matter of distinguished excellence shall appear in its pages and that will be very handsomely remunerated." The rate of pay was to range from $3 to $5 per page, "depending on the kind and merit of the writing." Hawthorne succumbed to these blandishments. Although he began to branch out and publish in a larger number of magazines, most of his tales and sketches after 1837 went to the *Democratic:* of approximately thirty-one pieces published between 1838 and 1845, nine were scattered among the *American Monthly,* the *Southern Rose,* the *Boston Miscellany,* *Sargeant's,* the *Pioneer, Godey's* and *Graham's,* while the remaining twenty-two appeared in O'Sullivan's journal. Hawthorne and the ingratiating O'Sullivan became warm friends, but the friendship on Hawthorne's side had repeatedly to withstand the severe strain of O'Sullivan's failure to keep his pecuniary promises.

The summer of 1838 found Hawthorne setting out on another extended journey, this time to western Massachusetts. It proved to be the last of its kind, for he was soon to have a good reason for staying at home, but it was the most profitable of all the summer excursions if one may judge from the records which have survived. Leaving Salem on July 23, he went by stage to Boston and took the afternoon train to Worcester, where he stopped at the Temperance House. He resumed his journey the next morning on the Northampton stage, riding outside nearly all day, as he recorded in his notebook, and being "very sociable with the driver and another outside passenger." Toward night he enjoyed the talk of an essence peddler (who was later to contribute to the portrait of Holgrave in *The House of the Seven Gables*), and observed of the class that "peddlers find satisfaction for all contumelies in making good bargains out of their customers." Leaving Northampton between one and two o'clock in the morning, the stage traveled on through the night. The passengers were silent during the dark hours, when nothing was visible except "the gleam of the lanterns on wayside objects," but they were revived at dawn by an excellent breakfast consisting of "newly caught trout, salmon, ham, boiled eggs, and other niceties." They were soon riding through "quite a romantic country, with mountains on all sides." The road appeared hazardous, but "the driver, a merry fellow, lolled on his box, with his feet protruding horizontally, and rattled on at the rate of ten miles an hour." The journey continued with éclat to North Adams, where Hawthorne arrived on the morning of July 26 and made his headquarters until September 11.

The North Adams journal, which runs to over 25,000 words, is one of the most interesting of Hawthorne's compositions. As a descriptive record of life a century ago in the interior of New England, it would be difficult to find its equal in literature. The journal abounds in "remarkable characters," closely observed and delineated—the decayed village lawyer, now a soapmaker, the blacksmith, the traveling surgeon-dentist, country doctors, peddlers and wrestlers at the Williams College commencement, the proprietor of a caravan of animals (whose exhibition was forbidden by the selectmen of North Adams on the grounds that the factory girls would be absent from their work and spend their money foolishly), and many others. Hawthorne enjoyed especially the conviviality and confidences of the tavern bar. He described the people he saw so accurately that as late as 1893, according to Bliss Perry, the subjects of his descriptions were readily identifiable by the older residents of the place. The North Adams setting and some of the villagers were to appear in "Ethan Brand."

Again, as in the case of the Augusta journal, there was a mixture of motives. Hawthorne was unquestionably having a good time. He participated in the life around him as much perhaps as was possible for an outsider. He marched in a meager funeral procession. His heart "warmed," he said, to the Williamstown students, who took him back to his own college days. He listened sympathetically to Mr. Leach's story of a girl's confession of unchastity.

But as he listened he was thinking, too, of the literary possibilities of the story: "Much might be made of such a scene—" he wrote in his journal; "the lover's astoundment at discovering so much more than he expected." After all, it was his primary business as a writer of fiction to study life and to see it clearly. If the writing often appears coldly objective, the reason is not so much the absence of natural feeling as the presence of artistic control. The North Adams journal should be regarded primarily as an artist's sketchbook and not as a diary of private emotion. The emotion, however, sometimes breaks through the restraint, for the man was never completely subdued by the artist.

Shortly after his return from North Adams in September, 1838, the natural man vigorously asserted himself for a time. Hawthorne met and fell in love with Miss Sophia A. Peabody, and she returned his love. It is significant that during the courtship of nearly four years his productivity fell off sharply. There were other reasons to be sure—his employment in the Boston Custom House and at Brook Farm—but the free play of personal emotion seems to have been incompatible with artistic creation.

Born in 1811, Sophia was the daughter of Dr. Nathaniel Peabody, who practised dentistry in Salem and later in Boston. She had three brothers and two sisters: the brothers did not distinguish themselves, two dying prematurely; one sister, Mary, married Horace Mann, the founder of Antioch College; another sister, Elizabeth, became a famous bluestocking. Julian Hawthorne described his mother's abilities and attainments without much exaggeration as follows:

Her mental faculties were finely balanced and of great capacity; her taste was by nature highly refined, and was rendered exquisitely so by cultivation. Her learning and accomplishments were rare and varied, and yet she was always childlike in her modesty and simplicity. She read Latin, Greek, and Hebrew; she was familiar with history; and in drawing, painting, and sculpture she showed a loving talent not far removed from original genius.

The same writer's description of Sophia's appearance is also worth quoting, for it is the most authentic portrait that we have and it loses nothing by its filial devotion:

In person she was small, graceful, active and beautifully formed. Her face was so alive and translucent with lovely expressions that it was hard to determine whether or not it were physically lovely; but I incline to think that a mathematical survey would have pronounced her features plain; only, no mathematical survey could have taken cognizance of her smile. Her head was nobly shaped; her forehead high and symmetrically arched; her eyebrows strongly marked; her eyes, gray, soft, and full of gentle light; her mouth and chin at once tender, winning, and resolute. Beautiful or not, I have never seen a woman whose countenance better rewarded contemplation.

Unfortunately, Sophia was a semi-invalid—or perhaps fortunately, for she was of sensibility all compact, and her physical distress was a constant challenge to her robust suitor, stimulating his sympathies and the protective instinct. She suffered from a chronic nervous headache, which the heroic treatment of the day —even hydropathy and the application of leeches— failed to cure. Although the headaches abated after marriage, Sophia was never sturdy and was subject to frequently recurring illnesses, more or less serious, throughout her life.

The Hawthornes and Peabodys had been Salem neighbors for many years, but it was not until 1837–38 that an active interest was manifested on either side. After the publication of the *Twice-Told Tales* Elizabeth Peabody—always eager to discover genius— learned that the author of the anonymous stories which had attracted her interest for some time was the son of Mrs. Hathorne. She invited Nathaniel and his sisters to call, but when they came Sophia was unable to assist in receiving them, being confined to her chamber. During subsequent visits a friendship developed between Hawthorne and Elizabeth Peabody, in the course of which she told him much of her invalid sister and read to him from a journal which Sophia had kept while in Cuba a few years before. Thus was Hawthorne gently prepared for his fate. Eventually—one evening in the autumn of 1838 when Hawthorne was present in the Peabodys' parlor—Sophia came down. She came down—to continue in the words of Elizabeth Peabody's recollections— " . . . in her simple white wrapper, and sat on the sofa. As I said 'My sister, Sophia,' he rose and looked at her intently—he did not realize how intently. As we went on talking, she would frequently interpose a remark in her low, sweet voice. Every time she did so, he would look at her again, with the same piercing, indrawing gaze." Although Elizabeth emphasized, in her recollections, the "seclusion" and "eccentricity" of the Hawthornes as if to impress the world with the magnitude of her accomplishment, it was really not too difficult for the Peabody sisters to meet Hawthorne, and after the introduction to Sophia he was a frequent caller at the Peabody house.

Sophia recorded her impressions during the early days of her association with Hawthorne. On one of his visits, "he looked very brilliant." "What a beautiful smile he has! He has a celestial expression." On another occasion, "he looked extremely handsome, with sufficient sweetness in his face to supply the rest of the world and still leave the ordinary share to himself." And again, "he looked like the sun shining through a silver mist when he turned to say good-bye. It is a most wonderful face." She also noted that he talked freely when a third person was not present.

As for Hawthorne, he was scarcely the lonely hermit of romantic legend who was rescued from solitude by the good offices of the Peabodys. The evidence, in fact, points to a fair amount of social activity with possibly distracting complications in 1838. He apparently was a member of Miss Burley's coterie and attended her literary salon. In a letter to Miss C. C. Ainsworth of Boston he thought it worth while to deny, with apparent seriousness, the report that he was "engaged to two ladies." And Elizabeth Peabody's plans seem to have been thwarted on one occasion when she wrote to Louisa Hawthorne, "I wonder what sort of prepara-

tion he finds an evening of whist for the company of the Muse."
But whatever social distraction there may have been was soon
superseded by a new and single devotion.

Progress from friendship to love can be traced toward the end
of 1838. Sophia drew a sketch of Ilbrahim, which appeared as a
frontispiece to a new edition of "The Gentle Boy." The new edition, too, was dedicated to "Miss Sophia A. Peabody" and contained a preface which complimented her upon the drawing,
saying, "Whatever of beauty and of pathos the author had con-
ceived, but could not shadow forth in language, has been caught
and embodied in the few and simple lines of this sketch." Sophia
responded with a continuation of her Cuban Journal,* dated
December 6, 1838, and the following dedicatory introduction:

To Nath¹ Hawthorne Esqʳ
Whose commendation & regard
alone give value to the previous
Journal, this closing record
is inscribed by his true
and affectionate friend
"Sophie"

"Now does not that equal your Dedication?" she asked, "and sur-
pass it in being overshadowed by seclusion from the world—a
private testimony of friendship & deference from me to you, for
which the public is none the wiser?" She had made a sketch of
Hawthorne, too; it was beside her, she said, as she wrote these recollections of Cuba, and she wished the countenance would look
round at her. The recollections themselves consisted of dawns and
tropical vegetation, devoted native servants and their regal
Spanish masters, music and moonlight in Havana, and other
splendors—all rendered in delicate if slightly overwrought
description. Hawthorne's letters to Sophia show that they had
arrived at a complete understanding by the spring of 1839.

In January, 1839, Hawthorne was appointed to the office of

---

* The unpublished manuscript has been made available through the courtesy
of Manning Hawthorne.

measurer of salt and coal in the Boston Custom House—a position which he held for two years—at an annual salary of $1,500. It had been clear for a long while that he would have to eke out in some way the small income derived from his writing, and because of his friendly connections with men who were active in the Democratic party—with Bridge, Cilley, and Pierce, and with David Roberts, William B. Pike, and other Salem Democrats—he looked to a political appointment for financial aid. In 1837 Bridge and Pierce had made an unsuccessful attempt to secure Hawthorne's appointment as historiographer of Commodore Wilkes' exploring expedition to the South Seas. By 1839, when he was contemplating marriage to Sophia Peabody, the financial need was even more urgent. The biographical sketch of Cilley, which appeared in the *Democratic Review* in September, 1838, attracted favorable political notice and made the time opportune for a renewal of effort. The successful outcome was owing in part to Elizabeth Peabody's recommendation to George Bancroft, collector of customs at Boston.

Hawthorne wrote to Longfellow with a good deal of enthusiasm for his new prospects: "I have no reason to doubt my capacity to fulfill the duties, for I don't know what they are; but, as nearly as I can understand, I shall be a sort of Port-Admiral, and take command of vessels after they enter the harbor, and have control of their cargoes." He jokingly proposed a series of sketches, based on his new employment, with such titles as "Passages in the Life of a Custom-House Officer," "Scenes in the Dock," "Voyages at Anchor," "Nibblings of a Wharf-Rat," "Trials of a Tide-Waiter," "Romance of the Revenue Service," and "an ethical work in two volumes on the subject of Duties." He assured Longfellow that there was no pleasanter expectation connected with his change of residence than that of seeing him more often. But Hawthorne did not write any such sketches nor did he see Longfellow very often, for during his employment at the Boston Custom House he was occupied almost exclusively by the tasks of his office and the composition of beautiful letters to his fiancée. The letters are an ample source of biographical information between March, 1839, the date of the earliest extant letter, and July, 1842, when he and Sophia were married. For this period there are 102 surviving letters comprising approximately 70,000 words.

They are a rich and revealing record, though the reader must make some allowance for the hyperbole of love and the natural tendency of the lover to exalt his present bliss by contrasting his former misery. The loved one "positively has no faults." She is "too delicate and exquisitely wrought in heart, mind, and frame to dwell in this world." Her letters are a "heavenly language": "It is like one angel writing to another angel; but alas! the letter has miscarried, and has been delivered to a most unworthy mortal." His soul was formerly a dark cloud but it is now brightened by a beam of heavenly sunshine. Her influence humanizes and ennobles him and gives him a new faith:

Thou hast taught me that I have a heart. . . . Indeed, we are but shadows till the heart is touched. . . . Thou keepest my heart pure, and elevatest me above the world. Thou enablest me to interpret the riddle of life, and fillest me with faith in the unseen and better land, because thou leadest me thither continually. . . . It is a miracle worthy even of thee to have converted a life of shadows into the deepest truth by thy magic touch. . . . God gave you to me to be the salvation of my soul.

Hawthorne was intensely sincere; he was also deeply in love for the first time in his life, and one may reasonably doubt whether his former spiritual state was quite as desperate as these letters represent it.

But the love letters are by no means so deadly serious and solemn throughout. They are brightened by delicate fantasies. The gentle West Wind assumes the characteristics of his beloved and, armed with her angelic power, triumphs over the fiendlike East Wind. Some "broad-winged and magnificent butterflies" recently seen on Long Wharf, he tells Sophia, are "the lovely fantasies of your mind, which you send thither in search of me." He imagines that Sophia, his dove, has flown into the clouds, and when he attempts to launch himself in pursuit from the mast of a salt ship, he falls to the deck. The fantasy is more "Hawthornesque" when he speaks of a great ink blot which at the moment, on the writing paper before him, reflects his face in its mirror . The blot will have dried to a dull black when she receives the letter, but the "talisman" of her kiss on the page will cause his image to reappear.

The letters are also enlivened by badinage and mocking humor. He writes half a page of nonsense about Sophie Hawthorne's nose —"she hates so much to have it kissed." He pretends to be too busy to write: "Thou canst not expect that a man in eminent public station will have much time to devote to correspondence with a Dove. I will remember thee in the intervals of business, and love thee in all my leisure moments." He even pokes fun at the solitary chamber where fame was won. Pilgrims to that shrine in future generations, he tells her with mock eloquence, will exclaim:

There is the very bed in which he slumbered. . . . There is the washstand, at which this exalted personage cleansed himself from the stains of the earth and rendered his outward man a fitting exponent of the pure soul within. There is the dressing-glass, which often reflected that noble brow, those hyacinthine locks, that mouth bright with smiles or tremulous with feeling, that flashing or melting eye, that— in short, every item of the magnanimous phiz of this unexampled man! There is the pine table—there the old flag-bottomed chair—in which he sat, and at which he scribbled, during his agonies of inspiration! There is the old chest of drawers. . . . There is the closet. . . . There is the worn-out shoebrush. . . .

Hawthorne was capable of a healthy alternation of mood even when such serious matters as love and authorship were concerned. The burlesque of the sacred chamber deserves to be remembered as well as the more famous sentimental treatment of the same theme.

Worshipful, imaginative, and humorous are these letters of courtship. One other characteristic, and not the least important, their ardent passion, which was long obscured by Mrs. Hawthorne's deletions in the manuscripts, can now be fully shown.

Many passages, recently restored,* allude to the little intimacies of lovers. He has silently given himself to her while holding her in his arms. He has sheltered her in his arms against the hateful East Wind and rendered her "invulnerable with kisses." His heart is "thirsty" for her kisses; "they are the dew which should restore its freshness every night." He has felt deep peace when her head was on his bosom and when his head was on hers. Other passages express a growing desire for the consummation of their love. He is lonely and cold in bed. "What a cold night this is going to be!" he exclaims in the midst of a Salem winter. "How I am to keep warm unless you nestle close, close into my bosom, I do not by any means understand. Not but what I have clothes enough on my mattress, but a husband cannot be comfortably warm without his wife." And again he writes from his bachelor couch: "Dearest, my heart yearns for thee mightily, but it is a joyful yearning that I feel . . . now and continually. My desire is full of warmth and hope; and though now I press my arms to my bosom and find thee not within them, yet I know that thou art destined there to be, and there to have thy abiding place."

Sophia to Hawthorne was quite obviously a woman as well as an angel. His physical nature could not be satisfied by soul food alone. The earthly elements were necessary to balance and give substance to the heavenly. "You looked like a vision," he wrote, "with the width of the room between us—so spiritual that my human heart wanted to be assured that you had an earthly vesture on, and your warm kisses gave me that assurance." In the divine scheme of things, physical love might very well be only a rung on the ladder which leads to celestial affection, but Hawthorne was unwilling to think even of love in heaven as entirely divorced from physical elements: "Shall there be no holy kisses in the sky?"—he asked unbelievingly—"Shall I not still hold you in my arms when we are angels together?"

But it is too early in this narrative to translate Hawthorne to

* A fuller account is given in my article "Letters to Sophia," listed in the biographical sources, p. 268.

heaven. At the moment of writing the love protestations just quoted, he was still measurer of salt and coal at the Boston Custom House, and his letters to Sophia tell a good deal of the nature of his work and his reactions to it. There were long days of exposure to the elements—the heat of summer and the cold of winter—while he superintended the unloading of vessels and computed the duties on their cargoes. There were moments of amusement, when, "engaged all the forenoon in measuring twenty chaldrons of coal," he was diverted "by frequent brawls and amicable discussions with a crew of funny little Frenchmen from Acadie"; or of exhilaration, when he was conscious of the freshness of air unbreathed in advance by the inhabitants of the city, and of the beauty of ships bounding over the waves "while a sheet of foam broke out around them"; or of creative stimulus, when he observed "a little Mediterranean boy from Malaga, who was not more than ten or eleven years old, but already a citizen of the world, and seemed to be just as gay and contented on the deck of a Yankee coal-vessel as he could be while playing beside his mother's door." There was satisfaction, too, in assuring himself that certain practical and social benefits would accrue to him from this kind of employment: "From henceforth forever," he declared, "I shall be entitled to call the sons of toil my brethren, and shall know how to sympathize with them, seeing that I, likewise, have risen at the dawn, and borne the fervor of the mid-day sun, nor turned my heavy footsteps homeward till eventide. Years hence, perhaps, the experience that my heart is acquiring now will flow out in truth and wisdom."

For the most part, however, his employment was a "grievous thraldom," from which he was eager to escape and which he endured only because of his pecuniary need. "I am convinced," he wrote in May, 1840, "that Christian's burthen consisted of coal; and no wonder he felt so much relieved when it fell off and rolled into the sepulchre. His load, however, at the utmost, could not have been more than a few bushels; whereas mine today was exactly one hundred and thirty-five chaldrons and seven tubs." Hawthorne continued to carry his burden until January 1, 1841, when he resigned. Presumably he could have continued longer, for the newly elected Whigs did not remove Bancroft and other Democratic incumbents in the Boston Custom House until the following November; but two years, he thought, were enough.

When Hawthorne left the Custom House, the air of Boston and its environs was electric with Transcendentalism. Emerson's *Nature*, the bible of the new philosophy, had appeared in 1836, and the *Dial*, its literary organ, had begun under the editorship of Margaret Fuller in 1840. The Peabody sisters were closely associated with the movement. Elizabeth Peabody's bookstore on West Street was a center of activity, dispensing both George Ripley's translations of modern European literature and shares in Ripley's utopian experiment, Brook Farm, which would embody plain living and high thinking in a communal economy. Hawthorne was a convert to neither the Transcendentalism nor the social philosophy despite a good deal of persuasive pressure from the Peabody ladies. He stood his ground as well as he could without being impolite or damaging the tender bond with Sophia. Not sharing her opinion (expressed some years earlier) that "Mr. Emerson is the greatest man—the most complete man—that ever lived," he declined the gift of a ticket to one of Emerson's lectures. "My evenings are very precious to me," he told Sophia, which was another way of saying that he would rather write to her than attend a lecture. He avoided not only Emerson, the priest, but Margaret Fuller, the priestess, declining an invitation to meet that lady at Bancroft's house: "Providence," he told his fiancée, "had given me some business to do, for which I was very thankful." (Sophia would secretly applaud his lack of interest in Margaret.) For a while he appeared more tractable in the matter of German, the study of which was a prerequisite for admission to the best Transcendentalist circles. But after attending a few sessions of a class at the Peabodys' and rummaging a bit in a dictionary borrowed from Longfellow, he gave up the struggle. "He said he wished he could read German," Sophia reported, "but could not take the trouble." As for socialism, Hawthorne once declared it to be his lifelong "creed" that "a man has no claim upon his fellow creatures, beyond bread and water, and a grave, unless he can win it by his own strength or skill." Moreover, he doubtless foresaw what he pointed out later, that, in its relation to society at large, Brook Farm would stand "in a position of new hostility rather than new brotherhood." But despite his lack of sympathy with the guiding spirits of Brook Farm and their ideology, Hawthorne joined the community in April, 1841, investing $1,000 of his hard-earned savings in the joint stock of the enterprise. His reason for so doing was the hope that membership in Brook Farm would provide the means of supporting a wife. His engagement had been protracted for more than two years and there was still no adequate financial basis for marriage. Believing that the community might be the solution of his problem, he wrote to Sophia on April 13: "Think that I am gone before to prepare a home for my Dove, and will return for her, all in good time." He liked to visualize their enchanting life together at West Roxbury. "There is a brook," he wrote on April 16, "so near the house that we shall be able to hear its ripple in the summer evenings, and whenever we lie awake in the summer nights." Hawthorne continued to view the prospect hopefully for several months, but by August 22 he was questioning the practicality of their idyllic plan. He was exhausted at the end of each day's labor, and besides, the community appeared not to be a financial success. "Thou and I must form other plans for ourselves," he wrote to Sophia, "for I can see few or no signs that Providence purposes to give us a home here. I am weary, weary, thrice weary of waiting so many ages. Yet what can be done? Whatever may be thy husband's gifts, he has not hitherto shown a single one that may avail to gather gold."

After a brief visit to Salem in September, Hawthorne returned to the community, not as one of Ripley's farmhands—the position hitherto held—but as a man of leisure, a "boarder." The change would enable him, he told Sophia on September 22, to "see these people and their enterprise under a new point of view, and perhaps . . . to determine whether thou and I have any call to cast in our lot among them." He would devote his time to writing instead of ploughing. But he soon discovered that the lack of perfect seclusion, which he had always required for creative work, was an insuperable obstacle. Unwilling to resume ploughing and unable to write, he abandoned in November an enterprise which appeared financially unsound and was ill adapted to his needs. "It is my opinion," he declared, "that a man's soul may be buried and perish under a dung-heap or in a furrow of the field just as well as under a pile of money." Even the Custom House "was not such a thraldom and weariness," and he was again reminded of Christian's burden.

Aside from his own *Blithedale Romance*, the literary classics of Brook Farm are the letters which Hawthorne wrote there. Epistolary literature contains nothing more delightful for picturesqueness and humor than his accounts of the "transcendental heifer, belonging to Miss Margaret Fuller"; the hay chopping, which he performed with such "righteous vehemence" that he broke the machine; his farmer's costume; his labor in the inexhaustible manure pile, euphemistically styled the "gold mine"; and many other subjects pertaining to the community and his share in its life. Brook Farm lives today chiefly in these Bucolics and Georgics of Hawthorne. His experiences there were real enough while they lasted, but after his departure from the farm they took on an air of unreality. "The real Me," he said, "was never an associate of the community; there has been a spectral Appearance there, sounding the horn at day-break, and milking the cows, and hoeing potatoes, and raking hay, toiling and sweating in the sun, and doing me the honor to assume my name"—so out of character seemed this episode in his life.

The marriage of Hawthorne and Sophia had to be still longer deferred. It is not surprising that a lover of normal passions should have become restive. For an unconscionably long while he had sublimated his desire in literary fantasies or contented himself perforce with chaste embraces. "We have left expression," he wrote frankly in January, 1842, "at least, such expression as can be achieved with pen and ink, far behind us. Even the spoken word has long been inadequate. Looks—pressures of the lips and hands—the touch of bosom to bosom—these are a better language; but, bye-and-bye, our spirits will demand some more adequate expression even than these." Marriage had become a necessity, whether with or without money. Being a literary artist by inner compulsion, Hawthorne resolved to return to his art and to rely upon it for financial support. Since the only opportunity for remuneration still was, or appeared to be, the magazines, he went to Albany in March, 1842, to see O'Sullivan, editor of the *Democratic Review*, with whom he presumably reached an understanding as to future contributions to that periodical and the rate of pay. Although Hawthorne had ample reason from his past experience to be dubious of the income derived from the magazines, his conference with O'Sullivan must have been reassuring up to a point—the more readily so because he wanted to be reassured. He returned from Albany resolved to make the venture.

In June Hawthorne told his mother and sisters of his approaching marriage. It is a curious instance of New England reticence that this should have been their first intimation of the sort from him. Elizabeth Hawthorne wrote Sophia a stiffish note beginning "Your approaching union with my brother makes it incumbent upon me to offer you the assurances of my sincere desire for your mutual happiness" and continuing with censure of her brother for "keeping us so long in ignorance of this affair." But matters were not as difficult as Elizabeth's letter would suggest, for Hawthorne assured Sophia on June 9, "Our mother had seen how things were, a long time ago. At first, her heart was troubled . . . but gradually and quietly God has taught her that all is good; and so, thou dearest wife, we shall have her fullest blessing and concurrence. My sisters, too, begin to sympathize as they ought, and all is well. God be praised!" The Old Manse in Concord, lately made available by the death of the venerable Ezra Ripley, D.D., was rented for an indefinite term. The Rev. James Freeman Clarke was engaged to perform the marriage ceremony. Margaret Fuller wrote a letter of congratulation to Sophia, saying, "If ever I saw a man who combined delicate tenderness to understand the heart of a woman, with quiet depth and manliness enough to satisfy her, it is Mr. Hawthorne." Emerson reported that the garden at the Old Manse made fine progress. Everything, in short, was in readiness, but the tension was almost too much for Sophia. Her health, always precarious, trembled in the balance, and a week's postponement of the marriage seemed advisable. Hawthorne resolved to be patient, offering, if need be, to go to the Old Manse and live there alone until his bride should be ready. In the urgency of his desire he consented to the limited use (short of being put to sleep) of the "magnetic" or hypnotic treatment of Sophia's headache, though he had previously been adamant in his objection to "magnetic miracles" as a violation of the sacredness of the individual; they were, he said, an "intrusion into the holy of holies." If the therapy so objectionable to Hawthorne was employed, it was reasonably successful, for Sophia recovered sufficiently to be married, at the house of her parents, number 13 West Street, Boston, on July 9, 1842. Immediately after the ceremony Hawthorne and his bride rode in a carriage out to Concord. There was a thunderstorm in the course of the journey, and Hawthorne remarked facetiously that the thundering sound came from cannon announcing their approach.

The life of the newly married pair at the Old Manse is the classic of American marital idyls. It is amply recorded in the Old Manse journal, in the writing of which—as Julian Hawthorne expressed it—"first one and then the other held the pen in lovely strophe and antistrophe." Sophia's health improved. Hawthorne had been sure all along that he could impart a portion of his own physical vigor. In an early letter he had enjoined upon her, "Partake of my health and strength, my beloved. Are they not your own, as well as mine?" His confidence was justified by the event despite Sophia's lapses into nervous debility. Years later he generalized about American women on the basis of his own marital experience: "Slight as they look," he said, "they always prove themselves sufficient for the whole purpose of life."

The happiness of husband and wife was as nearly perfect as human limitations permit. Sophia's portion of the Old Manse journal describes the rapture of the first summer in the following lyrical vein:

We penetrated the pleasant gloom & sat down upon the carpet of dried pine leaves. Then I clasped him in my arms in the lovely shade, & we laid down a few moments on the bosom of dear mother earth. Oh how sweet it was! There was a very slight diamond shower without any thunder or lightning & we were happiest. We walked through the forest, & came forth into an open space, whence a fair broad landscape could be seen, our old Manse holding a respectable place in the plain, the river opening its blue eyes here & there, & waving, mountainous ridges closing in the horizon. There we plucked whortleberries & then sat down. There was no wind & the stillness was profound. There seemed no movement in the world but that of our pulses.

And in the following spring she wrote in even greater ecstasy:

My heart is so full—it rises to so high a mark—it overflows so bountifully, that were there not another heart to receive my boundless love, I should feel sad & aimless. Oh lovely God! I thank thee that I can rush into my sweet husband with all my many waters, & sing & thunder with all my waves in the vast expanse of his comprehensive bosom. How I exult there—how I foam & sparkle in the sun of his love—how I wish for no broader region, because I have as yet found no limit to this. I myself am Spring with all its birds, its rivers, its buds, singing, rushing, blooming in his arms. I feel new as the earth which is just born again. I rejoice that I am, because I am his, wholly, unreservedly his. Therefore is my life beautiful & gracious. Therefore is the world pleasant as roses.

Hawthorne's journal was objective and restrained, with here and there a passage revealing his happiness. The following entry was written on the first anniversary of their marriage:

Life now heaves and swells beneath me like a brim-full ocean; and the endeavor to comprise any portion of it in words is like trying to dip up the ocean in a goblet. We never were so happy as now—never such wide capacity for happiness, yet overflowing with all that the day and every moment brings to us. Methinks this birthday of our married life is like a cape, which we have now doubled, and find a more infinite ocean of love stretching out before us. God bless us and keep us; for there is something more awful in happiness than in sorrow—the latter being earthly and finite, the former composed of the texture and substance of eternity, so that spirits still embodied may well tremble at it.

The routine at the Old Manse was comparatively simple. Hawthorne was busy mornings in his study (except in the summer months) writing for the magazines. After dinner, which came in the early afternoon, he walked to the village post office, and on his return stopped for an hour in the reading room of the Athenaeum. After supper, or tea, Hawthorne and Sophia sat together in his study while he read aloud from the English classics, beginning with Shakespeare and Milton. For exercise Hawthorne hoed vegetables in the summer and shoveled snow and chopped wood in the winter, while his wife marveled that a "seraph" could perform such mundane tasks. He liked the swimming and fishing, the boating and skating afforded by the Concord River, which flowed near by. There was always abundant walking. When conditions permitted, Sophia accompanied him on rambles through the surrounding woods and meadows.

The life of the Hawthornes at the Old Manse has been called a solitude *à deux;* actually it was surprisingly hospitable. Louisa Hawthorne and the members of Sophia's family paid extended visits. At one time or another George Hillard and his wife, with whom Hawthorne had lived while employed in the Boston Custom House, were week-end guests, as were George Bradford, a Brook Farm associate, David Roberts, a Salem friend of Hawthorne's whom his wife found uninteresting, and Anna and Sarah Shaw, friends of Sophia's whom Hawthorne received with great gallantry. Emerson, Thoreau, and Ellery Channing were frequent callers. Other visitors (for longer or shorter stays) were Margaret Fuller, Elizabeth Hoar, Sam Ward, the Rev. Barzillai Frost, Horatio Bridge, H. L. Conolly, Mr. and Mrs. Samuel Gridley Howe, Frank Farley, George W. Curtis, Stephen Longfellow, and Franklin Pierce—and more besides. Indeed, a guest book (if one had been kept and were extant) would suggest the necessity of a writer's barricading himself in his study if he hoped to meet his engagements with the magazines. Not that Hawthorne was forced to resort to any such measure—but the Old Manse was a sufficiently social place.

With the literary men of Concord Hawthorne was on friendly, though not intimate, terms. Not being a Transcendentalist, he was not in agreement with the tenets of the Concord School. He could hardly subscribe to Emerson's opinion that Margaret Fuller was "the greatest woman of ancient or modern times"; Hawthorne later decided that "she had stuck herself full of borrowed qualities." Channing, another protégé of Emerson's, seemed to him "an original in a small way" and likely to become "more dull and commonplace than even those who keep the ordinary pathway of life." Alcott he called "a great mystic innovator": "There is the spirit of a system in him," he thought, "but not the body of it." And as for Emerson himself, while admiring him, he said, "as a poet of deep beauty and austere tenderness," he "sought nothing from him as a philosopher." Hawthorne had a higher regard for Thoreau than for the others and expressed regret at Thoreau's leaving Concord in 1843. "On my own account," he wrote in his journal, "I should like to have him remain here, he being one of the few persons, I think, with whom to hold intercourse is like hearing the wind among the boughs of a forest-tree; and with all this wild freedom, there is high and classic cultivation in him too." Years later Hawthorne said that while Thoreau was "not an agreeable person" his books were "the work of a true man and full of true thought."

An early convert to Concord Transcendentalism, Sophia was at first inclined to look askance at her husband's critical view of its exemplars. But Hawthorne enjoyed an easy victory on this score, as well as on all other scores where Sophia was concerned, for in November, 1843, she wrote of her husband's insight and philosophical position: "It is so refreshing to find one person without theories of any kind, without party or sectarian tendency. . . .

He does not meddle with Truth & it lays upon him like the blessed sunshine, full & broad. . . . When men nail platforms over the depths of soul, we cannot get farther than the platform. But to be drawn forever into lower deeps, seeing only space beyond space, this is the true enchantment."

Though critical of the Concord illuminati, Hawthorne was by no means ungracious to them nor did he fail to enjoy their society. There were pleasant times with Emerson, as when he came "with a sunbeam in his face" and they talked about Margaret Fuller, Ellery Channing, Henry Thoreau, and Charles King Newcomb, or when he took Hawthorne on a walking tour of two days to the Shaker community at Harvard, Massachusetts. There were fishing trips with Channing, when Hawthorne enjoyed "the evanescent spray" of Ellery's talk. There were tramps and boating excursions with Thoreau, who opened up fascinating glimpses into the secrets of flora and fauna and thereby quickened Hawthorne's appreciation of nature. There was good talk with Margaret Fuller, Hawthorne reported, about "Autumn, the pleasures of getting lost in the woods, crows, the experiences of early childhood, the sight of mountains from a distance and the view from their summits." (The topics sound a little professional, as if the lady were rehearsing for one of her "Conversations.") Hawthorne could enjoy Margaret's company and her ideas without feeling, as some moderns have supposed, a sexual interest: such a supposition is incompatible with his marital happiness.

The Old Manse was paradise, and Hawthorne and Sophia were the new Adam and Eve. Or this would have been the case had there not been such unpleasant realities as house rent and grocer's bills. Hawthorne was embarrassed by the difficulty of meeting his financial obligations. "The Magazine people do not pay their debts," he wrote in his journal March 31, 1843, "so that we taste some of the inconveniences of poverty, and the mortification— only temporary, however—of owing money, with empty pockets. It is an annoyance; not a Trouble." But the situation steadily grew worse. Hawthorne kept on writing for the magazines, and the editors continued to be delinquent in their payments. The receipt of $100 from O'Sullivan on December 18, 1843, was sufficiently surprising and important to be recorded by Sophia in a letter to her mother. Even if the sums due had been paid fully and promptly, the total amount would not have been a living wage. "Drowne's Wooden Image," for example, went to *Godey's* for $25, and Hawthorne could hardly turn out more than ten or twelve such pieces in a year. The birth of their first child—named Una after Spenser's heroine—in March, 1844, brought joy to the parents but increased their financial anxiety.

A political appointment, once more, seemed to be the only means of making a living. Hawthorne hoped that the Democrats would be returned to power and, despite his uncongenial experience at the Boston Custom House, that he might obtain a lucrative post. Upon the election of Polk in November, 1844, Hawthorne wrote to his wife from Salem, where he was in conference with his political friends, "We have a right to expect that our difficulties will vanish in the course of a few months." But the wheels of the political machine turned slowly. Although powerful allies were active in his behalf—Bridge, now an officer in the Navy; O'Sullivan, editor of the chief magazine of the party; and Pierce, now United States Senator—the needed appointment was delayed until April, 1846.

Meanwhile, in the fall of 1845, the owner of the Old Manse, Samuel Ripley, son of the late clergyman, decided to take over the house for his own use. Carpenters were soon busy about the place making renovations. The Hawthornes left Concord in October, accommodations having been arranged for in the house of his mother at Salem. The departure was the end of a beautiful epoch. In writing at Salem several months later the famous autobiographical essay entitled "The Old Manse," Hawthorne remembered with tender nostalgia "the river, with its delightful solitudes, and the avenue, the garden, and the orchard, and especially the dear Old Manse, with the little study on its western side, and the sunshine glimmering through the willow branches."

Between 1837, the year of the *Twice-Told Tales*, and 1846, when *Mosses from an Old Manse* appeared, Hawthorne brought out three volumes: *Grandfather's Chair* (1841), a second edition of the *Twice-Told Tales* (1842), and the *Journal of an African Cruiser* (1845), edited from the manuscripts of Horatio Bridge.

In 1838 Hawthorne proposed to Longfellow that they collaborate in writing stories for children, saying that he believed such a project would prove remunerative. As Longfellow did not fall in with the plan, Hawthorne proceeded to try his hand independently. The result was *Grandfather's Chair*, a juvenile history of New England through the Revolution. Written while he was at the Boston Custom House, it was the kind of book which he could do with comparative ease and which did not require the full concentration of his powers.

The new edition of the *Twice-Told Tales* was in two volumes. Volume I reprinted the 1837 edition of eighteen titles and added one title which had appeared since that date. Volume II consisted of twenty titles, none of which had been collected before. Fourteen of these had appeared in magazines since the publication of the first edition; six had appeared before 1837 and had been passed over by the author when he made up his first collection. It is curious to find in the latter group such general favorites as "Endicott and the Red Cross" and "The Ambitious Guest." The publisher was James Monroe of Boston.

The *African Cruiser* was a journalistic task which Hawthorne undertook partly to gratify Bridge, partly to please himself, and partly to make a little money. As Volume I in E. A. Duyckinck's new "Library of American Books," published by Wiley and Putnam of New York, it sold well, going into a second edition within a few months. Hawthorne's share of the royalty is not known but Bridge can be depended upon to have made a generous division. The book consisted of Bridge's observations along the west coast of Africa while he was purser on an American frigate. Of the editorial labor Hawthorne wrote Duyckinck, "I have re-modelled the style, where it seemed necessary, and have developed

Bridge's ideas, where he failed to do it himself, and have put on occasional patches of sentimental embroidery—at the same time avoiding to tamper with his facts, or to change the tenor of his observations upon them."

In 1846 *Mosses from an Old Manse*, Hawthorne's third collection of tales, appeared in two volumes in the series so auspiciously inaugurated by the *African Cruiser*. The collection contained twenty-three pieces, seventeen of which were written at the Old Manse. Four antedated 1837. Among these were two tales— "Roger Malvin's Burial" and "Young Goodman Brown"—which most readers today would rank near the top of his productions in this kind and which Hawthorne had twice passed over in making collections of his work. Possibly he had feared that the unrelieved gloom of these stories would damage the reception of the earlier volumes, or possibly his judgment was curiously fallible where the relative worth of his own writings was concerned.

Hawthorne's reputation—though not his income—grew steadily in the 1840's. The second edition of the *Twice-Told Tales* evoked praise (to name a few examples) from the faithful Longfellow in the *North American*, from Orestes A. Brownson in the *Boston Quarterly*, from E. A. Duyckinck in *Arcturus*, and from Poe in *Graham's*. Poe's review, which was to become the *locus classicus* of his rationale of the short tale, is easily the most notable. "Mr. Hawthorne's distinctive trait," Poe said, "is invention, creation, imagination, originality—a trait which, in the literature of fiction, is positively worth all the rest. . . . Mr. Hawthorne is original at *all* points." The magazine pieces appearing during 1843–44 attracted a good deal of attention—especially "The Celestial Railroad," which was twice reprinted in pamphlet form. Poe invited Hawthorne to contribute to the *Stylus*, a periodical which unfortunately never came into being. Bryant called Hawthorne's English "the best written on either side of the Atlantic."

Mosses from an Old Manse was elaborately praised by Chorley in the London *Athenaeum*, by C. W. Webber in the *American Whig Review*, and by others. But the praise did not produce large sales. There seemed to be a good deal of truth in Poe's remark that Hawthorne was "the example, *par excellence*, in the country of the privately-admired and publicly-unappreciated man of genius." Poe's own attitude toward Hawthorne changed radically after his earlier critique. Reviewing the *Mosses* in *Godey's* for November, 1847, Poe now declared that Hawthorne was "peculiar and *not* original" and that he was "infinitely too fond of allegory." He concluded the article with this forthright advice: "Let him mend his pen, get a bottle of visible ink, come out from the Old Manse, cut Mr. Alcott, hang (if possible) the editor of 'The Dial,' and throw out of the window to the pigs all his odd numbers of 'The North American Review.' "

Poe grossly misjudged Hawthorne when he identified him with Alcott and the *Dial* or with the *North American*, and his reversal of opinion seems inconsistent. But he obviously felt that Hawthorne's work had deteriorated during the years at the Old Manse. Melville later felt the same thing. Discovering the *Twice-Told Tales* after having extravagantly praised the *Mosses*, he told Duyckinck that the "earlier vintage far exceeded" the later. Hawthorne himself may have had a sense of deterioration, for in the introductory essay to the *Mosses* he spoke of the volumes as the last collection of tales which he intended to publish. "Unless I could do better," he said, "I have done enough in this kind." If there was a falling off, was it because of his "satisfied heart," to which he attributed his unusually good health at the Old Manse, or because of too large an infusion of another's mind and spirit? Elizabeth Hawthorne feared that "the mingling of another mind" would "spoil the flavor of his genius," and believed that discontent was a more effective source of literary inspiration to her brother than happiness.

But whatever the causes in Hawthorne's creative life, most readers will agree with Poe and Melville in giving a higher rank, in general, to the earlier work. There is an artificiality in some of the later pieces. "The Gentle Boy" (1832) is authentic New England history and therefore credible, while "Rappaccini's Daughter" (1844) is fantasy and therefore less easy to accept. Likewise "Young Goodman Brown" (1835) is deeply imbedded in New England folklore, while "Earth's Holocaust" (1844) is an arbitrary fabrication. Still more artificial and farther removed from his New England world are pieces like "The Christmas Banquet" and "The Hall of Fantasy." Poe could have objected to the artifice and thinness of the later allegories more properly than to allegory per se.

But despite Poe's disapproval of them, there is something to be said for the allegories written at the Old Manse. Though possibly less convincing artistically than some of the earlier compositions, they reflect a growing awareness of the contemporary world and an increasing disposition to deal critically with the social problems of the author's own time. The atmosphere of Concord was more contemporaneous than that of Salem. On many accounts a man after marriage is less likely to be indifferent to the present state of the world. And the *Democratic Review,* in which most of his writings during these years appeared and which in the preface to "Rappaccini's Daughter" he praised for its "defense of popular rights," undoubtedly helped to draw Hawthorne into the current of social discussion.

A number of social questions were touched on cursorily but pointedly in the sketches composed at the Old Manse. "The New Adam and Eve" protested against "the world's artificial system" as seen in a modern city. The author pointed out the ugliness and deformity of city blocks, the worldliness of the metropolitan church, the perversion of justice in the courts in order that the wealthy might be favored, the shrewd practices of the capitalists, the growing economic inequality in American society. He condemned the desire for gold as "the mainspring, the life, the very essence of the system that had wrought itself into the vitals of mankind and choked their original nature in its deadly gripe." That a few should be "rolling in luxury, while the multitude was toiling for scanty food" he called a "great and miserable fact." "The New Adam and Eve" shows a widening social outlook.

In "The Procession of Life" the author examined the class system prevalent in modern society and the leveling forces which make for democracy. Physical disease is a leveling force, "embracing high and low, and making the king a brother of the clown." Intellectual gifts are another: a "silkgowned professor of languages" (like Longfellow) takes the arm of a "sturdy blacksmith" (like Elihu Burritt, the learned blacksmith) and is honored by the association. Sorrow and guilt are universal levelers. But love is, or ought to be, the greatest of all forces working for human brotherhood. The author paid a tribute to the "apostles of humanity" whose labors reached to "the prison, the insane asylum, the squalid chamber of the almshouse, the manufactory where the demon of machinery annihilates the human soul, the cotton field where God's image becomes a beast of burden, and every other scene where man wrongs or neglects his brother."

Hawthorne was clearly not indifferent to the world or its social improvement. But he doubted the permanence of the benefits conferred by many reforms, bringing forward in "Earth's Holocaust" the Puritan argument that the purification of individual souls is a necessary condition of a better world. The reformers themselves, moreover, were too often little better than crackpots and monomaniacs. "Here were men," he said in "The Hall of Fantasy," "whose faith had embodied itself in the form of a potato, and others whose long beards had a deep spiritual significance. Here was the abolitionist, brandishing his one idea like an iron flail." The juxtaposition of the abolitionist with Shakers and vegetarians must have been shocking to some, but from Hawthorne's point of view the abolitionist, like the others, made the mistake of concentrating on only one aspect of the problem, and that aspect a superficial one.

He was skeptical, too, of Concord Platonism because, for one thing (he seemed to see this clearly in the light of his own new happiness), it did less than justice to the solid satisfactions of this life. While his Transcendentalist neighbors regarded earthly joys as imperfect means to perfect ends, Hawthorne in "The Hall of Fantasy" dwelt upon them as legitimate ends in themselves:

The fragrance of flowers [he wrote] and of new-mown hay; the genial warmth of sunshine and the beauty of a sunset among clouds; the comfort and cheerful glow of the fireside; the deliciousness of fruits and of all good cheer; the magnificence of mountains and seas and cataracts, and the softer charm of rural scenery; even the fast falling snow and the gray atmosphere through which it descends . . . the country frolics; the homely humor; the broad, open-mouthed roar of laughter, in which body and soul conjoin so heartily! I fear that no other world can show us anything just like this.

Hawthorne was obviously unwilling to embrace the Platonism of Emerson and Alcott; he was too much in love with this world to be eager, as he put it, to pass into "a state in which the Idea shall be all in all."

The years from 1837 to 1845 greatly enriched Hawthorne's experience of life. The summers at Augusta and North Adams, the two years in the Boston Custom House, and the six or seven months at Brook Farm enlarged his knowledge of the world and of men. His courtship and marriage taught him all that a passionate, devoted love can teach. He experienced the joys and trials of parenthood; he felt (all the more acutely because of the pinch of poverty) the responsibilities belonging to the head of a family; he profited, like other men, from what Francis Bacon called "the discipline of humanity." The Concord scene afforded new experiences, and delightful ones, in husbandry and nature lore. Thoreau gave him eyes for the minutiae of field, stream, and forest. Emerson and Channing were stimulating and none the less so when they called forth opposing thoughts and attitudes.

If some of the tales and sketches composed in the Old Manse study seem less successful as works of art than many pieces written during the Salem years, they often reflect a growing concern for the state of the world. And if at the end of the period Hawthorne had still failed to achieve a financial success in his chosen career as writer, the blame must be placed not so much on the writer himself as on the current state of letters in America. Hawthorne's subsequent work was to succeed better financially and reflect more fully the rich experience of these years.

CHAPTER V

SALEM AND THE SCARLET LETTER, *1846–1850*

As early as March, 1843, Hawthorne spoke of the "prospects of official station and emolument, which would do away with the necessity of writing for bread." His friends had been active in his behalf on two previous occasions: in 1837 they had tried unsuccessfully to have him named historian of the expedition to the South Seas, and in 1839 they had secured his appointment as measurer in the Boston Custom House, having brought him forward as "the biographer of Cilley." Despite the fact that the incumbency of the Whigs made success unlikely, activities were resumed in 1843 after Tyler had formed a coalition with the Calhoun Democrats. O'Sullivan urged Hawthorne's appointment as postmaster of Salem in an eloquent letter to Henry A. Wise, one of Tyler's chief supporters. The letter argued that it was the duty of the government to give patronage to distinguished writers regardless of their party affiliation, and concluded with an account of Hawthorne's connection with the late Jonathan Cilley —a not too delicate hint that Wise, who had transmitted the challenge of William J. Graves (in a duel with whom Cilley had been killed), should be eager to make the small amends of a kindness to Cilley's friend. But the appeal was fruitless. It was not until after the election of Polk in the autumn of the following year that Hawthorne's supporters began in earnest to roll up the snowball of political influence.

Aside from the terrific competition for offices, the chief obstacle to success was the fact that Hawthorne had not been an active party man. Concord Democrats reported that he had not even voted during his residence in their town, and Seth Thomas passed the report on to George Bancroft, Polk's Secretary of the Navy and arbiter of patronage in New England. But O'Sullivan was indefatigable and resolute. He told Bancroft in April, 1845, that

Hawthorne was "in a state of extreme anxiety, not to say distress." An appointment, he said, would reflect "eminent credit" on the administration, and he suggested a position at the Watertown Arsenal. In May he wrote, "Hawthorne is dying of starvation and I, of anxious suspense on his behalf," and went on to mention the stewardship of Chelsea Hospital. O'Sullivan continued to bombard Bancroft with letters through the summer and fall. Bancroft proposed a Washington clerkship or a position on Santa Rosa Island, each of which O'Sullivan peremptorily rejected. "Some place of independent position, and no great amount of clerical drudgery, somewhere near Boston," he told Bancroft, "is what he ought to have." "The honor of the country and my Party," O'Sullivan passionately declared, "I hold deeply compromised by the cruel wrong and shame of neglecting such a man." Bancroft then offered a clerkship at the Charlestown Navy Yard, but Hawthorne himself rejected this. Bancroft was prolific in suggestions (another one being the position of naval storekeeper at Portsmouth), but he seemed unable to produce what Hawthorne wanted—a good post at Salem—possibly because he was afraid of the political situation there and possibly because he had, despite his protestations of friendship, no real desire to help Hawthorne. Sophia and her husband, at any rate, distrusted him. "Mr. Bancroft," Sophia had written upon first meeting him in 1839, "is not a man but a Gnome. I should never wish to be within three feet of him. I cannot express how disagreeable his effect was & I had no intention of not being pleased with him beforehand. It was my instinct to be repelled." In the private language of the Old Manse Bancroft was known by the Spenserian name, the "Blatant Beast."

Meanwhile Pierce and Bridge had swung into action. "If Hawthorne is not provided for in some way," Pierce wrote Bancroft, "it will fill me with regret and I shall never cease to feel that a thing has been omitted that was due from *this* Administration." He urged the Salem postmastership, which could easily be made available, he said, by the removal of Browne, a Tyler appointee. Bridge's campaign was more astute and contributed most, Hawthorne believed, to ultimate success. In the summer of 1845 Bridge entertained in his bachelor quarters at the Portsmouth Navy Yard the New England Senators Pierce, Atherton, and Fairfield with their wives and the Hawthornes, his object being, he said in his *Personal Recollections,* "to bring Mr. and Mrs. Hawthorne into social relations with some of my influential friends and their wives." With the enlistment of the wives, one may be sure, the campaign rapidly gained momentum. In October Fairfield urged upon Bancroft and Polk the importance of action. In January, 1846, Charles Sumner implored Mrs. Bancroft to remind, and again remind, her husband of Hawthorne's need. Bancroft assured Sumner in reply that he had been "most perseveringly Hawthorne's friend." The fact was that the Salem Democrats were torn by dissension, and Bancroft, being a shrewd politician, was waiting for the local caucus to reach an agreement.

The delay seemed interminable to Hawthorne, who had brought his family to Salem in October, 1845, and taken quarters in his mother's house. He needed money so desperately that he borrowed $150 from Bridge, dunned Duyckinck repeatedly for his share of the royalty from the *African Cruiser,* and instructed his attorney, George Hillard, to sue Ripley for the $530 still due him from his investment in Brook Farm.* Hawthorne's financial anxiety was increased by his wife's pregnancy. "What a devil of a pickle I shall be in," he wrote Bridge in February, 1846, "if the baby should come and the office should not." To his wife during her absence in Boston, he wrote, "Providence must take our matters in hand very speedily." But adversity served only to strengthen the domestic ties and deepen the domestic affections. He was solicitous of Sophia's safety on the crowded ferryboat which she must take on the return journey: "Thy poor dear little big body," he joked, "is not to be trusted in such a tumult." "God bless thee, dearest!" he continued, "and blessed be our daughter, whom I love next to thee! and blessed be the child which thy heart is brooding over! It shall be welcome to me in poverty or

---

* Ripley, a utopian, thought the plaintiff was a hard man.

riches. . . . Wouldst thou wast safe home again, eating thy potatoes and glancing sideways at me with thy look of patient resignation."

The office finally came in April, but not until after George Hood of Lynn had reported to Bancroft (on March 6) that Hawthorne's appointment would "harmonize the schisms" in the ranks of the Salem Democrats, and Marcus Morton, long the Democratic standard-bearer of Massachusetts, had assured Bancroft that Hawthorne was the choice of the Essex organization. No matter how much pressure was brought to bear in Washington, local party members could not be ignored. The office, in the last analysis, depended more upon their consent than upon support in high places or grandiloquent phrases about the nation's obligation to men of letters. For several months preceding his appointment Hawthorne was in close touch with the Salem politicians and the ensuing success testifies to his skill. Most of the details have passed into the limbo of secret caucuses, but the following passage from his letter to Bridge on March 1 shows a knowing strategist at work:

If you could authorize me to communicate to a few persons here in Salem the intelligence contained in your penultimate letter, I might use it so as to induce them to signify their assent to Hoyt's appointment, as their second choice, in case Howard could not succeed; and this would probably be sufficient, as Bancroft is so evidently anxious in Hoyt's behalf. Otherwise, I am convinced that I must go into the Naval Office. If you are at liberty, and think it advisable, to take the above course, write me such a letter as may be shown to the Postmaster and one or two others, giving the intelligence anew, and without reference to your former letter, the reception of which, as it has been concealed so long, cannot now be acknowledged. Nothing need be said as to the authority on which you make your statements. If you consider yourself not authorized to do what I have here suggested, then I had rather you would not write at all, just at present; for my friends here bother me to death, whenever I am known to have received a letter either from you or O'Sullivan—and it is difficult to conceal it, the Postmaster being one of the junto. You may depend upon my discretion. I have grown considerable of a politician by the experience of the last few months.

On April 3, 1846, Polk signed Hawthorne's appointment as "Surveyor for the District of Salem and Beverly and Inspector of the Revenue for the Port of Salem." The salary was $1,200 per annum. The pinch of poverty would soon be eased if not entirely removed. Hawthorne's chief thought, however, in the hour of success was one of gratitude to those who had worked so tirelessly in his behalf. With pride and thankfulness he said to Bridge, "I have as true friends as any man."

The Salem *Advertiser* of April 22 announced that the new surveyor had been officially installed two days before. The work apparently was not too strenuous. Salem was a decaying port, much of its former commerce having been transferred to Boston and New York. The Custom House (like many government enterprises) employed more people than were absolutely necessary. Hawthorne spent some three hours of the forenoon in the surveyor's office, where he described himself as usually "pacing from corner to corner, or lounging on the long-legged stool, with his elbow on the desk, and his eyes wandering up and down the columns of the morning newspaper." But perhaps the autobiographical essay, "The Custom House," exaggerated somewhat the surveyor's idleness and the somnolence of the entire establishment. At least one appointee, Zachariah Burchmore, was efficient, and Hawthorne declared of himself that he was "as good a Surveyor as need be." As executive head of the Custom House, he was responsible for the conduct of subordinate officers and the collection of imposts. He signed the official documents and saw to it that his name was stamped, he said, "with a stencil and black paint on pepper-bags, and baskets of anatto and cigar boxes and bales of all kinds of dutiable merchandise," thereby certifying that the necessary duties had been paid. The merchandise so stamped, he reflected, became a "queer vehicle of fame."

He was moving in a world where his fame as a writer had

scarcely penetrated. Most Salem merchants and Custom House pensioners were ignorant of the *Twice-Told Tales* and the *Mosses from an Old Manse*. Such people, as a rule, knew Hawthorne only as the surveyor of the port. For the time being he had stepped out of his life as author and could enjoy new associates and experiences. He took great delight (he recorded in "The Custom House") in old General Miller, now collector of the port and erstwhile hero of Lundy's Lane, whose " 'I'll try, Sir' breathed the soul and spirit of New England hardihood"; in Burchmore, the clerk, whose expert attention to business gave him "a new idea of talent"; in the veteran shipmaster, who had marvelous gifts as a storyteller; in the venerable gourmand, whose chief disappointment in life had been a very promising goose which, after being cooked, proved too tough to eat. Hawthorne was proud of his ability to mix easily with men so far removed from a literary atmosphere; it seemed to him to indicate a versatility and balance which many writers lacked. The change from writer's study to surveyor's office, he thought, contributed to health of mind and breadth of experience. In "The Custom House" he contrasted his present way of life with earlier, more literary ways:

After my fellowship of toil and impracticable schemes with the dreamy brethren of Brook Farm; after living for three years within the subtle influence of an intellect like Emerson's; after those wild, free days on the Assabeth, indulging fantastic speculations, beside our fire of fallen boughs, with Ellery Channing; after talking with Thoreau about pine-trees and Indian relics, in his hermitage at Walden; after growing fastidious by sympathy with the classic refinement of Hillard's culture; after becoming imbued with poetic sentiment at Longfellow's hearth-stone,—it was time, at length, that I should exercise other faculties of my nature, and nourish myself with food for which I had hitherto had little appetite. Even the old Inspector [the gourmand mentioned above] was desirable, as a change of diet, to a man who had known Alcott.

If the Custom House was beneficially distracting, so was his domestic life, which became more and more engrossing during the years of the surveyorship. The devoted husband and father found much at home to occupy his time and attention. Una, born in March, 1844, and Julian, born in June, 1846, not only evoked parental admiration but made practical demands as well. Sophia regretted, in a letter to her mother, that "the heaven-gifted seer should spend his life between the Custom House and the nursery." And to her husband she wrote in July, 1847: "Thou, beloved, oughtst not to be obliged to undergo the wear and tear of the nursery. It is contrary to thy nature and to thy mood. Thou wast born to muse and to be silent and through undisturbed dreams, to enlighten the world." It was not the first or the last attempt to re-create Hawthorne in the image of a romantic poet. But Hawthorne better understood himself and his relation to the world. In the "nursery" he was learning—as he plainly put it a few years later—that "when a man has taken upon himself to beget children, he has no longer any right to a life of his own." This was not said with bitterness or deprecation, for no man was ever more fully aware of the parental compensations.

Both parents wrote much about the children. Their attitudes, and hence their accounts, were complementary. Sophia was ecstatic: the children were unfallen angels to her. While loving and admiring them not a bit less, Hawthorne had a strong sense of fact and a strong sense of humor. Sophia often blinked at fact and was not amused by humor which appeared to be at the children's expense. After her husband's death, she inked out many passages in his letters and journals which dealt honestly or humorously with Una and Julian. But whatever her apprehensions for the opinion of posterity may later have been, passages like the following would mislead no intelligent reader to suppose that their author was other than a very human and devoted father:

Una has already smiled once, on the sixteenth morning of her existence. I was inclined to attribute it to wind, which sometimes produces a sardonic grin; but her mother, who was the sole witness of the phenomenon, persists that it was a veritable smile out of the child's mouth and eyes.

Una is a dear little thing in spite of her snub-nose and red hair.

Mamma says Julian likes the best book in the house—I say, he likes the book that is kept from him.

The children seem very good and beautiful at this distance [written from New York].

During Una's babyhood, Hawthorne refrained from keeping a journal of her life: "not because there is not much to record," he explained to a friend, "but because I seem to comprehend and feel it better while it remains unwritten. It would be dangerous to meddle with it." But in 1848, when Una was four and Julian two, he began a journal which continued at intervals for more than a year. If the danger which Hawthorne sensed in such an undertaking lay in the conflict between the artist and the parent— the one seeing clearly and the other with blurred vision—the danger was put aside and the conflict resolved through the mastery of the artist, for the journal shows an eye for the ludicrous and unlovely as well as the amiable and beautiful in the children's behavior. On Sundays or on afternoons after his return from the Custom House, Hawthorne sat in the midst of the domestic activities and attempted to record the ever-changing manifestations of the two children. Despite a rapid and facile pen, he could not catch everything: "Una has just come in," he wrote at the very beginning, "and puts me so far behind my subject that I am almost tempted to give it up in despair." But no other writer, perhaps, has succeeded so well in describing the protean behavior of children at play—the rompings and quarrels, the childish babble, the dramatic impersonations. The record is equally objective, whether the subject is conventionally beautiful: "Una's auburn curls come down over her shoulders with extreme grace; and as to her delicate little phiz, its spirit, grace, and sensibility elude the pen that would describe them," or unlovely and absurd: "I went to take a walk, leaving Una preparing for bed, and running about the room in her chemise, which does not come down far enough to serve the purpose of fig-leaf. Never were seen such contortions and attitudinizing—prostrating herself on all-fours, and thrusting up her little bum as a spectacle to men and angels, being among the least grotesque." Hawthorne was happy with his children—entering into their games, or improvising stories, or holding one or the other on his knee while the pen hurried forward.

He was happy, too, with his wife. For him marital love did not diminish with the coming of children and the passing of years but grew steadily deeper and stronger. When Sophia took the children for extended visits with the Peabodys in Boston or with the Horace Manns in West Newton, the husband was utterly forlorn and miserable. "Never did I miss thee so much," he wrote to his wife on one of these occasions, "at bed and board, and in all other incidents of daily and nightly life, as during this separation. But for the idea of thee, my existence would be as cold and wintry as the weather is now, and with a cloudy gloom besides, instead of the dazzling sunshine. . . . The thought of going to bed is hateful to me; especially these polar nights, when my body shivers like my heart. Hast thou slept warm?" The season, however, was beside the point, for in summer he lamented "our great, lonesome bed, at night—the scene of so many blissful intercourses—now so solitary." And during still another separation he told Sophia how dependent he was upon his family for the well-being of body and soul: "I cannot bear the loneliness of the house. I need the sunshine of the children; even their little quarrels and naughtinesses would be a blessing to me. I need thee, above all, and find myself, at every absence, so much the less able to endure it. It is misery to go to bed without thee. Come home! Come home!" But despite his great need Hawthorne could take an unselfish view of the matter. He often urged his wife—under the circumstances, one of the greatest of heroisms—to remain longer in Boston where she could be near her favorite physician, or in West Newton where the children could continue to enjoy the benefits of the open country.

Like all tender husbands, he sympathized with the wife who was bound down by domestic cares. "After a woman has become a mother," he said, with a touch of pathos, "she may find rest in Heaven, but nowhere else." During a visit in the relatively affluent household of Horatio Bridge, recently married, he lamented his inability to provide similar comforts: "Thou didst much amiss," he wrote to Sophia, "to marry a husband who cannot keep thee like a lady, as Bridge does his wife, and as I should so delight to keep thee, doing only beautiful things, and reposing in luxurious chairs, and with servants to go and to come. Thou hast a hard lot in life; and so have I that witness it, and can do little or nothing to help thee." But Sophia was far from repining at her lot; on the contrary, she too was supremely happy in her marriage. "I am so happy," she told her mother in 1848, "that I require nothing more. No art nor beauty can excel my daily life, with such a husband and such children, the exponents of all art and beauty."

As engrossing in their respective ways as Hawthorne found the Custom House and the family circle, his life during these years extended itself somewhat beyond the confines of home and business.

As secretary of the Salem Lyceum, he devoted a good deal of time to the affairs of that institution. He may have felt a little awkward in this position, for a few years earlier he had glanced satirically, in "The Celestial Railroad," at the "innumerable lecturers, who diffuse such a various profundity, in all subjects of human or celestial science, that any man may acquire an omnigenous erudition without the trouble of even learning to read." He had no illusions as to the benefits of the New England Lyceum; but he went about the task, nevertheless, of securing lecturers, arranging for their entertainment, and attending to the publicity with commendable diligence. On one occasion he traveled to West Newton in a rainstorm to engage the services of Horace Mann. Other distinguished lecturers who appeared during Hawthorne's secretaryship were Webster, Sumner, Emerson, Thoreau, and Alcott. Emerson was entertained by the Hawthornes during his stay in Salem, as was Thoreau, who lectured

twice during the 1848-49 season. Sophia described Thoreau's discourses as "enchanting": they were, she told her mother,

such a revelation of nature in all its exquisite details of wood-thrushes,
squirrels, sunshine, mists and shadows, fresh, vernal odors, pine-tree
ocean melodies, that my ear rang with music and I seemed to have been
wandering through copse and dingle. Mr. Thoreau has risen above all
his arrogance of manner, and is as gentle, simple, ruddy, and meek as
all geniuses should be; and now his great blue eyes fairly outshine and
put into shade a nose which I once thought must make him uncomely
forever.

When applying to Thoreau in February, 1849, for a return engagement, Hawthorne wrote that a portion of the manuscript then
in the printer's hands (*A Week*), or the "Indian lecture" which
Thoreau had mentioned to him, or "a continuation of the Walden
experiment," or "indeed anything else," would be welcomed by
the audience. Hawthorne while in Salem seems to have been more
appreciative of the Concord men, and more willing to attend their
lectures, than while living in their midst. If he was so in fact, it was
an experience that often comes with the perspective of distance.

Hawthorne continued to see something of his old friends and to
maintain cordial relations with them. Bridge came up from the
Portsmouth Navy Yard and Hawthorne returned the visit. He and
Hillard met on friendly terms in Boston and in Salem. Longfellow
dined with Hawthorne at the Essex House in Salem and recorded
in his private journal (October 10, 1846) that "no German village
with a dozen houses in it could have furnished so mean a dinner."
But the fault was the hotel's and Salem's rather than his host's. The
dinner was infinitely better at the Craigie House a fortnight later,
one may be sure, when Longfellow entertained Hawthorne and
Hawthorne's quasi friend Horace Conolly, and Longfellow (as he
put it in his journal) was "more and more struck with Hawthorne's manly beauty and strange, original fancies." It was probably on this occasion that Longfellow heard from Hawthorne and
Conolly (for Conolly was its originator) the story of Evangeline.

There were friendly meetings too, during these years, with political associates like William B. Pike, David Roberts, and Benjamin F. Browne. Such meetings were likely to be enlivened by cigars and potations of gin and water. Hawthorne could meet the local Democratic leaders on their own grounds; moreover, he had a genuine liking for some of them. He did Browne the kindness of editing his "Dartmoor" papers for the *Democratic Review*; he hospitably received Roberts in his home even though Roberts was distasteful to Sophia; he had an affection for Pike and a high opinion of Pike's intellectual and spiritual capacities, which, he thought, had been damaged by a political career. By and large, Hawthorne would not have subscribed to the second part of Emerson's proposition that "the Democrats have the best principles, the Whigs the best men." He felt a loyalty to the men who espoused "the best principles." When he went to Boston to see the fireworks on July 4, 1848, very probably he was in the good company of Salem Democrats. The party of Jefferson and Jackson regarded the Fourth of July with a special proprietorship, and Hawthorne could privately reflect that the Glorious Fourth was, incidentally, his natal day.

The Whig victory in the presidential election of November, 1848, meant that Hawthorne and his Democratic friends would lose their jobs. Despite protestations to the contrary, the Whigs applied the spoils system as relentlessly as the Democrats. Hawthorne received his notice of dismissal on June 8, 1849. It came as a great blow to him. For one thing, he needed the surveyor's salary to live on and to pay old debts; as late as 1848 he had given a note for the balance of rent still due the Ripleys in Concord. For another, he had been assured by those who were supposed to know that, whatever the result of the election, his tenure was secure. President Taylor had declared that officeholders would not be removed except for incompetence or malfeasance. Local politicians had made the points that Hawthorne had not displaced a Whig, his predecessor having been a "Tyler Democrat," and that he had not received his appointment for political services but for his standing in the world of letters. Goaded by financial necessity and fortified by what appeared to him to be his rights in the matter, Hawthorne resolved not to surrender his office without a fight.

The Salem Whigs, headed by the Rev. Charles W. Upham, charged that Hawthorne had been guilty of corruption in office: the Whig inspectors, they said, had received smaller salaries than the Democratic inspectors and the difference had been confiscated for party purposes. They charged, moreover, that Hawthorne had sacrificed the immunity derived from his literary position by political action: he had written political articles for the press, served as a member of party committees and delegations, and marched in torchlight processions. Hawthorne attempted to answer these charges in a letter which was addressed to his friend Hillard, a Whig, and published in the Boston *Daily Advertiser* of June 21. He proved that his predecessor, Nehemiah Brown, was not a Whig but a Tyler Democrat. He asserted that the pay of the Custom House officers had been determined by the Whig collector of the port. He asserted, moreover, that his contributions to the press had been nonpolitical, that he had not taken an active part in the Democratic organization, and that he had never marched in a torchlight procession.

Hawthorne's contentions were valid enough, but appearances were against him. There had apparently been some irregularities at the Custom House in the allotment of wages and the collection of party subscriptions. Hawthorne admitted privately that there may have been "an operation to squeeze an assessment out of recusant Inspectors," but maintained that such machinations were outside his jurisdiction and were perpetrated without his connivance. Possibly there was a legitimate question as to the extent of the surveyor's responsibility. Hawthorne had contributed occasionally to the Salem *Advertiser*, a rather obstreperous organ of the Democratic party. His contributions had been purely literary —they were chiefly reviews of current books—but his connection with the paper gave color to the Whig charge that he had written political articles—a charge not easily refuted because of the fact that contributions to the *Advertiser* were unsigned. Once more, Hawthorne's name had several times appeared in the *Advertiser* as a member of the Democratic "Town Committee" and on one occasion as a member of the Salem delegation to the Democratic State Convention in Worcester. The Whigs professed to find it difficult to believe that he had not gone to Worcester and that he had performed no duties for the Town Committee.

Hawthorne called upon his Whig friends for support since his old Democratic allies could exert no influence on the new administration, and George Hillard, Horace Mann, and others labored earnestly in his behalf. The dismissal of Mr. Surveyor Hawthorne became a *cause célèbre* throughout New England. Arguments and counterarguments, charges and countercharges filled the metropolitan and country presses during the summer months of 1849. "Mr. Hawthorne's name," Sophia told her mother, "is ringing through the land. All the latent feeling about him now comes out, and he finds himself very famous." But despite the justice of his cause and the valiant defense of friends, he failed of reinstatement. Upham had succeeded in making his charges stick in Washington, and the Taylor administration stood pat.

Hawthorne was the victim of an ambiguous relationship. As a man of letters who had been honored by a political appointment, he might be considered exempt from the vicissitudes of national elections, but as a member of a party organization and a beneficiary of party patronage, he was subject to the same liabilities as other political appointees. It was difficult, if not impossible, to play a double role. If Hawthorne was not nearly as active politically as his associates wanted him to be—so inactive, in fact, that they could fairly call him a poor party man—he was nevertheless identified with the Democratic party of Salem and that identification gave the Whigs all the leverage they needed. For clarity's sake, he should have been either a complete party man or none at all. His dismissal, interestingly enough, had the effect of strengthening his feeling of party loyalty, and of dispelling the theory, preached by his supporters and half believed by himself, that he could expect political preferment by virtue of his position in literature. The experience was a down-to-earth lesson in practical politics. "The late Surveyor," Hawthorne wrote in "The Custom House," "was not altogether ill-pleased to be recognized by the Whigs as an enemy, since his inactivity in political affairs . . . had sometimes made it questionable with his brother Democrats whether he was a friend. Now, after he had won the crown of martyrdom . . . the point might be looked upon as settled."

The unceremonious dismissal, and the underhanded way in which it had been brought about, aroused a vindictive mood. He was resolved, he told Longfellow, to "select a victim, and let fall one little drop of venom on his heart, that shall make him writhe before the grin of the multitude for a considerable time to come." Fortunately Hawthorne thought better of his intention—or at least postponed its execution well beyond the heat of the moment. He merely told his wife that Upham was "the most satisfactory villain that ever was," and stored him away for future use. There seems little doubt of Upham's villainy. Sumner referred to him contemptuously as "that smooth, smiling, oily man of God," and Longfellow described him as "a fat, red, rowdy chap." No one knew better than Upham himself the falsity of the charges against Hawthorne, but he relentlessly pursued his course for reasons of political expediency. Nearly two years later Hawthorne presumably pilloried Upham in the character of Judge Pyncheon. "There he stands for all time," Julian Hawthorne declared, "subtle, smooth, cruel, unscrupulous." Doubtless so; but Upham bears about the same relation to Judge Pyncheon that Shaftesbury bears to Dryden's Achitophel. The prototype of real life has been translated into the realm of the universal.

The summer of 1849 was for Hawthorne, as he himself later described it, a time of "great diversity and severity of emotion." He was angry at his political enemies and chagrined and frustrated by his inability to defeat them. He was very properly anxious about the support of his family. He was distressed, moreover, by the rapidly failing health of his mother and was grief-stricken at her death on July 31. One of the most moving passages in all his writings is the following account from his notebook of a visit to his mother's bedside two days before her death:

At about five o'clock, I went to my mother's chamber, and was shocked to see such an alteration since my last visit, the day before yesterday. I love my mother; but there has been, ever since my boyhood, a sort of coldness of intercourse between us, such as is apt to come between persons of strong feelings, if they are not managed rightly. I did not expect to be much moved at the time—that is to say, not to feel any overpowering emotion struggling, just then—though I knew that I should deeply remember and regret her. Mrs. Dike was in the chamber. Louisa pointed to a chair near the bed; but I was moved to kneel down close by my mother, and take her hand. She knew me, but could only murmur a few indistinct words—among which I understood an injunction to take care of my sisters. Mrs. Dike left the chamber, and then I found the tears slowly gathering in my eyes. I tried to keep them down; but it would not be—I kept filling up, till, for a few moments, I shook with sobs. For a long time, I knelt there, holding her hand; and surely it is the darkest hour I ever lived. Afterwards, I stood by the open window, and looked through the crevice of the curtain. The shouts, laughter, and cries of the two children had come up into the chamber, from the open air, making a strange contrast with the death-bed scene. And now, through the crevice of the curtain, I saw my little Una of the golden locks, looking very beautiful; and so full of spirit and life that she was life itself. And then I looked at my poor dying mother; and seemed to see the whole of human existence at once, standing in the dusty midst of it. Oh what a mockery, if what I saw were all,—let the interval between extreme youth and dying age be filled up with what happiness it might! But God would not have made the close so dark and wretched, if there were nothing beyond; for then it would have been a fiend that created us, and measured out our existence, and not God. It would be something beyond wrong—it would be insult—to be thrust out of life into annihilation in this miserable way. So, out of the very bitterness of death, I gather the sweet assurance of a better state of being.

So overwhelming was the accumulation of misfortunes that Hawthorne suffered (his wife reported to her mother) a "brain fever,"
or something dangerously close to it.

Financial anxiety was not new to Hawthorne but it was present
now in a more acute form than before. It must have been in a spirit
of desperation that he sat down once more to try to make a living
with his pen. Meanwhile, the pressure was mercifully relieved by
the efforts of his wife and several friends. Having saved each
week, without her husband's knowledge, an amount drawn from
her allowance for household expenses, Sophia now produced the
accumulated sum. To eke out her savings she turned her artistic
talent to making articles for sale. Her select clientele (Mr. Froth-
ingham and the Misses Maria and Lydia Chase are mentioned)
liked her decorated lamp shades and hand screens, paying $5 for a
shade and $10 for a screen. Hawthorne could bless his stars, Julian
Hawthorne justly remarked, for sending him such a wife. Hawthorne's friends, too, came to his relief. The contributors are not
known, except that Hillard and Longfellow were among them;
nor the amount, though it was substantial. Hillard's letter inclos-
ing the money, Hawthorne said in his reply, brought water to his
eyes. "The only way," he added, "in which a man can retain his
self-respect, while availing himself of the generosity of his friends,
is by making it an incitement to his utmost exertions."

During the years of the surveyorship Hawthorne had been unable to apply himself steadily to creative writing. He seemed to
require a solitary chamber, and this was not available either in the
old family mansion in Herbert Street, where the Hawthornes
lived with Nathaniel's mother and his two sisters in 1845–46; or
in the house occupied for a short time in Chestnut Street, where
they lived alone. Accommodations were better at 14 Mall Street,
whither they removed in September, 1847, for although the
mother and sisters again shared the house, there was a separate
apartment for them and a study removed from all commotion for
Hawthorne. His wife recorded that he began retiring to the
study every afternoon in the autumn of 1847. About this time he

wrote to Longfellow: "I am trying to resume my pen; but the influences of my situation and customary associates are so anti-literary, that I know not whether I shall succeed. Whenever I sit alone, or walk alone, I find myself dreaming about stories, as of old; but these forenoons in the Custom House undo all that the afternoons and evenings have done. I should be happier if I could write." The distractions of the Custom House job, perhaps more than anything else, prevented sustained composition. Such had been his experience in Boston in 1839–40; such was to be his experience again in Liverpool in the years from 1853 to 1857.

The literary output during the four years between the autumn of 1845, when Hawthorne left the Old Manse, and the autumn of 1849, when he settled down to write *The Scarlet Letter*, was indeed small. During the winter of 1845–46 he edited B. F. Browne's "Papers of an Old Dartmoor Prisoner" for the *Democratic Review*, and wrote the introductory essay to the *Mosses* and brief notices of Melville's *Typee* (which he called "a very remarkable work") and four other books for the Salem *Advertiser*. In 1846–47 (Hawthorne's productive year—like an academic year—normally consisted of autumn, winter and spring, for he was habitually averse to writing during the summer) and 1847–48, his writing fell off still more in amount: some pages of the notebook and a few notices for the *Advertiser* are all that can be placed certainly in these years. One of the notices sang the praises of *Evangeline* and its author: "Let him stand, then," Hawthorne said, "at the head of our list of native poets, until someone else shall break up the rude soil of our American life, as he has done, and produce from it a lovelier and nobler flower than this poem of Evangeline."

The year 1848–49 was much more productive, for though "Main Street," "The Great Stone Face," and "Ethan Brand" may have been written, or at least begun, earlier, it is plausible to assign them to these months. "Main Street," a historical study of early Salem, appeared (along with Thoreau's "Civil Disobedience") in Elizabeth Peabody's *Aesthetic Papers* in 1849. Hawthorne would not accept any money for his contribution to a volume sponsored and published by his sister-in-law. "The Great Stone Face" was a story with an Emersonian moral—the power of an ideal to shape an individual life. The *National Era*, in which the story appeared in January, 1850, paid the author $25; Whittier, an editor of the *Era*, apologized to Hawthorne for the "inadequate compensation." In December, 1848, Hawthorne sent "Ethan Brand" to C. W. Webber, another magazine editor, with a grim account of the story's genesis: "At last, by main strength," he said, "I have wrenched and torn an idea out of my miserable brain; or rather, the fragment of an idea, like a tooth ill-drawn, and leaving the roots to torture me." The story was an illustration of intellectual pride, which Hawthorne called the "unpardonable sin." The circumstances of publication are mysterious, for Webber's magazine failed before it had begun, and "Ethan Brand" appeared in January, 1850—more than a year after the manuscript had left Hawthorne's hands—in the Boston *Museum*. The editor of the *Museum* had apparently rescued the work from some limbo of discarded manuscripts, and so far as he knew (he testified), the author had never been paid. It was indeed true, as Hawthorne told Hillard, that writing for the magazines was "the most unprofitable business in the world." Under the circumstances there was small monetary incentive to produce the kind of literature in which Hawthorne had achieved excellence. There was, to be sure, the artist's incentive, which Hawthorne felt to an extraordinary degree or he would not have written the three works just named, the average remuneration for each of which was $8.33. From the standpoint of earning a livelihood, obviously, his literary future was discouraging unless he could hit upon something more profitable than the short tale. This Hawthorne did, fortunately, in *The Scarlet Letter*.

Exactly when he began the composition of his greatest book is not known, but by September 27, 1849, he was at work on it both mornings and afternoons. Mrs. Hawthorne estimated the daily stint at nine hours. "He writes immensely," she told her mother;

"I am almost frightened about it. But he is well now and looks very shining." Progress was so rapid that by January 15, 1850, only three chapters remained to be written. Julian Hawthorne said that all of *The Scarlet Letter* was in the printer's hands within six months after the author had begun to write, and this seems a conservative estimate, so intensive was Hawthorne's application to his task.

On January 15 Hawthorne sent the completed portion, together with "The Custom House," to James T. Fields, junior partner in Ticknor, Reed, and Fields, with the following deprecatory comment: "Perhaps you will not like the book nor think well of its prospects with the public. If so (I need not say) I shall not consider you under any obligation to publish it." But the deprecation was wide of the mark, for Fields liked the book enormously. While visiting Hawthorne in Salem several weeks earlier, he had borrowed a portion of the manuscript ("the germ," he called it in his reminiscences) and had urged Hawthorne to finish the story. Fields, indeed, soon became and continued to be a valuable friend, adviser, and encourager: the last especially, for like many other men—even those with less genius and fewer compunctions —Hawthorne sometimes required the tonic of encouragement. The need was supplied by Bridge in 1836, and by Fields in generous quantity in 1849 and thereafter.

Hawthorne planned to bring out a collection of tales, for which he suggested the title "Old Time Legends; together with Sketches, Experimental and Ideal." *The Scarlet Letter*, he estimated, would take up about half of the proposed volume. The rest of the book would consist of the introductory "Custom House" and a number of uncollected tales—presumably some of those collected later in *The Snow Image and Other Twice-Told Tales*. When Fields, with prophetic insight, recommended the separate publication of *The Scarlet Letter*, Hawthorne was skeptical, though willing to abide by Fields' decision:

If the book is made up entirely of "The Scarlet Letter" [he wrote on January 20, 1850], it will be too sombre. I found it impossible to relieve the shadows of the story with so much light as I would gladly have thrown in. Keeping so close to its point as the tale does, and diversified no otherwise than by turning different sides of the same dark idea to the reader's eye, it will weary very many people and disgust some. Is it safe, then, to stake the fate of the book entirely on this one chance? A hunter loads his gun with a bullet and several buck-shot; and, following his sagacious example, it was my purpose to con-join the one long story with half a dozen shorter ones, so that, failing to kill the public outright with my biggest and heaviest lump of lead, I might have other chances with the smaller bits, individually and in the aggregate. However, I am willing to leave these considerations to your judgment, and should not be sorry to have you decide for the separate publication.

He went on to say, as if the question had already been decided as Fields had advised, "If 'The Scarlet Letter' is to be the title, would it not be well to print it on the title-page in red ink? I am not quite sure about the good taste of so doing, but it would certainly be piquant."

Hawthorne finished *The Scarlet Letter* on February 3, 1850. On the evening of that day he read the latter part of the book to his wife who—as always—had religiously refrained from any in-quiry or intermeddling during the process of composition. "It broke her heart," Hawthorne wrote to Bridge, "and sent her to bed with a grievous headache, which I look upon as a triumphant success." Of his own reactions on that memorable evening, Haw-thorne recalled several years later "my emotions when I read the last scene of the Scarlet Letter to my wife, just after writing it—tried to read it, rather, for my voice swelled and heaved, as if I were tossed up and down on an ocean, as it subsides after a storm." The emotion attests the author's sincerity (if attestation were needed), the more so because Hawthorne was not in the habit of breaking down. The present scene and the scene, already de-scribed, at the bedside of his dying mother are the only recorded instances of uncontrolled emotion.

The book was published on March 16 without the other tales which Hawthorne thought necessary for variety. In addition to

The Scarlet Letter the volume contained only "The Custom House," and the title, as the author had suggested, was printed in red ink on the title page. The sale surpassed the author's expectations. The first edition of 2,000 copies was exhausted in ten days, and a second edition of 3,000 copies was going well a month after publication. But the sales soon dropped off. Two years later the publishers advertised *The Scarlet Letter* as being in its "sixth thousand." If we suppose that 6,000 copies were sold in two years (the price per copy was $.75), then the author's royalty of 10 per cent for that period amounted to only $450. It was a small financial return for a best seller, and masterpiece to boot, but it was much better than Hawthorne had been able to do up to that time.

The leading critics were lavish in their praise. Writing in *The Literary World*, E. A. Duyckinck said that "The Custom House," like its predecessor "The Old Manse," was among "the most charming of Hawthorne's compositions." The novel itself he declared to be "a sounder piece of Puritan divinity than we have been of late accustomed to hear from the degenerate successors of Cotton Mather." E. P. Whipple (who was henceforth to be Hawthorne's favorite American critic) said in *Graham's* that "the deep-seeing eye of the novelist had mastered the whole philosophy of guilt," and that *The Scarlet Letter* had "utterly undermined the whole philosophy" of the French school of Sue, Dumas, and George Sand. Chorley wrote in the London *Athenaeum*, "If Sin and Sorrow in their most fearful forms are to be represented in any work of art, they have rarely been presented with loftier severity, purity, and sympathy than in Mr. Hawthorne's 'Scarlet Letter.' " The praise was more than enough to satisfy an author's legitimate craving.

Two objections, however, were repeatedly expressed. One was that the gloom of *The Scarlet Letter* was unrelieved. Shakespearean criticism in the early nineteenth century had often pointed out the advantage of mingling the comic with the tragic and the principle was applied to Hawthorne's present work. "The Custom House," as well as many other writings, showed that he did not lack the comic spirit, but *The Scarlet Letter* was wholly tragic. If, some critics complained, he could only combine the two attitudes in a single work—like Shakespeare! Whipple concluded his review by saying, "In his next work, we hope to have a romance equal to *The Scarlet Letter* in pathos and power, but more relieved by touches of that beautiful and peculiar humor, so serene and searching, in which he excels almost all living writers." Hawthorne was in complete agreement with this criticism: he felt the unmitigated gloom of the tale to be both an obstacle to popularity and an artistic defect as well. But if it was a defect, it was one which in this instance at least he had been powerless to correct. "*The Scarlet Letter,*" he told Bridge, "is positively a hellfired story, into which I found it almost impossible to throw any cheering light."

While this objection was being suggested by sympathetic critics, a group of hostile critics were violently proclaiming another —namely, the gross immorality of the book. Orestes A. Brownson led the attack in *Brownson's Review.* "There is an unsound state of public morals," he declared, "when the novelist is permitted, without a scorching rebuke, to select such crimes, and to invest them with all the fascination of genius, and all the charms of a highly polished style." "Is the French era actually begun in our literature?" A. C. Coxe asked in the *Church Review*—and went on to illustrate the corrupting influence of *The Scarlet Letter* by citing the giggling conversation of some schoolgirls whom he had overheard in a stagecoach. *The Scarlet Letter* was enjoying something approaching a success of scandal. Hawthorne was not above relishing such attacks, or (needy that he was) taking satisfaction in their value as advertising. But he was not in sympathy with them as criticism, even though the novel's position on the moral question might, with some show of justice, be called equivocal. To Fields he had said, " 'The Scarlet Letter' is rather a delicate subject to write upon, but in the way in which I have treated it, it appears to me there can be no objections on that score." He had indeed treated an unchaste subject chastely, and though extenuating the sin of Hester and Arthur, he had not permitted them to be happy.

While *The Scarlet Letter* was scandalizing certain quarters of New England, "The Custom House" was stirring up a furor in Salem. The following attack in the Salem *Register* of March 21, 1850, may be taken as representing the attitude of the Whig portion of the Salem community:

Hawthorne seeks to vent his spite . . . by small sneers at Salem, and by vilifying some of his former associates, to a degree of which we should have supposed any gentleman . . . incapable. . . . We almost began to think that Hawthorne had mistaken his vocation . . . he would have been more at home as a despicable lampooner. . . . The most venomous, malignant, and unaccountable assault is made upon a venerable gentleman, whose chief crime seems to be that he loves a good dinner. . . . Why this gentleman should be dragged so rudely and abusively before the public and his and his children's feelings outraged so unjustifiably is a mystery beyond our power to fathom. . . . This chapter has obliterated whatever sympathy was felt for Hawthorne's removal from office. . . . If we had any doubt before, we have not a single scruple remaining in regard to the full justification of the Administration in relieving him.

"The Custom House" hardly warranted such violent language as that employed by the *Register*, but the satire, if not exactly Swiftian, was sharp enough. Hawthorne wisely refrained from making a public reply. At first surprised and then defiant and embittered, he wrote to Bridge on April 13 concerning his situation:

As to the Salem people, I really thought that I had been exceedingly good-natured in my treatment of them. They certainly do not deserve good usage at my hands after permitting me to be deliberately lied down—not merely once, but at two several attacks—on two false indictments—with hardly a voice being raised on my behalf; and then sending one of the false witnesses to Congress, others to the Legislature, and choosing another as the mayor.

I feel an infinite contempt for them—and probably have expressed more of it than I intended—for my preliminary chapter has caused the greatest uproar that has happened here since witch-times. If I escape from town without being tarred and feathered, I shall consider it good luck. I wish they would tar and feather me; it would be such an entirely novel kind of distinction for a literary man. And, from such judges as my fellow-citizens, I should look upon it as a higher honor than a laurel crown.

The outraged Salemites offered no violence, but Hawthorne had become *persona non grata* in his native city and was to remain so, to an astonishing degree, for half a century. It is not the only instance of a writer's incurring the displeasure of the people whom he had truthfully described.

Hawthorne was understandably eager to get out of Salem. His change of residence at this time, however, was not so much caused as hastened by the unfriendliness of his neighbors, for in the preceding autumn he had engaged a house at Lenox, in the Berkshires, for occupancy during the coming summer. Pressed by the untoward developments in Salem, he removed his household possessions from 14 Mall Street about the middle of April and installed his family with Mrs. Hawthorne's parents in Boston. He then slipped off to Portsmouth for a fortnight's visit with Bridge. Upon his return he spent another fortnight in Boston, stopping at a boardinghouse out of deference to the crowded state of the Peabody household. During this interval he freely explored the city —"I take an interest in all the nooks and crannies and every development of cities," he declared in his notebook—and enjoyed himself generally. He sat for his portrait to Cephas G. Thompson; visited the Athenaeum, where he looked over the newspapers and magazines; called on George Ticknor at his fine house on Beacon Street; went to the theater and found the audience "more noteworthy than the play"; dropped in at Parker's "grog shop" for a friendly meeting with Burchmore and Pike. In his growing reputation Hawthorne could well afford to dismiss from his mind his political defeat and the ill will of Salem: Fields told him—he recorded in his journal of May 5—that two London publishers had already advertised *The Scarlet Letter* as in press. He would receive no royalty from these pirated publications, but the fame was gratifying.

Late in May the Hawthornes moved into the Little Red House at Lenox. The change was a happy one. Hawthorne was glad to be rid of politics and political strife. For a few weeks perhaps, he fought the old battles over again. He asked Burchmore to ferret out a suspected stratagem of the enemy's which was still undisclosed. He indulged in a gloating letter to Conolly, who had turned traitor and joined Upham's forces. "The seed of Evangeline was yours," he wrote, "and The Scarlet Letter would not have existed unless you had set your mischief-making faculties at work. If not a literary man yourself, you are certainly the cause of literature in other people." But the rancor gradually died away, and Hawthorne recovered his self-possession. Situated in the hills of Berkshire, he could once more mock at fate and care. His literary reputation was at last established beyond all cavil. Though he was still hard pressed for money, his new fame had improved his financial prospects. Like his own "artist of the beautiful," he could enjoy the inner satisfaction of artistic achievement. He was still free to give his entire energies to creative work.

CHAPTER VI

WITH MELVILLE IN THE BERKSHIRES, 1850–1851

In June, 1850, the Hawthornes were busy getting settled in the Little Red House overlooking the Stockbridge Bowl. Sophia exercised her talents to their utmost toward making attractive the interior of their incommodious dwelling. The resulting arrangements can be visualized from her description in a letter to her mother:

Will you enter the drawing-room? Between the front windows stands the beautiful antique ottoman, the monument of Elizabeth's loving-kindness, covered with woven flowers. In the corner at that side stands crosswise the fairy tea-table—a Hawthorne heirloom—and on an embroidered mat upon it lies my pretty white greyhound. In the other corner, on the same side, stands Apollo, whose head I have tied on! Diagonally opposite Apollo stands the ancient carved chair, with its tapestry of roses. Opposite the ottoman is the card-table, with the alabaster vase, and over the vase hangs Correggio's Madonna. Rafael's Transfiguration is over the ottoman. Opposite the door you have entered stands the centre-table; on it are books, the beautiful India box, and the superb India punch-bowl and pitcher, which Mr. Hawthorne's father had made in India for himself. In another corner stands the ancient Manning chair with its worked cover. The scarlet-tipped chair wanders about the room. The black haircloth rocking chair was much abused in moving and one of the rockers is off. It has not yet been mended; and when it is mended, the hall is to be its place. Over the centre-table hangs Endymion, and over the fireplace Leonardo da Vinci's Madonna in bas-relief. You cannot think how pretty the room looks, though with such a low stud that I have to get acclimated to it, and still fear to be crushed.

The bathroom was adorned with two pictures of Psyche—"about to bathe and about to be dressed." The dining room and the "boudoir" commanded a magnificent view of meadow, lake, and mountain, as did Hawthorne's study upstairs, which was furnished with a secretary, a red upholstered ottoman, and a center table a bit wobbly for having lost a foot on the journey from Salem to Lenox. Hawthorne sometimes wished for a richly furnished room in which to write—"a soft, thick Turkey carpet upon the floor, and hung round with full crimson curtains so as to hide all rectangles," he specified on one occasion—but he managed to get along without such a luxury. The important requirements were the seclusion and the elevation afforded by an upstairs room.

The Hawthornes made the red "shanty" their home from May, 1850, until November, 1851—a period comprising one winter and two summers—and the children reveled in the outdoor life in all seasons. Early in the first summer their father reported them to be "as brown as berries." During the ensuing winter they played constantly in the snow, enjoying themselves even more than in summer, and were entirely free from colds. Hawthorne doubted if there were two other children in all New England who enjoyed such splendid health.

Hawthorne himself began his Berkshire residence somewhat run-down in mind and body. He was still—his wife said—"dragging *Salem* at his ankles." But the new environment soon wrought a happy change. He cultivated a vegetable garden, built a hennery, converted furniture crates into bookshelves and clothes' closets, and made various other improvements in the house and grounds. These labors attended to, he found leisure to play with the children. Julian Hawthorne wrote with eloquence and feeling of the sports which he and Una enjoyed with their father in the Berkshires:

Hawthorne made his children boats to sail on the lake, and kites to fly in the air; he took them fishing and flower-gathering, and tried (unsuccessfully for the present) to teach them swimming. . . . In the autumn they all went nutting. . . . The children's father displayed extraordinary activity and energy on these nutting expeditions; standing on the ground at the foot of a tall walnut-tree, he would bid them turn their backs and cover their eyes with their hands; then they would hear, for a few seconds, a sound of rustling and scrambling, and, immediately after, a shout, whereupon they would uncover their eyes and gaze upwards; and lo! there was their father—who but an instant before, as it seemed, had been beside them—swaying and soaring high aloft on the topmost branches, a delightful mystery and miracle. And then down would rattle showers of ripe nuts, which the children would diligently pick up, and stuff into their capacious bags. It was all a splendid holiday; and they cannot remember when their father was not their playmate, or when they ever desired or imagined any other playmate than he.

In a less strenuous mood Hawthorne would lie under a tree while Una and Julian covered his face with long blades of grass, making him look (to the admiring wife and mother who described the scene) "like the mighty Pan."

Hawthorne himself has written exquisitely of this phase of his life in "Twenty Days with Julian and Little Bunny," a diary kept between July 28 and August 16, 1851, when he and Julian were left alone in the Little Red House, the rest of the family having gone to West Newton to visit the Manns. It is no small undertaking for the male parent to attend to the needs of a five-year-old child for a period of three weeks, but Hawthorne made a creditable showing. Feeling lonely for his wife, and wishing also to be relieved of his responsibility, he told her that there had been no enjoyment during her absence—there had been only "doing and suffering." But the diary tells of many experiences which were obviously pleasurable both in themselves and in their recording, as the following excerpt will show:

After dinner, we walked down to the lake. On our way, we waged war with thistles, which represented many-headed dragons and hydras, and on tall mulleins, which passed for giants. Arriving at the lake, Julian dug most persistingly for worms in order to catch a fish. Then we threw innumerable stones into the water, for the pleasure of seeing the splash; also, I built a boat, with a scrap of newspaper for a sail, and sent it out on a voyage; and we could see the gleam of its sail, long afterwards, far away over the lake.

I went and lay under an apple tree. Julian climbed up into the tree and sat astride of a branch. His round merry face appeared among the green leaves, and a continual stream of babble came dripping down upon me like a summer shower. He said he should like to live always in the tree, and make a nest of leaves. Then he wanted to be a bird, so that he might fly far away; and he would go to a deep hole, and bring me back a bag of gold; and he would fly to West Newton and bring home mamma on his back; and he would fly to the Post Office for letters.

After a while, we chanced upon a remarkable echo. It repeated every word of his clear little voice at his usual elevation of talk; and when either of us called loudly, we could hear as many as three or four repetitions—the last coming apparently from far away beyond the woods, with a strange, fantastic similitude to the original voice as if beings somewhat like ourselves were shouting in the invisible distance. . . . What a strange, weird thing is an echo, to be sure!

If the summer was indolent, the winter prove active enough. There were paths to be shoveled, wood to be cut, and the mail to be fetched from the Lenox Post Office two miles away, often through heavy snow, or mud ankle-deep. But Hawthorne found the winter even more enjoyable than the summer. "The country," he wrote to Duyckinck in April, 1851, "has undoubtedly most to offer in the late autumn and winter. I never spent a pleasanter winter than this last one, with a twenty-mile breadth of snow-storm drifting against my old red farm-house." The Berkshire regimen restored to Hawthorne much of his earlier physical vigor. Fields described him enthusiastically for Miss Mary Russell Mitford in England after Hawthorne's visit to the Corner Bookstore in September, 1851: "He is young, I am delighted to say. His hair is yet untinged by Time's silver. His form is only second to Daniel Webster's in robustness, and his step is like a war horse tramp." Although the simile may have been overdrawn, Fields' description is a vivid testimony to Hawthorne's good health at forty-seven.

The interior of the red shanty was especially agreeable during the autumn and winter, which were pre-eminently for Hawthorne the seasons of literary labor. "I am never good for anything in the literary way," he said to Fields in October, 1850, "till after the first autumnal frost, which has somewhat such an effect on my imagination that it does on the foliage here about me." The mornings were devoted to writing in the upstairs study, where he was secure against interruption. In the statement often recurring in Sophia's letters, "Mr. Hawthorne has retired to his study," there is something impressively inviolate. The afternoons were free for chores, and after tea and an early bedtime for the children, the long winter evenings were given over to reading, Hawthorne usually reading aloud to his wife. Borrow's *Lavengro*, Hawthorne told Duyckinck, "filled up a week of happy evenings." Other works which Hawthorne read aloud during the winter of 1850–51 were G. W. Curtis' *Nile Notes of a Howadji*, *Paradise Regained* and *Samson Agonistes*, Pope's *Epistles*, a good deal of Southey and De Quincey, and *David Copperfield*. Sophia delighted in these readings, especially in her husband's rendering of Dickens. "I cannot tell," she wrote in her diary, "how much I enjoy *David Copperfield* made vocal by him. He reads so wonderfully. Each person is so distinct; his tones are so various, apt, and rich. . . . It is better than any acting I ever saw on the stage."

Lenox was a sociable place, and the Hawthornes especially enjoyed the social expansiveness after the morgue-like atmosphere of old Salem. "It is very singular," Sophia remarked, "how much more we are in the center of society in Lenox than we were in Salem." Except for the years abroad, the Hawthornes never saw so many people or experienced so much social activity. Berkshire was already a fashionable summer resort; it was also something of a literary community, in which Hawthorne, now famous, could hardly avoid conspicuousness.

Many callers were strangers who wanted to see the author of *The Scarlet Letter* and, in some cases, the letter itself. A Miss Phelps of New York, whose face seemed hard and pitiless to

Sophia, stopped to have a look at the great writer. Sophia noted how she "devoured" Hawthorne with her eyes, and was shocked further at the lady's boldness in calling Julian "superb" in one breath and in the next "the image of his father"—all being, no doubt, a distressing example of New York manners. A more agreeable admirer was Elizabeth Lloyd, a friend of Whittier's, whose visit Hawthorne recorded in "Twenty Days." "She had a pleasant smile," he wrote, "and eyes that readily responded to one's thought; so that it was not difficult to talk with her;—a singular, but yet a gentle freedom in expressing her own opinions; —an entire absence of affectation. . . . She did not bore me with laudations of my own writings, but merely said that there are some authors with whom we felt ourselves privileged to be acquainted, by the nature of our sympathy with their writings." So delighted was Hawthorne with Miss Lloyd that he declared her visit the only pleasant one he had thus far experienced in his capacity as author.

Relatives, friends, and acquaintances visited or called at the Red House in considerable number. Louisa Hawthorne and Dr. and Mrs. Peabody came at various times for protracted visits. The faithful Bridge, helping the while with the household chores, was a guest for several days, as was the exuberant O'Sullivan, who contributed éclat by introducing the Hawthornes to the Dudley Fields, the Henry Sedgwicks, and other socially prominent persons in the neighborhood. Sophia prolonged a visit to the Fields by spending the night, but Hawthorne preferred to return to the Red House. Fanny Kemble, the actress, more than once rode up to the door on a strong black horse, and on one occasion took Julian for a gallop, holding him astride the pommel of her saddle. L. W. Mansfield, whose poem "The Morning Watch" Hawthorne had carefully criticized in manuscript, called to show his appreciation. Upon Hawthorne's refusal of money for his critical services, Mansfield sent a case of champagne, which proved very useful in the entertainment of guests. Among many other visitors were G. P. R. James, the English novelist, who lived near by, E. P. Whipple, the Boston critic, Miss Fredrika Bremer, the Swedish novelist, Burrill Curtis, who made a drawing of the porch of Tanglewood, James Russell Lowell, and Oliver Wendell Holmes. The last named drove a skittish horse, and when Hawthorne put a restraining hand on the bridle, the Doctor exclaimed, "Is there another man in all America who ever had so great an honor as to have the author of *The Scarlet Letter* hold his horse?" One looks in vain for evidence of social isolation in the Berkshires.

The most frequent visitor, and the most enjoyed, was Herman Melville, who resided at Pittsfield, about six miles distant. Hawthorne and Melville first met on August 5, 1850, when they were members of a party of literary people who climbed Monument Mountain and scrambled through the Ice Glen. It was a jolly occasion. Dr. Holmes served champagne in a silver mug. Melville astonished the group by his agile and bold mountain climbing. In the darkness of the Ice Glen Hawthorne called out ominous warnings—in fact, according to James T. Fields' report, he was "among the most enterprising of the merry-makers." During a thunder-shower Hawthorne and Melville took shelter under a great rock and so had a special opportunity of getting acquainted. "I liked Melville so much," Hawthorne wrote Bridge two days later, "that I have asked him to spend a few days with me."

Prior to this auspicious meeting the two men had not been unknown to each other, for each had read with admiration the other's books. Hawthorne had praised *Typee* in the Salem *Advertiser* in 1846, and had read Melville's subsequent books, as he told Duyckinck, "with a progressive appreciation of the author." "No writer," he had gone on to Duyckinck, "ever put the reality before his reader more unflinchingly than Melville does in 'Redburn' and 'White Jacket.' 'Mardi' is a rich book, with depths here and there that compel a man to swim for his life. It is so good that one scarcely pardons the writer for not having brooded long over it so as to make it a great deal better." Melville, on the other hand, had only recently discovered Hawthorne's writings (the flyleaf of his copy of the *Mosses*,* the first of Hawthorne's books which he read, bears the date July 18, 1850), but his reaction had been even more enthusiastic. He had marked his copy of the *Mosses* heavily and copiously and had written in the margin such comments as "Exquisite!" "What can be finer!" "What a revelation!" Shortly before meeting Hawthorne Melville had written an article entitled "Hawthorne and His Mosses," which appeared anonymously on August 17 and 24 in Duyckinck's *Literary World*, and in which he had gone so far as to compare Hawthorne with Shakespeare. The article naturally pleased both Hawthorne and his wife. "The writer is no common man," Hawthorne said to Duyckinck, "and, next to deserving his praise, it is good to have beguiled or be-witched such a man into praising me more than I deserve." Sophia saw no extravagance in the praise. "At last," she wrote her mother, "some one speaks the right word of Mr. Hawthorne. I have not before heard it. I have been wearied and annoyed hitherto with hearing him compared to Washington Irving and other American writers, and put, generally, *second*. At last some one dares to say what in my secret mind I have often thought—that he is only to be mentioned with the Swan of Avon." Although Melville's au-thorship was unknown to the Hawthornes at the time, his undis-guised admiration and his way of expressing himself must have re-vealed the secret after a brief acquaintance.

All of the Hawthornes found Melville extremely likeable and stimulating. On one occasion he told so graphically of a fight be-tween savages which he had witnessed in the Pacific that the Haw-thornes afterward supposed that he had brandished an actual club during the narrative—but Melville had no club when he left and it was nowhere to be found in the house. Sophia wrote percep-tively to her mother of their new friend:

A man with a true, warm heart, and a soul and an intellect,—with life to his fingertips; earnest, sincere, and reverent; very tender and mod-

* Melville's copies of Hawthorne's works are preserved in the Houghton Library of Harvard.

est. And I am not sure that he is not a very great man. . . . He is tall and erect, with an air free, brave, and manly. When conversing, he is full of gesture and force, and loses himself in his subject. . . . Once in a while, his animation gives place to a singularly quiet expression . . . an indrawn, dim look, but which at the same time makes you feel that he is at that instant taking deepest note of what is before him. It is a strange, lazy glance, but with a power in it quite unique.

Sophia was sometimes made uneasy by this strange, hypnotic glance of Melville's, but the uneasiness was transient and did not seriously interfere with the general enjoyment. She regularly recorded the visits of "Mr. Omoo" as "very agreeable and entertaining."

Hawthorne and Melville also enjoyed more private meetings, at which Sophia and the children were not present, both at the Red House and at Arrowhead, for Hawthorne sometimes went to Melville's house, and would have gone oftener if he had had his own horse (as Melville had) and if he had not been reluctant to leave his family unprotected. He reported to Duyckinck from Arrowhead in March, 1851, that Melville made himself and his guests "snug and comfortable," and a month later he told G. W. Curtis that Melville, besides being "an admirable fellow," had an ample supply of "excellent old port and sherry wine." The Red House furnished hospitality to match, when Melville was a guest. Mansfield's champagne, gin * supplied by William B. Pike, brandy obtained at an apothecary's in the village, and cigars (a quarter of a thousand sent by Burchmore from Salem) were freely drawn upon. On one occasion, when Sophia was absent at West Newton, Hawthorne and Melville—Hawthorne confessed in "Twenty Days"—"smoked cigars even within the sacred precincts of the sitting-room." Such an exceptional liberty—exceptional because of Sophia's aversion, perhaps allergy, to tobacco fumes—suggests an especial friendliness on Hawthorne's part.

There is little record of the talk which accompanied the cigars,

---

* Which Hawthorne regarded as "both wholesomer and more agreeable" than champagne.

gin, and champagne beyond Hawthorne's statement in "Twenty Days" that, on the occasion just referred to, it concerned "time and eternity, things of this world and of the next, and books, and publishers, and all possible and impossible matters," and that it "lasted pretty deep into the night." The conversation was obviously free, metaphysical, and wide ranging, with the more exuberant fancy of the younger man (Hawthorne was forty-seven, Melville only thirty-two) taking the lead. But there is no reason to suppose that Hawthorne lagged far behind. All told, it was the most congenial talk which either Melville or Hawthorne had ever experienced, nor would either know its like again. So pleased was Melville by these conversations that he wrote lyrically of their continuation in the next world:

If ever, my dear Hawthorne, in the eternal times that are to come, you and I shall sit down in Paradise, in some little shady corner by ourselves; and if we shall by any means be able to smuggle a basket of champagne there (I won't believe in a Temperance Heaven), and if we shall then cross our celestial legs in the celestial grass that is forever tropical, and strike our glasses and our heads together, till both musically ring in concert,—then, O my dear fellow-mortal, how shall we pleasantly discourse of all the things manifold which now so distress us,—when all the earth shall be but a reminiscence, yea, its final dissolution an antiquity.

Although the passage suggests a greater abandon than was probably attainable in the Hawthorne parlor even during Sophia's absence, it could hardly have been written if the celestial meeting so described was entirely out of keeping with the earthly one.

Melville's letters to Hawthorne (which are among the most remarkable of his compositions) express a soul affinity with a frankness which might well prove embarrassing to a man of Hawthorne's reserve. Toward the end of their fifteen months' association, Melville wrote characteristically:

Whence come you, Hawthorne? By what right do you drink from my flagon of life? And when I put it to my lips—lo, they are yours and not mine. I feel that the Godhead is broken up like the bread at the Supper, and that we are the pieces. Hence this infinite fraternity of feeling. . . . I shall leave the world, I feel, with more satisfaction for having come to know you. Knowing you persuades me more than the Bible of our immortality.

Although Hawthorne's letters to Melville have not survived, they must have been free and cordial, if more restrained, for in one of his replies Melville spoke of "your easy-flowing long letter which flowed through me and refreshed all my meadows"; and in another, of "your plain, bluff letter," which was also, in a different connection, "joy-giving and exultation-breeding." The two men, indeed, had much in common: an intellectual honesty and disinterestedness, a skepticism, a distrust of fashionable panaceas, a sense of the humor as well as the tragedy of life, and an appreciation also of life's good things. Both could be at once Olympian and down to earth. Although Hawthorne was temperamentally less ebullient than Melville and philosophically less rebellious, and although the two men were separated by the distance between middle age and youth, their friendship, by any reasonable standards, was an eminently successful one.* In England, five years later, Melville and Hawthorne talked again (Hawthorne recorded in his notebook) of "Providence and futurity, and of every thing that lies beyond human ken," and Hawthorne testified in his journal to Melville's "very high and noble nature." Nor did Melville's admiration wane with separation and the passing of time, for he continued to read and annotate Hawthorne's works during their author's lifetime and even after his death. "Nothing can be finer than this," Melville wrote beside a passage in "The Celestial Rail-

* Lewis Mumford's *Herman Melville* (1929) did great damage to the truth concerning Hawthorne and Melville by representing Hawthorne, through cold unresponsiveness, as the villain in Melville's personal tragedy. This view was supported chiefly by the assumption that Hawthorne portrayed Melville in "Ethan Brand." The assumption proved to be incorrect, for "Ethan Brand" was published six months before Hawthorne met Melville and was fully outlined in his journal two years before the publication of Melville's first book (see my "Ethan Brand," listed in the biographical sources, p. 267).

road" above the date "May 1865"; Hawthorne had been in his grave a year but he and his *Mosses* had lost none of their first charm.

It is impossible to determine precisely the effects which the friendly association of Hawthorne and Melville had upon their literary productions, but it seems certain that each stimulated the other to the happiest exertion of his creative powers. During the winter of 1850–51 Melville was writing *Moby Dick*, and when the book appeared in the autumn of 1851 it bore a dedication to Hawthorne. "What a book Melville has written!" Hawthorne exclaimed to Duyckinck. It was after reading *Moby Dick* that Hawthorne sent the letter which Melville found "joy-giving and exultation-breeding." During the same months Hawthorne was writing *The House of the Seven Gables*, for which he repeatedly expressed a preference over *The Scarlet Letter:* "It has more merit than *The Scarlet Letter*," he told his sister Elizabeth, and it was a work "more characteristic" of his mind, he said to Bridge, "and more proper and natural" for him to write. Melville, too, thought that the *Seven Gables* surpassed the other works of the author "for pleasantness of running interest." "It has delighted us," he wrote Hawthorne; "it has piqued a reperusal; it has robbed us of a day, and made us a present of a whole year of thoughtfulness; it has bred great exhilaration and exultation." Such a mutuality of interest and admiration must be credited with no small share in the production of two American masterpieces. Melville reached his peak in *Moby Dick*, and if *The House of the Seven Gables* was not Hawthorne's greatest work, he enjoyed writing it more than any other.

The writing had begun, after a summer of relaxation and recuperation, in late August, 1850. "I religiously seclude myself every morning (much against my will)," Hawthorne wrote to Fields, who was eager to follow up the success of *The Scarlet Letter*,

and remain in retirement till dinner-time [in the early afternoon], or thereabouts. But the summer is not my natural season for work; and

I often find myself gazing at Monument Mountain, broad before my eyes, instead of at the infernal sheet of paper under my hand. However, I make some little progress; and shall continue to lumber along with accelerated velocity; so that I should not much wonder if I were to be ready by November. If not, it can't be helped. I must not pull up my cabbage by the roots, by way of hastening its growth.

Hawthorne was not ready by November, but the acceleration came as predicted, for by December he was writing every day (Sophia noted) from breakfast till four. On December 9 he came to a "standstill," he told the importunate Fields, "having written so fiercely for some days past." In such a state of affairs he proposed to "keep quiet" for a while. But the creative urge soon returned and the book was finished on January 26, 1851. Several days earlier, in the evening, Hawthorne had begun to read the manuscript to his wife. "Oh joy unspeakable!" Sophia wrote in her diary. "Before he told me he should read, I was anticipating a drowsy time on the couch"—she was five months' pregnant—"but the spell of his voice and the power of the book kept me marvellously awake till ten." While Sophia did her sewing during the following day, she could think only of Maule's Well. And after she had listened on successive evenings to the story's progress and close, she wrote: "There is unspeakable grace and beauty in the conclusion, throwing back upon the sterner tragedy of the commencement an ethereal light, and a dear home-loveliness and satisfaction."

Published in April, 1851, *The House of the Seven Gables* was even more enthusiastically received than *The Scarlet Letter*. Whipple in *Graham's* praised the humorous admixture, which *The Scarlet Letter* had lacked. To Chorley of the London *Athenaeum*, *The House of the Seven Gables* gave gratifying evidence of its author's "fertility in humours and characters." Writing in the *Southern Literary Messenger*, H. T. Tuckerman likewise regarded the work as a "more elaborate and harmonious" production than its predecessor. In an age when Shakespeare provided the standard of the highest literary achievement, it was natural that critics should prefer variety of tone to a severe uniformity. Mrs. Kemble wrote that the *Seven Gables* had produced a greater sensation in England than any other book since *Jane Eyre;* at home, Lowell said it was the most valuable contribution to New England history ever written. The *Seven Gables* sold more rapidly than *The Scarlet Letter,* for in May, 1852, Ticknor and Fields advertised each book as in its "sixth thousand."

Hawthorne could afford to relax a bit after such a success, but about June 1 he resumed his pen and during the following six weeks wrote his famous retelling of the classical myths entitled *A Wonder-Book.* "Unless I greatly mistake," he had said to Fields in May,

these old fictions will work up admirably for the purpose; and I shall aim at substituting a tone in some degree Gothic or romantic, or any such tone as may best please myself, instead of the classic coldness, which is as repellent as the touch of marble. . . . The book, if it comes out of my mind as I see it now, ought to have pretty wide success amongst young people; and, of course, I shall purge out all the old heathen wickedness, and put in a moral wherever practicable.

The writing came easily, apparently, for the complete manuscript was shipped to Fields on July 15. In the course of composition Hawthorne read the stories—trying them out, as it were—to his own children with reassuring success. Julian Hawthorne testified that he and his sister could repeat much of the book by heart before it was in the printer's hands. This happy augury has been confirmed by the continued popularity of *A Wonder-Book* among young readers down to the present time.

Aside from "Twenty Days with Julian and Little Bunny" and a few additional pages in the notebooks, only three other writings of importance belong to the Berkshire period—"Feathertop," and the prefaces to the *Twice-Told Tales* (third edition) and to *The Snow Image and Other Twice-Told Tales.*

"Feathertop," a satirical masterpiece exposing the inanities of a "stuffed-shirt," was written in the early autumn of 1851. The story appeared in the *International Magazine* in two installments, in January and February, 1852, and Rufus W. Griswold, the editor, paid Hawthorne $100 for it. The amount was the largest which Hawthorne had ever received for a tale or sketch. "I cannot afford it for less," he told Griswold, "and would not write another for the same price." "Feathertop" was, in fact, Hawthorne's last short piece of fiction. "The thought and trouble expended on that kind of production," he explained to Griswold, who had asked for twelve tales, "is vastly greater, in proportion, than what is required for a long story." And the remuneration much smaller, he might have added. Henceforth he was to do only the long work in fiction.

The preface to the new edition of the *Twice-Told Tales*, which Fields had taken over from Monroe (on whose shelves a remnant of the 1842 edition had been languishing), was dated January 11, 1851. The tone of the preface was quasi-deprecatory: in a mood half serious, half whimsical, the author underrated the merits of the tales. The underrating, however, was an indulgence which the famous author of *The Scarlet Letter* might pardonably allow himself. He was aiming at a piquant effect, and a lack of complete seriousness is implied by his calling the preface, in a letter to Fields, "a very pretty one."

The preface to *The Snow Image and Other Twice-Told Tales* —cast in the form of a dedicatory letter to Horatio Bridge and dated November 1, 1851—was more forthright, being largely an expression of warm and grateful friendship. Writing from the happy vantage point of a second success which had quickly followed the first, the author of *The Scarlet Letter* and *The House of the Seven Gables* gracefully recalled the encouragement and active aid which he had received from Bridge ever since their college days. The volume contained four pieces which had been written since the collection of the *Mosses* in 1846: "The Snow Image," "The Great Stone Face," "Main Street," and "Ethan Brand." Most of the other pieces—eleven in all—were of early composition and had been passed over by the author when he collected from the magazines the first and second editions of the *Twice-Told Tales* and the *Mosses from an Old Manse*. Among these thrice-rejected selections were "The Canterbury Pilgrims" and "The Devil in Manuscript"—stories which most readers today would not regard as having less than average interest among Hawthorne's writings. The author promised the public that he would not inflict upon it "any more of these musty and mouse-nibbled leaves of old periodicals," because in all probability, he said, no more uncollected stories could be found there. "If a few still remain," he added, "they are either such as no paternal partiality could induce the author to think worth preserving, or else they have got into some very dark and dusty hiding-place, quite out of my own remembrance, and whence no researches can avail to unearth them. So there let them rest." Hawthorne did not quite keep his promise. Persuaded by Fields' insistence that he reclaim any writings still uncollected, he added to the second edition of the *Mosses* in 1854 two pieces which antedated 1837 and which therefore had been passed over four times. Nor did this end the long process of reclamation, if indeed it is finished now. G. P. Lathrop was able to include in the Riverside Edition of the "Works," published in 1883, several uncollected compositions of unquestionable authenticity, and since that date researchers have proposed, usually without convincing authority, still further additions to the Hawthorne canon culled from the pages of old magazines.

It was good business, of course, to bring out as many volumes as possible while the success of the two novels was still fresh in the public mind. *The Snow Image and Other Twice-Told Tales* and the new edition of the *Twice-Told Tales* appeared in 1851; *A Wonder-Book*, early in 1852. A thousand copies of *The Snow Image* were sold within a few days after publication. James T. Fields, who was not only a warmhearted friend of Hawthorne's but also one of the most expert book promoters America has ever produced, worked manfully to make Hawthorne a popular writer. He never quite succeeded despite his intimate connection with and indefatigable cultivation of booksellers, newspaper editors, magazine reviewers, and distinguished authors at home and abroad. But thanks to his efforts as well as to the merits of the books themselves, Hawthorne's financial condition showed a marked improvement. On the flyleaf of one of his notebooks Hawthorne itemized receipts from Ticknor and Fields totaling $1,430 for the year 1851. The sum is not staggering but it was much larger than that received from his writings in any previous year.

For the first time Hawthorne could view his financial responsibility as head of a growing family with something approaching equanimity. He could not afford life insurance, having never seen the year, since he was married, when he could have spared even a hundred dollars from the necessary expenses of living—he explained to Elizabeth Peabody, who had urged upon him the importance of such a provision—but he hoped to be able to provide for Sophia and the children, he told his solicitous, meddlesome sister-in-law, by being as industrious in literature as was compatible with his good health. Beyond that, he added, "we must take our chance, or our dispensation of Providence."

The birth of a third child, Rose, on May 20, 1851—"the brightest," her father reported to her aunt Louisa, "and best-conditioned baby in the world"—increased, of course, the family expense. But the Hawthornes practised a simple mode of life, and living costs in the Berkshires in 1851 were low, as Mrs. Hawthorne's itemized account bears witness: "milk, three cents a quart; butter, fourteen cents a pound; eggs, eleven cents a dozen; potatoes, two shillings a bushel; buckwheat, sixty-two cents for twenty-four pounds; wood, three dollars a cord; charcoal, eight cents a bushel; veal, six cents a pound; mutton, five cents; beef, nine cents." An economy of abundance, a golden age! Equally suggestive of such an age was the domestic service, performed by Mrs. Peters, a Negro ("grim" and "angelic" were Hawthorne's adjectives for her), whom Sophia, in their infrequent moments of leisure, instructed in the mysteries of reading, writing, and ciphering.

By and large the Hawthornes were, or seemed to be, happily situated in the Berkshires. But by the summer of 1851 Hawthorne was expressing dissatisfaction with his residence there. In "Twenty Days" he complained of the uncertain and variable climate: "This is a horrible, horrible, most hor-ri-ble climate; one knows not, for ten minutes together, whether he is too cool or too warm; but he is always one or the other; and the constant result is a miserable disturbance of the system. I detest it! I detest it!! I detest it!!! I hate Berkshire with my whole soul, and would joyfully see its mountains laid flat." The Red House, too, no longer pleased him; it was, he told Louisa in July, 1851, "the most inconvenient and wretched little hovel" that he had ever put his head in. If one is a little dismayed at the reversal of attitude, one must remember that Hawthorne—like most men of genius, and like some who do not have the excuse of genius—was subject to changing moods.

Like all migrators westward, too—whether to California or to western Massachusetts, for the distance of migration does not so much matter—Hawthorne began to feel the pull back to the East where the current of life seemed to run swifter. Berkshire, he told Bridge, was "too much out of the way." "I have learned pretty well [he went on] the desirableness of an easy access to the world. . . . It will do well enough to play Robinson Crusoe for a summer or so, but when a man is making his settled dispositions for life, he had better be as near a railroad station as possible." Hawthorne's letters in the summer and autumn of 1851 continued in this vein, for having set his face toward eastern Massachusetts he could think of many reasons why a change of residence was desirable. "I do not feel at home among these hills," he wrote to Pike, "and should not like to consider myself permanently settled here. I do not get acclimated to the peculiar state of the atmosphere, and, except in midwinter, I am continually catching cold, and am none so vigorous as I used to be on the seacoast. The same is the case with my wife; and though the children seem perfectly well, yet I rather think they would flourish better near the sea." It was the sea especially which Hawthorne missed in the Berkshires—the sea and city streets. Cities—particularly Boston and later London —interested him greatly. Even in the summer, when most people would prefer the country, he wrote feelingly to Duyckinck of urban advantages: "There is always the shady side of the well-watered street," he said, "and awnings on the sunny side; not to speak of ice-creams and all kinds of iced liquors, which are greatly preferable to the luke-warm basin of a brook, with its tadpoles and insects mingling in your draught." It was pleasant and stimulating to walk on pavements and feel the pulsing life of crowds. Hawthorne and Melville talked of making an excursion together to New York but never got around to it. The ideal place of residence, Hawthorne thought, would be within easy access to a city and, equally important, near the seacoast. He asked Pike to keep on the lookout for a house by the sea which could be purchased for about $2,000.

Whether he was fully aware of it or not, his thoughts on a change of residence suggest the profound influence of Salem—situated as it is near Boston and on the seacoast—though there were insuperable objections to his returning to his native town. Julian Hawthorne pointed out that after leaving Salem in 1850 Hawthorne soon wearied of any particular locality. The roots proved ineradicable. With a perspective clarified by distance, he had given to old Salem in the *Seven Gables* something approaching final literary treatment but, as his later works were to show, he had not done with it. While in the Berkshires, too, he longed for the companionship of Salem friends—the political, unliterary, and from a cultivated point of view somewhat plebeian men with whom he had been associated in the Custom House. He had no desire to return to political office: "God bless General Taylor!" he declared heartily. But he continued to have a lively interest in Salem politics and he missed the political talk. He inquired eagerly of Burchmore, "Do you see anything of C[onolly]? What are you doing? How are the black ducks? Are you still a teetotaler? How does Eph[raim Miller] stand with the present administration? In short, what is the news generally and particularly?" "I do long to see you," he wrote Pike, "and to talk about a thousand things." He sent complimentary copies of the *Seven Gables* to

Pike, Roberts, Conolly, Miller, and Browne—the members of the old Salem junto—though Pike was the only one of the group who was seriously interested in Hawthorne's writings and whose literary opinion Hawthorne cared about.

Despite a growing restlessness Hawthorne had become reconciled to spending another winter in the Berkshires when a misunderstanding with the Tappans, the owners of the Red House, seemed to necessitate an immediate change. It was one of those little quarrels which, almost inevitable between even the best-intentioned neighbors, take on at the time an exaggerated importance. The question in dispute was whether the Hawthornes were entitled to the fruit which grew in an adjoining orchard. Although their rights had not been clearly defined when they rented the house, they had supposed that the fruit was theirs, and their appropriation of it had not been challenged during the previous season. But in September of the second year Mrs. Tappan hinted that the fruit was the Hawthornes' only if she chose to give it to them. Hawthorne wrote the lady a sharp letter in which he said that he preferred rights to favors. "This is a world of bargain and sale," he declared with hardheaded realism, "and no absurdity is more certain to be exposed than the attempt to make it anything else." The quarrel was patched up by Mr. Tappan's assuring the Hawthornes that the fruit was of course theirs by right, but Hawthorne felt that neighborly relations had been spoiled and the feeling made him all the more eager to leave.

He had already been looking for a house to buy and had enlisted the aid of Pike and Bridge, but nothing suitable had turned up. Bridge had suggested the old family home of the Sparhawks at Kittery Point, which was then for sale, but Hawthorne had rejected it as "too much out of the way." At this critical juncture Sophia's sister, Mrs. Horace Mann, came forward with the suggestion that the Hawthornes take the Manns' house in West Newton during the absence of Congressman Mann and his family in Washington. The arrangement was only temporary, to be sure, but it would provide a means of escape from Berkshire and would facilitate the search for a permanent residence. "It strikes me," Hawthorne wrote his wife, "as one of those unexpected, but easy and natural solutions wherewith Providence occasionally unknots a seemingly inextricable difficulty." Although the rent of $350 per annum was more than they could afford, he thought, perhaps within a few months they would find a desirable house to buy, and toward that end Ticknor and Fields had promised a liberal advance of money should they need it.

The Hawthornes left the Red House on November 21 in a snow storm and boarded the cars at Pittsfield. It would be good to get back to eastern Massachusetts, Hawthorne and his wife felt, where they naturally belonged. Hawthorne returned hopefully to the center of his New England world, for thanks to *The Scarlet Letter*, *The House of the Seven Gables*, and James T. Fields, his position as a man of letters was much improved both in prestige and in dollars and cents.

The passing months obliterated recollections of the harsh climate, Mrs. Tappan, and other irritations, and in retrospect Hawthorne was soon able to think of his residence in the Little Red House as an altogether happy chapter in his life. Subsequent visits by Melville reminded him of their pleasant association in the Berkshires. And the natural beauties of the region were never to him as a landscape to a blind man's eye. While touring the Scotch Highlands several years later, he remembered the Berkshire hills with pride and nostalgia and thought that in cloudy, misty weather, at least, they looked grander than the Highlands.

CHAPTER VII

WEST NEWTON AND THE WAYSIDE, 1851–1853

DURING the winter of 1851–52 at West Newton, Hawthorne was busy writing *The Blithedale Romance*, which was based upon his experiences at Brook Farm ten years earlier. He had chosen this subject and begun work while still at Lenox, for in the summer of 1851 he was reading Fourier with a view, he said, to his next romance. His intention, he told Bridge, was "to put an extra touch of the devil into it" because he doubted whether he could do two "quiet" books in succession without losing ground with his public. "My facility for labor," he added, "increases with the demand for it." *Blithedale* was finished on April 30, 1852, and the proof sheets began coming on May 14. The book was published by Ticknor and Fields on July 14.

Hawthorne directed Ticknor to send complimentary copies to Longfellow, Hillard, Holmes, Melville, Irving, H. T. Tuckerman, G. W. Curtis, G. P. R. James, L. M. Mansfield, Charles G. Atherton, Dr. Peabody (his father-in-law), and Mrs. Horatio Bridge. Eight copies were to go to Burchmore for distribution among his Salem friends. The list is by no means exhaustive, for some copies —those to Pierce and Whipple, for example—were delivered without the aid of the post. Hawthorne's presentation lists, in general, show that he was loyal to the friends whose adoption he had tried.

Despite his attempt to enliven *Blithedale* with a diabolical touch, the book was less enthusiastically received than either *The Scarlet Letter* or *The House of the Seven Gables*. Perhaps the Brook Farm community was too restricted in its appeal. Possibly, too, skepticism of social reform was an unpopular note to strike in 1852. Emerson thought the story "disagreeable" and the sketches "not happily" drawn. Hillard wished that Hawthorne could have concluded the novel "without killing Zenobia" or that she might have

had "a drier and handsomer death." Fields, who could praise for
business reasons if intrinsic ones were lacking, deviated from his
customary promotional practice when he wrote to Miss Mitford,
"I hope Hawthorne will give us no more Blithedales." Perhaps
Fields was especially chagrined at the lukewarm reception because
he had taken considerable trouble to secure the book's publication
by Chapman and Hall in London and had obtained £200 from
that source for the author. This was the first money which Hawthorne received from an English publisher (though London stalls
were loaded with pirated cheap editions of his previous works),
and Fields probably feared for the success of future attempts of
the kind since *The Blithedale Romance* appeared to be falling a
little flat. Later judges were to think more highly of *Blithedale*—
among them William Dean Howells, who preferred it to Hawthorne's other romances because of its greater "realism."

The use of Mr. Mann's house in West Newton being a temporary arrangement, the search for a permanent home continued
through the winter. In the spring of 1852 a place was found and
the decision made to purchase it. The property consisted of a
house and nine acres in Concord, for which Hawthorne paid
$1,500. It was not near the sea, but Concord held tender memories
from the Old Manse days. The Concord countryside was pleasant. The scenery in fact was preferable to that of Berkshire, Hawthorne thought, for unlike the mountains the "broad meadows
and gentle eminences" did not "stamp and stereotype themselves
into the brain, and thus grow wearisome with the same strong impression repeated day after day." A few months later he purchased thirteen additional acres at a cost of $313.*

To Duyckinck he wrote concerning his new residence:

It is no very splendid mansion, being originally a farm house of moderate size and ante-revolutionary date; but Mr. Alcott, the Orphic
Sayer, of whom I bought it, had wasted a good deal of money in fitting
it up to suit his own taste—all which improvements I get for little or

* I am indebted to Margaret M. Lothrop for information concerning the purchase of "The Wayside."

nothing. Having been much neglected, the place is the raggedest in the world; but it will make, sooner or later, a comfortable and sufficiently pleasant home. Alcott called it "Hillside," as it stands close at the base of a steep ascent; but as it also is in proximity (too nigh indeed) to the road leading into the village, I have re-baptized it "The Wayside"—which seems to me to possess a moral as well as descriptive propriety. It might have been called "Woodside"—the hill being covered with a growth of birch, locust-trees, and various sorts of pine.

At the Wayside, accordingly, the Hawthornes took up their abode in late May, 1852, and for the first time in his married life, Hawthorne said, he felt himself at home.

A good deal of refurbishing and redecorating was done to make the house more habitable and, as always, Mrs. Hawthorne directed the work with a lively interest and an artistic—if Victorian—taste. Prior to the improvements the house had seemed to her "fit only for a menagerie of cattle." But she was soon able to report to her mother "magical changes wrought inside the horrible old house by painters, paperers, and carpenters, and a little upholstery." Her wifely devotion expressed itself in special attention to Hawthorne's study, which she called "the temple of the Muses and the Delphic Shrine." She described the furnishings in detail to Mrs. Peabody. A rich carpet of lapis lazuli blue, recently purchased, laid "the foundation of its charms." The walls were adorned by a bust of Apollo, Mrs. Hawthorne's drawing of Endymion, a picture of the Transfiguration (a gift from Emerson), a picture of Luther and his family (a gift from George Bradford), and two drawings of Lake Como. The room was probably the most elaborately decorated study Hawthorne ever had. It would seem ironical that he was to write there only the *Life of Pierce* and the *Tanglewood Tales*.

During the summer and early autumn of 1852 Mrs. Hawthorne and the children (Una, eight; Julian, six; Rose, one and a half) as well as Hawthorne himself reveled in the Concord countryside. There were strolls to Walden Pond, to Sleepy Hollow, to the Old Manse. "All that ground," Sophia noted, "is consecrated to me by unspeakable happiness," and yet her present happiness she thought was even greater, for she was "ten years happier in time." The wooded hill back of the Wayside, which became Hawthorne's favorite retreat, was a constant invitation in good weather. On an October Sunday Mrs. Hawthorne and the children sat on the hill weaving wreaths of red leaves while the pine trees (she recorded in a diary) made a noise like the sea. The comparison was probably Hawthorne's, spoken as he lay at full length on a carpet of pine needles, for though he liked Concord well he preferred the seacoast and now derived comfort from the mere illusion.

At the Wayside, as at their other homes however temporary, the Hawthornes were a remarkably happy family. The children were an unfailing source of joy and delight. Mrs. Hawthorne often amused herself by writing descriptive sketches of their development. The following account of Rose, for example, was sent to Mrs. Peabody about this time:

I wish I could show you my Rosebud; she is wholly different from Una & Julian, very facetious, self relying, practical, observant of facts, and inconceivably naughty, and very bewitching, on her cheeks bloom the roses of Sharon, adown her neck float golden sunbeams, her eyes are blue, sagacious, with very long lashes, and a charming double row of snowy teeth shine when she laughs, her figure is round and rolling, but symmetrical, her face is too perfect a circle and she jumps straight up and down on two of the straightest, finest little legs ever seen, out of pure joy of existence, she sings like Jenny Lind, and judges us all like a Lord Chancellor. . . . She fails in reverence, and excels in wit, and so far is wholly irresponsible in her actions. . . . I never saw such a child in my life!

If Hawthorne was less voluble, his pride and affection were none the less great. He accompanied the children in explorations of the near-by woods and fields. Julian recalled particularly a huge snow-ball which his father helped him roll up on the front lawn and which lasted throughout the winter and well into the spring.

Outside the family circle the Hawthornes found agreeable society. Hawthorne enjoyed conversation with his next door neighbor, Ephraim Bull, the inventor of the Concord grape. The Emersons were cordial. Una made herself at home at the Emerson house, Julian rode on Edward Emerson's pony, and the Hawthornes joined the Emersons and others at neighborhood picnics. Several children of the community regularly gathered at the Wayside to receive (gratis), in company with the Hawthorne children, Mrs. Hawthorne's instruction in reading, geography, drawing, and the Bible. On a particular Sunday she recorded in her diary, "I read them the story of Balaam's ass, and about the death of Moses. They were much afflicted that Moses was not allowed to go to the Promised Land. I read that he looked down from Mount Pisgah and saw Canaan and the City of Palms, and showed them my Cuban sketch of a palm, describing exactly how they looked and grew, and the vision of the City of Palms became very beautiful to them." The Wayside was a lively and pleasant place. Hawthorne expressed his satisfaction in a letter to Bridge very simply: "We are quite comfortable in all respects."

In Concord, also, Hawthorne was able to see more of his Boston and Salem friends than he had been able to do while living in the Berkshires. William B. Pike of Salem, whom Julian Hawthorne described as a man "of remarkable depth of mind and tenderness of nature," came to Concord more than once upon Hawthorne's special invitation. Fields came from Boston, and strolled with Hawthorne along the banks of the river's sluggish stream, the two hiding in the tall grass when a passer-by seemed to threaten their privacy. If Ticknor was sometimes too busy with his accounts to accept Hawthorne's invitation, he compensated for his absence by sending cigars and claret. The cigars, Hawthorne told him, would keep his "memory fragrant for many a day to come," and the claret was "most excellent and acceptable." Other friends had sent sauterne, champagne, and sherry, and as Hawthorne had laid in a supply of brandy, he hoped, he said, to keep himself "pretty jolly, in spite of the Maine Law."

Not long after the Hawthornes arrived at the Wayside, a public event occurred which was to affect their future profoundly:

Franklin Pierce was nominated for the presidency by the Democratic National Convention in session at Baltimore. On June 8, 1852, three days after the event, Hawthorne heard of the nomination, and on the following day he wrote to Pierce offering his services as campaign biographer. He knew that he was not very well qualified to write a book of this kind. "It needs long thought with me," he told Pierce, "in order to produce anything good; and after all, my style and qualities as a writer are certainly not those of the broadest popularity." The editor of the Boston *Times*, Hawthorne suggested, would be a better choice. But he did not seek to evade the responsibilities of friendship: "Whatever service I can do you," he said, "would be at your command."

Pierce wanted Hawthorne to do the biography and Hawthorne consented, putting aside his plan to write another Wonder-Book during the summer and plunging at once into the task of gathering the necessary materials. By July 5 he was able to report progress: he had interviewed Senator Atherton of New Hampshire and other political associates of Pierce and had obtained a good deal of information from them, but he needed certain facts which Pierce himself would have to supply; Pierce's exploits in the Mexican War should be emphasized, but not so much as to overshadow the man of peaceful pursuits ("a statesman in your proper life," he wrote, thinking aloud, "a gallant soldier in the hour of your country's need—such is the best mode of presenting you"); although the slavery question was a "knotty point," he confessed, and he did not yet see his way clear, the subject was "not to be shirked nor blinked" but presented in such a way as to put Pierce "on the broadest ground possible, as a man for the whole country." Finally, he asked Pierce to come to Concord for "a long and quiet discussion" before he should put the biography into its final form.

Pierce came promptly, and the work was rapidly taking shape when Hawthorne was distracted, and temporarily paralyzed, by the sudden death of his sister Louisa. She had been invited to the Wayside in mid-June for a good long visit but had been prevented from coming, though Hawthorne had warned, as if with a sense of foreboding, that if she did not come at once something would intervene to prevent her coming at all that summer. About the middle of July Louisa had gone to Saratoga Springs in company with her cousin, John Dike of Salem, and later they had started on a journey down the Hudson to New York City on the steamer "Henry Clay." When the boat caught on fire from an explosion on July 27, Louisa jumped into the river and was drowned. Three days later, early in the morning, Pike brought the news to Concord. The entire family was grief-stricken, for Louisa had been an especial favorite not only with her brother but with Sophia and the children as well. "My husband," Sophia recorded, "shut himself in his study."

There is no recorded commentary by Hawthorne on this tragic event to set beside the notebook passage written during the last illness of his mother. But Mrs. Hawthorne's religious faith shone bright in this dark hour. She consoled the children, and perhaps Hawthorne too, by saying to them, "Aunt Louisa is with her mother, and is happy to be with her. Let us think of her spirit in another world." Writing to Mrs. Peabody a little later, she expressed her faith in immortality with full eloquence:

It is a positive bliss to me to contemplate Louisa and her mother together. If there is anything immortal in life, it is the home relations, and heaven would be no heaven without them. God never has knit my soul with my husband's soul for such a paltry moment as this human life! I have not loved my mother for one short day! My children do not thrill my heartstrings with less than an eternal melody! We know that God cannot trifle!

Three years earlier Hawthorne had reached the same conclusion at the deathbed of his mother, though with greater difficulty. He could not put aside the bitter cup hastily. He had dwelt upon the "dark and wretched close." He had at last attained an "assurance of a better state of being" but only after he had tasted the bitterness of death.

Hawthorne's grief-stricken state delayed the progress of the biography, but not for long. He returned to his task, and by August 6 he was appealing to Pierce for additional documents and promising to send on at least half of the biography within a week. The book had to be completed at once, of course, or it would appear too late to influence the election; Hawthorne betrayed nervousness when he wrote to Ticknor on August 22, "If not finished before the end of the week, I'll be d—d if I mean to finish it at all." Three days later he jokingly urged Ticknor to use a more flamboyant style of advertisement, suggesting the following in large capitals: "Hawthorne's Life of General Pierce; sanctioned by the General, drawn up from original documents, and with the General's Own Journals, as written in the Field. Together with a superb engraving from the best portrait of the General." "Go it strong," he urged; "we are politicians now, and you must not expect to conduct yourself like a gentlemanly publisher." With a great sense of relief, for the task had not been entirely congenial to him, Hawthorne sent the final pages of the biography to Ticknor on August 27.

On August 30 he left Concord on a journey which was to occupy about three weeks and which took him first to Brunswick to attend the semicentennial celebration of Bowdoin College and later to the Isles of Shoals, off the coast from Portsmouth, where he could enjoy the sea breeze and the pounding surf. It was the sort of excursion which he had often found recreational in times past after a period of concentrated labor and nervous strain. His favorite prescription, indeed, for nervous fatigue was going on a journey.

He had received a special invitation to the Bowdoin exercises from his old teacher, Professor Alpheus S. Packard, who had asked him to write something especially for the occasion—"an ode or a reminiscence or tale." Hawthorne's reply had expressed pleasure in accepting the invitation to be present but unwillingness to undertake a literary composition. His mind, he had said, was "a little worn and paralysed by pretty constant use" and he would "greatly prefer to be an unnoticed spectator and auditor." The refusal need not be construed as showing a lack of affection for his alma mater. He was preoccupied, as we have seen, with the biography of Pierce. Moreover, unlike Longfellow, Lowell, and Holmes, Hawthorne had no talent for the occasional piece or liking for public exhibitions.

Delayed in transit by heavy rains, he arrived in Brunswick after the completion of the program—fortunately, he felt, for he had been spared the embarrassment of hearing himself celebrated by orators and poets. His reaction to the Bowdoin homecoming was one familiar to many middle-aged alumni on similar occasions: his classmates proved to be, he said,

a set of dismal old fellows, whose heads looked as if they had been out in a pretty copious shower of snow. The whole intermediate quarter of a century vanished; and it seemed to me as if they had undergone this transformation in the course of a single night, especially as I myself felt just about as young as when I graduated. They flattered me with the assurance that time had touched me tenderly; but, alas, they were each a mirror in which I beheld the reflection of my own age.

Having returned to Portsmouth, Hawthorne voyaged from there to the Isles of Shoals on September 3. His observations and recreations during the ensuing fortnight are recorded in his journal in the vivid manner of the early journals kept at Augusta and North Adams. New England scenes and characters continued to impress him as subjects worthy of close scrutiny and careful description. The unpolished Yankee was often of greater interest to him than the polished—a fact which Mrs. Hawthorne, no doubt rightly, regarded as evidence of her husband's democratic sympathies.

On the voyage over, two passengers—a storekeeper from Danvers and a farmer from Hamilton—became seasick. The storekeeper, Hawthorne wrote, "lay along the boat, with his head over the side, longing (as he afterward said) for a little fresh water to be drowned in." Landing at Appledore Island Hawthorne went to Laighton's Hotel where, having presented a letter of introduction from Pierce, he obtained the best accommodations that were to be had. After dinner, which was good and abundant though homely in its style, Levi Thaxter, the husband of Celia Thaxter, the poetess (then just seventeen), and John Weiss, a Transcendentalist, showed Hawthorne some of the remarkable features of the island, which included (he noted in his journal) "a monument of rude stones said to have been erected by Captain John Smith, and the remains of a settlement that Cotton Mather speaks about." In the evening he joined a whist party, his partner being an agreeable young lady from Portsmouth.

The days continued to pass pleasantly as Hawthorne and his new acquaintances further explored the "remarkables" of Appledore and the near-by islands. Of particular interest to him were the records (dating back to colonial times) of the church at Gosport. A frequent entry, which he copied into his notebook as if to confirm the authenticity of *The Scarlet Letter*, recorded the "public confession of the breach of the Seventh Commandment." Pleasant also were the evenings, most of which were spent at the home of the Thaxters, where Hawthorne found the company enjoyable and the hospitality cordial. On several occasions, according to the notebook record, Thaxter served "hot gin and water, the gin being Schiedam, put up in a genuine Dutch jug, of the distillation of 1820 and very excellent stuff." On another occasion the company—made vocal by apple-toddy—sang glees and Negro melodies. Hawthorne had a warm, pleasurable feeling as he walked back to the hotel after a social evening at the Thaxters, for (the journal relates) "emerging into the open air, out of that room of song, and pretty youthfulness of woman, and gay young men, there was the sky, and the three-quarters waning moon, and the old sea moaning all round about the island."

Recreated by sea breezes and convivial experiences, Hawthorne returned to Concord September 17 and was embraced by his wife and children. The latter fact would hardly merit recording if the Hawthornes' homecomings were not so heartwarming to contemplate. During his brief absence husband and wife (now, respectively, forty-eight and forty-one and ten years married) had longed for each other. After enjoining her to kiss the children for him, Hawthorne had continued in a letter from Portsmouth, "Kiss thyself, if you canst—and I wish thou couldst kiss me." An equal deprivation was felt by those who stayed at home. "The children missed papa miserably," Mrs. Hawthorne wrote her mother, "and I could not bear the trial very well. I could not eat, sitting opposite his empty chair at table, and I lost several pounds of flesh." Each kept a journal for the other to read upon Hawthorne's return, so that as little as possible might be lost to each of the other's life during their separation. On the afternoon of his arrival Mrs. Hawthorne set the stage for a brilliant welcome, and the elements and chance happily conspired with her:

I put the vase of delicious rosebuds [she wrote Mrs. Peabody] and a beautiful China plate of peaches and grapes, and a basket of splendid golden Porter apples on his table; and we opened the western door and let in a flood of sunsetting. Apollo's "beautiful disdain" seemed kindled anew. Endymion smiled richly in his dream of Diana. Lake Como was wrapped in golden mist. The divine form in the Transfiguration floated in light. I thought it would be a pity if Mr. Hawthorne did not come that moment. As I thought this, I heard the railroad-coach—and he was here. He looked, as he wrote in one of his letters, "twice the man he was."

The biography of Pierce had been published during Hawthorne's absence, Mrs. Hawthorne having received twelve copies from Ticknor on September 10. Cooperating with the plans of the Democratic party for wide circulation, Hawthorne consented to the free distibution of five thousand copies in New York City. The Whig press, of course, attacked the book, accusing its author of venal motives and ridiculing its authenticity by calling it "Mr. Hawthorne's latest *romance*." The biography cost Hawthorne many admirers and well-wishers because of his position on slavery. The part which especially gave offense to the abolitionists read as follows:

Pierce fully recognized, by his votes and by his voice, the rights pledged to the South by the Constitution. This, at the period when he so declared himself, was comparatively an easy thing to do. But when it became more difficult, when the first imperceptible movement of agitation had grown to be almost a convulsion, his course was still the same. Nor did he ever shun the obloquy that sometimes threatened to pursue the northern man who dared to love that great and sacred reality—his whole, united, native country—better than the mistiness of a philanthropic theory. . . .

He considered, too, that the evil of abolition would be certain, while this good [emancipation] was, at best, a contingency, and (to the clear, practical foresight with which he looked into the future) scarcely so much as that, attended as the movement was and must be during its progress, with the aggravated injury of those whose condition it aimed to ameliorate, and terminating in its possible triumph—if such possibility there were—with the ruin of two races which now dwelt together in greater peace and affection, it is not too much to say, than had ever elsewhere existed between the taskmaster and the serf.

In sum, Pierce believed—and Hawthorne agreed with him—that slavery was entitled to protection under the Constitution, that the Union ("that great and sacred reality") was threatened with disruption by the activities of the abolitionists, and that the welfare and happiness of the Negro himself would be jeopardized by his emancipation. These were his real sentiments, Hawthorne told Bridge, and he did not regret that they were on record even though, as he put it, "hundreds of friends at the north dropped off" from him "like autumn leaves."

Hawthorne reviewed the whole subject of the biography and his relations with Pierce in a letter to Bridge in October. He had been "reluctant to undertake the work," he said, but "after a friendship of thirty years" he could not refuse to do his best in Pierce's behalf, "at the great pinch of his life." Pierce was pleased with the result, and Hawthorne thought the work "judiciously done": "without any sacrifice of truth, it puts him in as good a light as circumstances would admit." And, he added with a smile, "though the story is true, yet it took a romancer to do it."

Hawthorne was caught up in the excitement of the presidential campaign. Sometimes he pitied Pierce, whose hair was perceptibly whitening, and wished that the Democratic Convention had nominated "old Cass." At the same time he felt an almost superstitious regard for him as a man of destiny. Pierce, he thought, had "the directing mind"; he was "deep" in a political sense, and withal so lucky that it seemed nothing could ruin him. Now in the intensest blaze of celebrity he was playing for a tremendous stake, the alternatives being "a place in history" or "a forgotten grave." Mrs. Hawthorne, too, felt the excitement of the living drama which was being acted out before them. She rallied to the defense of her husband and her husband's friend despite the fact that her family and social connections were abolitionists. "As no instrument could wrench out of Mr. Hawthorne a word that he did not know to be true in spirit and in letter," she wrote Mrs. Peabody (who could be counted on to circulate Sophia's testimony), "so also no fear of whatsoever the world may attribute to him as motive would weigh a feather in his estimation." And in another letter, which was an elaborate defense of Pierce both as man and statesman, she declared, "If you knew General Pierce as we know him, you would be the first to respect him."

The biography out of the way, Hawthorne attempted to settle down, in October, to creative writing. "In a day or two," he wrote Bridge on October 13, 1852, "I intend to begin a new romance, which, if possible, I mean to make more genial than the last." Fields reported to Miss Mitford in England on October 24 that Hawthorne was at work on another romance: "From all I can gather from this silent genius," he said, "it will be in the Scarlet Letter vein." On November 5 Fields stated again to Miss Mitford that Hawthorne was busy with a new romance: "I feel it will be good," he declared, "better far than the B. Romance, for his wife says he looks happy about it." The work on which Hawthorne was engaged has not been identified, but if Fields was correct it is possible that Hawthorne was exploring the "Agatha" story offered him by Herman Melville.

In August Melville had sent to Hawthorne the story (recorded by a New Bedford lawyer) of Agatha Hatch who, residing on the New England coast, had married a shipwrecked sailor and had been deserted by him. Melville thought that the story had possibilities—the patient waiting of the wife, the awakening moral sense of the faithless husband and his consequent remorse—and that it was especially appropriate for Hawthorne. Thinking that Hawthorne was seriously considering the story, and was perhaps actually writing it, Melville sent on October 25 some suggestions for explaining the husband's behavior and moral development. Probably not long afterward—but the date is undetermined—Melville visited Hawthorne at the Wayside. During the visit the two men talked over the Agatha story. Hawthorne had apparently given some thought to the matter, for he mentioned the Isles of Shoals (of recent memory) as a suitable setting. The upshot of the conversation, however, was that Hawthorne seemed uncertain, and urged, or appeared to urge, Melville to do Agatha, for in a letter written soon after the visit Melville requested the return of the documents, with the addition of such suggestions as Hawthorne cared to make, since he himself had decided to write the story after all. It seems probable that Hawthorne was interested in the story of Agatha and had done some work on it when Melville came to Concord, but that his hesitation in accepting the gift of the story caused him to convey the impression that he did not want it. The fact that it dealt with marital unfaithfulness might have led Fields to describe it as being "in the Scarlet Letter vein," and if Hawthorne perhaps intended a reconciliation of the husband and wife, he might have regarded the story in prospect as "more genial" than *Blithedale*. (He had told of the reconciliation of a wife and her wayward husband in "Wakefield," of which the Agatha story reminded Melville.) Hawthorne's hesitation—if such it was—might have been prompted by his own regrets—if he had them—for having given Evangeline to Longfellow: at any rate he would not be in too great a hurry to accept another man's literary property. The event was that Hawthorne never wrote the Agatha story nor, so far as is known, did Melville.

Quite aside from the abortive attempts to put Agatha into fiction, it is pleasant to see the reunion of these Berkshire friends. A note by Mrs. Hawthorne written about this time doubtless refers specifically to Melville at the Wayside (the context develops the idea of Hawthorne's evocative sympathy): "So Mr. Melville," she wrote, "generally silent and incommunicative, pours out the rich floods of his mind and experience to him, so sure of apprehension, so sure of a large and generous interpretation, and of the most delicate and fine judgment." Before coming to Concord Melville had written, "Keep some champagne or gin for me," and after his return home he expressed great pleasure in his visit, sent greetings to the children, and asked Hawthorne's blessing upon his literary labors.

Not long after the election of Pierce Hawthorne found himself in the maelstrom of politics. As the campaign biographer and life-long friend of the President-elect, he had suddenly become a man of political importance. He was "as besieged by office seekers," he said, "as a prime minister." He was asked to give sage counsel and to exert influence. He was applied to for subordinate positions on his own staff, the assumption being that he himself would receive an important post and would therefore control a certain amount of patronage. Hawthorne responded almost zestfully to these new demands; it was not unpleasant to be in a position of power just four years after his ignominious ejection from the Salem Custom House; the whirligig of time had brought in its revenges. His days were soon filled with receiving visitors, writing letters, and journeying to Boston for deep sessions at Parker's grog shop. By November 12 he had decided to go to Boston in the future "incog," for he had hardly enjoyed a moment to himself during his last visit of two days. In the following March he hesitated to address more letters to the President: "There is so much of my paper now in the President's hands," he remarked, "that (as the note-shavers say) I am afraid it will be going at a discount." There was no overseriousness. Politics was a game and he could take an amateur's pleasure in playing it in his favored position. His attitude throughout was one of realism brightened by humor. In recommending Richard Henry Stoddard, the poet, to J. L. O'Sullivan, Hawthorne noted Stoddard's "claim" as the author of a magazine biography of his "distinguished self" and added with a twinkle, "Biographers of great men ought to be rewarded—and sometimes are."

It is no longer possible to reconstruct the local political situation in detail. Salem was a whirlpool of intrigue into which Hawthorne was inevitably drawn. His chief object was to help his old friends Pike and Burchmore and this he succeeded in doing: Pike eventually got the Salem collectorship, and Burchmore, who apparently had become a little disreputable from too much drink, a place in the Boston Custom House. In several letters Hawthorne gave strategic advice to the Salem politicians. "What do you think of a programme like this?" he wrote Burchmore on December 9, 1852:

In consideration of your withdrawing your claim to the Naval Office, Loring and his coadjutors shall pledge themselves to use all their influence to get you a situation in the Boston Custom House. Their strength, together with what you could otherwise obtain, would certainly give the fairest prospect of success,—*provided* you could be sure that they would not play you false. Should Loring be a party to the contract to the above effect, I think he would do his utmost to fulfill it—especially as all his supporters wish to get you out of the district. Unless I am mistaken in your views, you would not regret escaping from the Salem Custom House. Think over this matter, and consult with Dr. Browne about it, and take the course which you deem most advisable.

To Burchmore again on March 14, 1853, he said:

I advise you to try to make friends with the enemy, before proceeding to open war. Perhaps it may be a false alarm, after all. Do not force them into an attitude of hostility, if they have not already taken it. If you have an interview with the President, speak of them in a friendly way, and do not (unless compelled) act on the supposition that they are hostile to you. I must confess, I do not understand how they can proceed openly against you, after giving you their letters.

On May 31 Hawthorne reviewed Burchmore's situation once more and favored him with more sage advice:

I have already taken one step towards a negotiation with the enemy respecting your being restored to your old place. Of course, it was not to be expected that I should get a very favorable response, at first; but I have strong hopes of finding a soft spot in their gizzards, if not in their hearts.

Meantime, be quiet, and do not let them suspect you of founding your hopes upon any hostile section of the party. If you declare war against them, and try to fight your way in, I would not give a "whore's cuss" (to borrow an elegant phrase from the old General [General James Miller, late Collector at Salem]) for your chance of being reinstated.

The extent to which Hawthorne's advice was actually carried out is now probably past discovery, but it bears the marks of astuteness. He was hardly a babe in the political woods.

Hawthorne was active, too, beyond his immediate district. Being a citizen of the world of letters and having friends who resided outside the jurisdiction of Boston and Salem politics, he was glad of the opportunity to assist brother authors whose income from literature, like his own, required supplement. Hawthorne himself would have starved without political emolument, and he saw no good reason why he should not help others to eke out their incomes in a similar way. There were at least two writers whom he sought to make the beneficiaries of the new Democratic administration: Richard Henry Stoddard and Herman Melville.

Stoddard, Hawthorne thought, was naïve and needed advice. "Are you fond of brandy?" he inquired of the young office seeker. "Your strength of head," he continued,

(which you tell me you possess) may stand you in good stead at Washington; for most of these public men are inordinate guzzlers, and love a man that can stand up to them in that particular. It would never do to let them see you corned, however. But I must leave you to find your own way among them. If you have never associated with them heretofore, you will find them a new class, and very unlike poets.

Not only was strength of head necessary to the successful candidate but the abeyance of conscientious scruples. One might as well be realistic about it:

When applying for office [Hawthorne continued in his letter to Stoddard], if you are conscious of any deficiencies (moral, intellectual, educational, or whatever else), keep them to yourself, and let those find them out whose business it may be. For example, supposing the office of Translator to the State Department to be tendered you, accept it boldly, without hinting that your acquaintance with foreign languages may not be the most familiar. If this unimportant fact be discovered afterwards, you can be transferred to some more suitable post. The business is, to establish yourself, somehow and anywhere. . . . A subtile boldness, with a veil of modesty over it, is what is needed.

In the meantime, Hawthorne was writing to influential Democrats in Stoddard's behalf. The outcome was a clerkship in the New York City Custom House.

Hawthorne tried without success to secure an appointment for Melville. One can only conjecture the reason for his failure: it may have been Melville's lack of political connections or of any "claim" upon the party; or an equivocal reputation caused by his attacks on American missionaries in *Typee* and *Omoo* and his use of a forbidden theme in *Pierre*, just published; or, more probably, an opposition in Washington resulting from his angry exposure in *White Jacket* of brutal practices in the United States Navy. Melville was almost certainly "the friend" in whose behalf Hawthorne inquired concerning "the Roman charge-ship" in the contingency that Pierce would remove the present incumbent. He was also probably the friend to whom Hawthorne said he was "indebted for many kindnesses," and whose cause he advocated in Washington during his visit there in April. Melville wanted a consular appointment, and Hawthorne did his best. He was embarrassed and chagrined by his failure. When the two men met in England three years later, Hawthorne said that he "felt rather awkward at first"; but when he considered that he had "failed only from real lack of power to serve Melville," he concluded that "there was no reason to be ashamed."

There had never been any serious doubt that Hawthorne himself would be given a good appointment, though for a while there was some doubt as to what the appointment would be. In December Hawthorne jokingly asked Fields about Portugal—"as, for instance, in what part of the world it lies, and whether it is an Empire, a Kingdom, or a republic . . . and more particularly, the expenses of living there." "Any other information about foreign countries," he said, "would be acceptable to an inquiring mind." The uncertainty and the wealth of possibilities were tantalizing. Two months later the prognostication was the consulship at Liverpool. Fields had it from the President himself that Hawthorne would be given a post which would relieve him of financial anxiety, and the Liverpool consulate was the most lucrative office within the gift of the Administration. The expectation was soon realized. Pierce appointed Hawthorne consul to Liverpool and the appointment was confirmed by the Senate, March 26, 1853. On the floor of the Senate Charles Sumner, abolitionist though he was, shouted "Good! Good!" for he admired Hawthorne and his writings and was keenly sensible of his financial need.

Nor was there any doubt that Hawthorne would accept the Liverpool appointment—least of all in Hawthorne's own mind. For although he had resolved, when he undertook the biography, that he would accept no office from Pierce, he later decided that it would be folly rather than heroism to keep such a resolution.

In the first place he needed the money. He had a wife and three growing children whom he could not reasonably expect to support by his pen. (He must also contribute to the support of his sister Elizabeth, now living with a farmer's family near Beverly.) Although he had just written three successful novels in as many years, with a successful juvenile thrown in, the annual income from his books did not much exceed $1,000. The collections of tales, whose sale one might expect to be stimulated by the success of *The Scarlet Letter* and the other novels, were selling hardly at all. In February, 1853, G. P. Putnam sent a check for $144.09, the author's total income from the *Mosses* for one and one-half years. As a writer Hawthorne enjoyed a success of esteem, but he was convinced at last that it was impossible for him (however fabulous Washington Irving's or someone else's income from his books might be) to make a decent living by literature alone.

In the second place he had never been abroad, and he longed to see England especially. All of his literary confreres except Thoreau had been to Europe—some of them several times. Although Emerson might declare traveling to be a fool's paradise and counsel the wise man to stay at home, he himself had already been abroad twice. Longfellow had gone to Europe repeatedly and had traveled from one end of the continent to the other. And likewise with the others. Hawthorne was forty-nine, and if he did not take this opportunity he would never be able to go. He felt his ancestral ties deeply; felt deeply also his ties with English literature and history, English places and scenes. He would like to vivify his impressions and make them concrete through the physical senses. Moreover, as Fields told him and as letters from Miss Mitford, Barry Cornwall, De Quincey's daughter, and others testified, he was acquiring an English reputation. Such a reputation was an ambition cherished from boyhood: "How proud you would feel," to refer again to the early letter to his mother, "to see my works praised by the reviewers as equal to the proudest productions of the scribbling sons of John Bull!" Well, critical readers in England were now saying just that: a recent letter from Miss Mitford had praised "the fine tragic construction unsurpassed amongst living authors—the passion of the concluding scenes—the subtle analysis of feeling—the exquisite finish of style" in *Blithedale*, and had quoted the cleverest man she knew as saying, "Hawthorne's English is the richest & most intense essence of the language I know of." "Just at this time," Hawthorne wrote to Bridge with pardonable pride (pardonable because it was Bridge's early faith, he said, that was responsible for his being an author at all), "I rather think your friend stands foremost in England as an American fiction-monger." He had received, he added, "several invitations from English celebrities to come over there." In sum, the time was propitious for the journey.

Only a querulous soul would censure Hawthorne for accepting the Liverpool consulship. Such a censure occurs, interestingly enough, in the private journal of Thoreau, who wrote, "Better for me, says my genius, to go cranberrying this afternoon for the *Vaccinium Oxycoccus* in Gowing's Swamp, to get but a pocketful and learn its peculiar flavor, aye, and the flavor of Gowing's Swamp and of *Life* in New England, than to go consul to Liverpool and get I don't know how many thousand dollars for it, with no such flavor." If it was a question of indigenousness to New England, one might fairly reply, Hawthorne was as indigenous as Thoreau. He had assimilated life in New England for forty-nine years (no author ever assimilated his native region more lovingly or more completely) and he had given classic expression in literature to that assimilated life. Thoreau should have singled out another writer than Hawthorne to accuse of neglecting the native "flavor." If it was a question of money, there is no arguing with a man of Thoreau's opinions. "In his presence," Hawthorne said of him, "one feels ashamed of having any money, or a house to live in, or so much as two coats to wear."

Hawthorne's preoccupation with politics for many months past had left him little leisure or freshness of mind for creative writing. In the summer of 1852 the biography of Pierce had compelled him to defer the *Tanglewood Tales*, and in the autumn of that year political pressure (and possibly Melville's reclamation of the Agatha story) had led him to discontinue work on a new romance. Despite political distractions, however, he was able during the winter to resume the less difficult of the two. Exactly when he began the *Tanglewood Tales* is not known. Because of interruptions its writing probably required somewhat longer than that of *A Wonder-Book*. He recorded the completion of the stories of *Tanglewood* on March 9, 1853, and of the "Introduction" on March 13; and on March 15 he sent the manuscript to Ticknor, urging that it be put in press immediately. The book was published in August. Hawthorne remarked of the tales to Stoddard: "They are done up in excellent style, purified from all moral stains, re-created as good as new, or better, and fully equal, in their own way, to Mother Goose. I never did anything else so well as these old baby stories." Ever since *Grandfather's Chair* and earlier, Hawthorne had fancied himself, with justice, as a writer of stories for children. At one time he had envisaged the large-scale produc-tion of such works as an easy road to wealth. His writings in this kind—especially *A Wonder-Book* and *Tanglewood Tales*—early attained the rank of juvenile classics, and they were moderately popular. Julian Hawthorne tells of the "many entreaties from young people" (including no doubt the author's own children) for a second volume after the appearance of *A Wonder-Book*. But the sale of the juveniles did not much improve the author's finan-cial condition. Hawthorne gave Fields credit for a major achieve-ment when he managed to get £50 from Chapman and Hall for the English copyright of *Tanglewood*.

The "baby stories" finished, Hawthorne was free again to give his entire attention to the fascinating political scene. He had never been to the national capital, and the days immediately following the inauguration of the new President, when the Washington merry-go-round was liveliest, seemed a good time to go. Besides enjoying the spectacle, he hoped by such a trip to help some of his friends more effectively and perhaps to improve his own situation. Accordingly, plans were made for the journey. Late in March Hawthorne sent to his Boston tailor, through Ticknor, an order for a new suit of clothes: "My best dress-coat," he wrote Tick-nor, "is rather shabby (befitting an author much more than a man of consular rank); so, when you next smoke a cigar with our friend Driscoll, I wish you would tell him to put another suit on the stocks for me—a black dress-coat and pantaloons; and he may select the cloth."

Accompanied by Ticknor, who was himself apparently something of an old hand in politics, Hawthorne set out on a leisurely journey to Washington on the morning of April 14, leaving the Wayside—his wife recorded sadly—"in a dark rain." The travelers stopped for three days in New York, where Hawthorne was busily occupied with callers and engagements; he managed to have a talk with O'Sullivan, but it was unseasonably interrupted when other people joined them; he dined in Waverly-Place with Miss Anne Charlotte Lynch, famous bluestocking; he wished, he said, that he could be let alone to follow his own ideas of what was agreeable, and punned (in a letter to his wife) on the prospect of being "lynched." Like many another devoted husband and father —both before and since—at sea in the great metropolis, he was homesick for his family: "I am homesick for thee," he wrote Sophia. "The children, too, seem very good and beautiful at this distance. I hope Una will be very kind and sweet. As for Julian, let Ellen make him a pandowdy. Does Rosebud still remember me? It seems an age since I left home. No words can tell how I love thee. I will write again as soon as possible." From Philadelphia, where he stopped off for a day, he wrote his wife: "I enjoy the journey and seeing new places, but need thee beyond all possibility of telling. I feel as if I had just begun to know that there is nothing else for me but thou. The children, too, I know how to love, at last. Kiss them all for me." From Baltimore, on the day following: "Thus far in safety . . . With love a thousand times more than ever." And again from Washington, where he arrived a full week after leaving Concord: "My heart is weary with longing for thee. I want thee in my arms."

Hawthorne remained in Washington for nearly two weeks. He had not meant to stay so long but he was asked by the President to extend his visit. In a letter to his wife he summed up his accomplishments by saying: "It is very queer how much I have done for other people and myself since my arrival here." One known result of his presence in Washington was the addition of the consulship of Manchester to his original portfolio. Not all of his time, however, was spent in the business of politics. He was a good deal lionized, receiving more invitations than he could accept. On one occasion he accompanied the ladies of the President's family to Mount Vernon, whence he wrote to his wife of Virginia in April: "Thou never sawest such a beautiful and blossoming Spring as we have here."

Spring was beginning to come to Concord also by the end of April. Mrs. Hawthorne recorded in her diary that the peach trees and cherry trees were in bloom. But she could not enjoy the blossoms in her loneliness: "I looked about, as I sat down in our pine grove, and tried to bear my husband's absence, but it is desolation without him." She was busily occupied, though, with the children and with visitors. Mrs. S. G. Ward, splendid and radiant, drove up in the stagecoach, and was cruelly disappointed not to see Mr. Hawthorne. Emerson and Ellery Channing stopped by and took Julian with them to Walden Pond. Judge Rockwood Hoar congratulated the Hawthornes upon their going to England—"the only place fit to live in," the stalwart patriot said, "out of America." The prospect of England and of absence from the Wayside was now looming large, for the Hawthornes planned to sail in the early summer. Documents pertaining to the Liverpool consulate arrived from the State Department. The thought of leaving the Wayside was poignant to Sophia: "This is the sweetest place," she said; "I really cannot bear to leave it."

Soon after Hawthorne's return from Washington in early May he and his family were busy with preparations for the impending change. They had made many changes before but none so radical as this. Their residence abroad was to be of considerable duration: they were looking forward to a consul's term of four years at Liverpool with an additional year in Italy. Some possessions had to be packed for shipment, others had to be stored, and the house made ready for Mrs. Hawthorne's brother Nathaniel and his family, who were to occupy it during the Hawthornes' absence. Two incidents during these weeks of preparation called forth the following characteristic notes in Hawthorne's journal:

Cleaning the garret today (here at the Wayside) the woman found an immense snake, fat and outrageously fierce—thrusting out his tongue. Ellen killed it. She called it an adder, but it appears to have been a striped snake. It seemed a fiend, haunting the house. On further inquiry, Una describes the snake as plaided with brown and black.

I burned great heaps of old letters and other papers, a little while ago, preparatory to going to England. Among them were hundreds of Sophia's maiden letters—the world has no more such; and now they are all ashes. What a trustful guardian of secret matters fire is! What should we do without Fire and Death?

During the last weeks before his departure Hawthorne could not receive the visits or accept the invitations proffered him. It is pleasant to know, however, that he found time for a dinner in his honor at the Craigie House. Although Hawthorne and Longfellow had seen less of each other in recent years than either would have liked, Longfellow's hospitality—quite removed as it was from the political sphere—testified to the enduring warmth of their friendship: "Had a very pleasant farewell dinner for Hawthorne," Longfellow wrote in his Journal of June 14, "who sails for his Liverpool Consulship in a few weeks. Guests were Hawthorne, Emerson, Clough, Lowell, Charles Norton, and brother Sam. After dinner, we sat on the piazza chatting." And on the following day Longfellow wrote again in his journal: "The memory of yesterday sweetens today. It was a delightful farewell to my old friend. He seems much cheered by the prospect before him; and is very lively and in good spirits."

Accompanied by the faithful Ticknor, the Hawthornes sailed from Boston July 6, 1853, on the screw steamer *Niagara*, Cunard Line, Captain Leitch. James T. Fields, with beaming countenance, and Dr. Peabody, Mrs. Hawthorne's father, were among those who saw them off. As they moved out of the harbor the *Niagara's* cannon roared a long salute in recognition of the fact—Mrs. Hawthorne wrote her parents—that "Mr. Hawthorne, the distinguished United States Consul and author, was leaving the shore and honoring her Majesty's steamship with his presence."

CHAPTER VIII

ENGLAND, 1853–1857

THE voyage required ten days, the *Niagara* reaching Liverpool on July 16. Except for a sharp squall in midocean the weather was fine all the way. Once his family were fairly settled on board and the American shore, viewed regretfully, had vanished from sight, Hawthorne gave himself freely to the enjoyment of the voyage. It was his first extended sea journey and the enjoyment was hereditary, he must have reflected, because his forefathers for several generations had followed the sea. He spent much time on deck, never tiring of wind, waves, and sky. Meanwhile, Julian raced back and forth on the deck, Una sat reading an advance copy of *Tanglewood Tales*, and Mrs. Hawthorne talked with a young Englishman, Field Talfourd (brother of the author of *Ion*), whose "all-sided development"—she recorded— was "a lovely flower requiring more leisure and a deeper culture than Americans yet have." Throughout the voyage the Hawthornes had seats of honor at the captain's table. The voice, smile, and military air of Captain Leitch inspired complete confidence.

For the first month or so after their arrival in Liverpool the Hawthornes lived at the Rock Ferry Hotel. In September they took a house in Rock Park, about five miles up and across the Mersey from Liverpool. Hawthorne mused sadly in his new surroundings: "As I sat in this English house, with the chill, rainy English twilight brooding over the lawn, and a coal-fire to keep me comfortable on the first evening of September, and the picture of a stranger gazing down at me from above the mantel-piece, I felt that I never should be quite at home here."

He assumed office August 1, 1853, and on August 4 he recorded in his journal his first impressions of his new surroundings:

My apartment (about twelve feet by fifteen, and of a good height) is hung with a map of the United States, and another of Europe; there is a hideous colored lithograph of General Taylor, life-size, and one or two smaller engraved portraits; also three representations of American naval victories; a lithograph of the Tennessee State-house, and another of the Steamer Empire State. The mantel-piece is adorned with the American Eagle, painted on the wood; and on shelves there are a number of volumes, bound in sheepskin, of the laws of the United States and Statutes at Large. Thus the consular office is a little patch of America, with English life encompassing it on all sides. One truly English object, however, is the Barometer hanging on the wall, and which today for a wonder points to Fair.

The consulate was located near the Liverpool docks in the midst of a world of noise and traffic. From his office window he wrote, "across the narrow street, I have a view of a tall, dismal, smoke-blackened, ugly brick ware-house—uglier than any building I ever saw in America; and from one or another of the various stories, bags of salt are often being raised or lowered, swinging and vibrating in the air. There is a continual rumble of heavy wheels, which makes conversation rather difficult, although I am gradually getting accustomed to it."

The consulship proved to be a difficult and irksome assignment. Hawthorne often thought of resigning, but he stayed on doggedly at his post for a little more than the normal term of four years because he had accepted the appointment in order that he might accumulate a financial competence and at the same time see and assimilate England, and both of these objects required a maximum of time. Some people not well acquainted with Hawthorne (Samuel G. Ward, for example) questioned his ability to perform satisfactorily the duties of the office. But Pierce knew Hawthorne's mundane capacities better than the skeptics, who perchance knew him only by his writings and mistakenly supposed that the creator of Arthur Dimmesdale and Father Hooper would be as much out of place in the workaday world as some of his creations. The task was in many ways uncongenial, but Hawthorne showed a remarkable adaptability. When he turned the office over to his successor in the autumn of 1857, he viewed his consular record with satisfaction for, if such evidence were needed, he held in his hand a letter from the Secretary of State testifying to "the prudent and efficient manner" in which he had discharged his duties. But the outcome had hardly been a foregone conclusion to Hawthorne himself: "I thank God," he wrote Ticknor, "for bringing me through this consular business so well."

The new consul was immediately besieged by a horde of supplicants: "Every morning, I find the entry thronged with the most rascally set of sailors that ever were seen—dirty, desperate, and altogether pirate-like in aspect. What the devil they want here, is beyond my present knowledge; but probably they have been shipwrecked, or otherwise thrown at large on the world, and wish for assistance in some shape."

The routine business of the consulate—the keeping of accounts, the processing of documents and the like—was attended to by two experienced clerks, Peirce and Wilding, in whose ability and integrity Hawthorne had complete (and as the event proved a fully justified) confidence. While thus relieved of clerical chores, he was constantly occupied by importunities from the outside. The chief of these were from sailors who sought redress for injuries received on board American ships. The consul had a large responsibility to the members—both officers and crews—of the American merchant marine who came into Liverpool, and Hawthorne discharged the responsibility conscientiously. Conditions aboard the ships at the time were lawless often to the point of mutiny, and since the captain could enforce discipline only by physical violence, both officers and men were often the victims of brutal attack. Much of Hawthorne's time, consequently, was spent in police courts, assisting in the adjudication of conflicting claims; in hospitals, visiting the sick and wounded; and in coroners' offices, funeral parlors, and cemeteries—for there were many fatalities—attending to the multifarious business connected with death and burial.

Of the numerous accounts in Hawthorne's notebook describing experiences of this kind, the following passage dated November 16, 1855—which is at once objective and sympathetic—is quite typical:

I went to the North Hospital yesterday, to take the deposition of a dying man as to his ill-treatment by the second and third mates of the ship Assyria, on the voyage from New Orleans. . . . We went forthwith up two or three pairs of stairs, to the ward where the sick man lay, and where there were six or eight other beds, in almost each of which was a patient—narrow beds, shabbily furnished. The man whom I came to see was the only one who was not perfectly quiet; neither was he very restless. The doctor, informing him of my presence, intimated that his disease might be fatal, and that I was come to hear what he had to say as to the causes of his death. Afterwards, a Testament was sought for, in order to swear him; and I administered the oath, and made him kiss the book. He then (in response to Mr. Wilding's questions) told how he had been beaten and ill-treated, banged and thwacked, from the moment he came on board;—to which usage he ascribed his death. Sometimes his senses seemed to sink away, so that I almost thought him dead; but, by-and-by the questions would appear to reach him, and bring him back, and he went on with his evidence,—interspersing it, however, with dying groans, and almost death rattles. . . . He sank away so much, at one time, that they brought him wine in a tin vessel, with a spout to drink out of; and he mustered strength to raise himself in bed and drink; then hemmed, with rather a disappointed air, as if it did not stimulate and refresh him as drink ought. When he had finished his evidence (which Mr. Wilding took down in writing, from his mouth) he marked his cross at the foot of the paper; and we ceased to torment him with further question. . . . Before I left the dying sailor, his features seemed to contract and grow sharp. Some young medical students stood about the bed, watching death creep upon him, and anticipating, perhaps, that, in a day or two, they would have the poor fellow's body on the dissecting-table.

Although habitually distrustful of organized reform and professional reformers, Hawthorne was acutely conscious of the maritime evils every day thrust before his eyes and felt that something should be done toward their amendment. "There is a most dreadful state of things aboard our ships," he declared in his notebook; "Hell itself can be no worse than some of them; and I do pray that some New Englander, with the itch of reform in him, may turn his thoughts this way." If Hawthorne himself lacked "the itch of reform," he nevertheless took such steps as were within his power at the time to bring the subject to the attention of the proper authorities. He made repeated representations to the State Department and wrote Charles Sumner, offering to supply him with the facts and urging him to present the question before the Senate. When Sumner ignored the letter Hawthorne commented wryly to Ticknor, "Had he busied himself about this, instead of Abolitionism, he would have done good service to his country and have escaped Brooks's cudgel."

The first step toward improvement, Hawthorne thought, would be to legalize flogging on shipboard. "As in so many other instances," he said, "philanthropy has overshot itself by the prohibition of flogging, causing the captain to avoid the responsibility of solemn punishment, and leave his mates to make devils of themselves by habitual ill-treatment of the seamen." But a more fundamental need was the rehabilitation of maritime personnel, and in behalf of such a reform Hawthorne sent a dignified and explicit despatch to the State Department in June, 1857. He pointed out to the Secretary of State that not one in ten of the seamen employed on American vessels was a native-born or even a naturalized American, and that many of the men were not seamen at all but landsmen who had been impressed into service or had shipped for the purpose of accomplishing a voyage. It was inevitable that the regular seamen should abuse the landsmen for not doing (albeit through incapacity) their share of the work and that a feud should arise between the two classes. Hawthorne asserted also that the laws which purported to deal with the maritime situation were ineffectual and that most of the offenders went unpunished. Their escape, however, was not the fault of the consul, he maintained, but of a combination of circumstances over which the consul had no control. In a brief reply the Secretary exonerated Hawthorne for failure to bring offenders to punishment and concurred in the view that what was chiefly wrong with the merchant service was the lack of American seamen. But with the question of how that lack might be supplied or the evils corrected the Secretary was not at that time concerned. Having taken the question to the highest authority and having met there with indifference, Hawthorne made no further efforts as a maritime reformer, even though some Liverpool philanthropists continued to accuse him of dereliction. "They will hardly succeed in crowding me off my track," he told Ticknor, and he did not take up the subject again except to review it briefly in *Our Old Home.*

Not only aggrieved sailors but hundreds of other people came to the consulate with some kind of axe to grind. At one time Hawthorne resolved to put down in his notebook everybody who called at his office during a week, only to find that there were too many for record. Some were Americans stranded in Liverpool without money or friends. Others were Englishmen who pretended to be Americans the better to recommend themselves to the consul, and Hawthorne used very successfully, he thought (though its use would be less decisive today), "been" as a shibboleth. Still others were men without a country. "All exiles for liberty come to me," he wrote in his journal "—Hungarians, Poles, Cubans, Spanish Americans, French republicans—as if the representative of America were their representative." Of all appeals to the consul's charity, those of the "exiles," he said, were the hardest to refuse. To many applicants Hawthorne lent money, some of which was never repaid. His letters to Ticknor, who acted as his banker and broker, repeatedly inclosed I.O.U's. for collection. How much Hawthorne was out of pocket by financial aid which seemed to him imperative and which a remiss government had failed to provide for cannot be determined or even estimated; but more than once he quoted ruefully to Ticknor the old adage, "A fool and his money are soon parted."

The visits of Americans Hawthorne recorded in particular detail. It was with a peculiar feeling of having "lost the property of his own person" that he overheard American callers speaking of him as "my Consul." He felt that during the four years at the consulate he became better acquainted with American characteristics —the lunatic and vulgar as well as the commonsensical and refined —than in all his previous life. Day after day a variegated procession filed through his office—an unforeseen realization of his own "Procession of Life." There was William Lilley of Ohio, consul-elect to Pernambuco—"a very unfavorable specimen of American manners, an outrageous tobacco-chewer and atrocious spitter on carpets"; Hawthorne lent him money and succeeded in collecting it only after he had threatened to report the default to the State Department. On the same day came Stephen A. Douglas, whom Hawthorne described as "a very able man, with the Western sociability and free fellowship." There was the Reverend Mr. Richards of New Orleans, who turned up at the consulate in a disreputable condition after several days and nights in a Liverpool brothel. Hawthorne lectured him on his misconduct so sternly that the culprit shook in his shoes, but observed relentingly in his notebook, "In my opinion, he has incurred sin no farther than as a madman may." The consul assumed responsibility for the clergyman's passage to Boston and sent him thither in the company of a responsible custodian. Another visitor was Captain Walter M. Gibson, whose romantic adventures recalled Othello's and whose talk had "a strange oriental fragrance breathing through it, as if the smell of the Spice Islands were still in his garments." The captain was slow in repaying a loan (if he ever repaid it), as was Philip Richardson of Louisville, Kentucky, who had been at the Battle of New Orleans and whom Hawthorne liked for the "keen, strong sense at the bottom of his character." Sharply contrasted with such a person was the feeble-minded old man (his story reminded Hawthorne of Melville's *Israel Potter*) who had tried for many years and was still trying "to get home to Ninety-Second Street, Philadelphia." Hawthorne gave him money and with good judgment refused to send him back to a home which had long since forgotten him and which he himself would now find unrecognizable.

But it is not necessary to multiply examples. All told, the consulate was a rich education in human varieties and vagaries. The experience was a bit wearing too. "I have received, and been civil to, at least 10,000 visitors since I came to England," he wrote Ticknor, with a mixture of weariness and humorous exaggeration, in July, 1857, "and I never wish to be civil to anybody again."

Besides the round of visitors at the consulate and the many responsibilities which they entailed, Hawthorne was frequently called upon to make speeches at banquets and on other public occasions. Speechmaking was perhaps the most trying of all his official duties. Except for the declamations at college—which he had usually avoided to the point of incurring fines—he had probably never made a public speech before coming to England. But the American consul had to speak, and Hawthorne met the requirement manfully if not always brilliantly. As he acquired facility he was surprised at the pleasure (though the joy was three parts pain) which could be derived from such an exercise.

The most frequent demand came from the mayor of Liverpool, who gave banquets in the town hall at regular intervals. Within two weeks after taking office Hawthorne found himself seated at the mayor's banquet table in the midst of British dignity and splendor. "The rooms," he recorded in the notebook, "were beautiful; gorgeously painted and gilded, gorgeously lighted, gorgeously hung with paintings, gorgeously illuminated—the plate gorgeous, the dinner gorgeous." The guests included the judges of England, who, during the assize then being held, had (royalty excepted) the highest rank in the kingdom. As he sat awaiting his turn with nervous apprehension, the notebook continues,

By-and-by came a toast to the United States and me as their representative. Hereupon, either "Hail Columbia" or "Yankee Doodle," or some other of our national tunes (but Heaven knows which) was played; and at the conclusion—being cornered, and with no alternative—I got upon my legs and made a response. They received me and listened to my nonsense with a good deal of rapping; and my speech seemed to give great satisfaction. My chief difficulty lay in not knowing how to pitch my voice to the size of the room; as for the matter, it is not of the slightest consequence. Anybody may make an after-dinner speech, who will be content to talk onward without saying anything. My speech was not more than two or three inches long;—and considering that I did not know a soul there, except the Mayor himself, and that I am wholly unpractised in all sorts of oratory, and that I had nothing to say, it was quite successful. I hardly thought it was in me; but being once on my legs, I felt no embarrassment, and went through it as coolly as if I were going to be hanged.

A diffident beginner, Hawthorne continued to speak not only at lord mayors' dinners but before boards of trade, at the launching of ships, and at the laying of cornerstones. Perhaps the high point of his public appearances was the speech delivered at a dinner given by the lord mayor of London in April, 1856. "I rose," Hawthorne wrote in his journal, "so screwed up to the point that I did not care what happened next. The Lord Mayor might have fired a pistol, instead of a speech, at me, and I should not have flinched." A few moments before he had confided his fears to his neighbor-at-table, Samuel Carter Hall, who proved to be an incomparable artist in "whip-syllabub and flummery." "I took some of Mr. Hall's flummery," the journal continues, "and clothing it in my own words, it really did very well indeed; and this I joined and interwove with two or three points of my own, and thus tinkered up and amalgamated a very tolerable little speech, which was much helped along by the cheers that broke in between the sentences." Hawthorne's letters, as well as his notebook, contain many humorous references to his speeches. He wrote Bridge of one postprandial occasion, "I had missed no opportunity of gulping down champagne, and so had got myself into that state of pot-valor which (as you and Pierce know) is best adapted to bring out my heroic qualities."

How good the speeches were it is perhaps impossible to determine. "I don't in the least admire my own oratory," he said to Ticknor, "but I do admire my pluck in speaking at all." The speeches, nevertheless, were more than perfunctory performances.

Despite some private reservations Hawthorne elected to throw the weight of his consular and personal influence on the side of Anglo-American good will, and it is reasonable to believe that he brought the point home effectively at a time when the relations between the United States and England were not entirely cordial. The London *Examiner* summarized the speech at the mayor's dinner in part as follows: "Mr. Hawthorne said that there was never yet a moment when America was not ready to extend her hand to meet the hand of England outstretched in earnestness and good faith, and that it would be strange, indeed, if it were not so, for Providence had connected the two countries by indissoluble ties." The London correspondent of the New York *Tribune* reported that Hawthorne had made "a capital appearance" on this occasion.

Although the consular duties were in many ways uncongenial, Hawthorne performed them well. Meanwhile he found solace and happiness as always in his wife and children, and rich compensation in the opportunity which his situation afforded for the study of English scenes and manners. The desire to see as much of England, Scotland, and Wales as possible, the precarious health of Mrs. Hawthorne, and the usual difficulties in finding satisfactory lodgings resulted in a migratory mode of life. During the four consular years the Hawthornes had no permanent residence but repeatedly moved from place to place, the consul sometimes commuting considerable distances to keep in touch with official business. In the latter half of his term he felt free to absent himself from Liverpool for longer intervals—a week or two at a time—in order to go on a tour or enjoy his family wherever they might be. Hawthorne characteristically speculated on "the moral effect of being without a settled abode." "It is a strange, vagabond, gypsy sort of life, this that we are leading," he wrote in his journal, "and I know not whether we shall finally be spoilt for any other, or shall enjoy our quiet Wayside as we never did before, when once we reach it again." "What sort of character," he wondered, "will it form in the children, this unsettled, shifting, vagrant life, with no central home to turn to, except what we carry in ourselves?"

Though never quite domesticated at Rock Park, the Hawthornes found the house—except for the inconvenience of commuting to Liverpool by steamboat and the harmful effect of the river damp on Mrs. Hawthorne's health—an agreeable place of residence. The building was a stone structure of three stories, of castellated design, and with large pleasant rooms. It was surrounded by a smooth-shaven lawn and a trim garden. The rent, furnished (the furniture being only mediocre), was £160 a year. Rock Park contained a number of other handsome modern houses, all designed for the upper middle class of merchants and professional people. It was a semiprivate area, with a policeman stationed at the entrance. Since the policeman collected a toll from carriages and admitted no vagrants, the total effect was one of quiet seclusion. Hawthorne thought Rock Park "an improvement on anything, save what the very rich can enjoy, in America."

Though he had less time for his family than formerly they continued to be a delight to him and he to them. He soon resumed the practice of reading aloud in the winter evenings. During the first winter he read—to the especial delight of his young auditors— *Robinson Crusoe*, *Don Quixote*, and *The Lady of the Lake*. He amused the children too by playing games and improvising stories. He taught them to make paper boats, and Julian's bureau was covered with papers intricately folded into the shapes of hulls, decks, and sails. Battledore and shuttlecock was a favorite pastime and, after Julian had taken lessons, fencing. "Papa plays with the foil in a very funny way," Julian told his older sister; "he whirls it round and round and then pokes away so fast that I have to laugh so that he generally hits me." Blindman's buff was another source of merriment; Hawthorne's youngest daughter recalled the blindfolded father's "gentle laughter and happy-looking lips during these bouts" and "the pulsing grasp of his great hands." Hawthorne gave his fancy free reign in spinning yarns for the children's amusement. Julian remembered particularly the mythical tale of "General Quattlebum," one episode of which he recounted as follows:

Hawthorne and Quattlebum had intrenched themselves on opposite sides of a deep valley, about a mile in width, and all was ready for the bombardment to begin—the cannon loaded and primed, and the aim taken. But the heroes, like two accomplished duellists about to engage with the small-sword, could not begin the conflict without having exchanged those graceful courtesies which should always accompany a truly heroic antagonism. Accordingly each mounted upon his largest cannon, and, standing at the very extremity of the muzzle, touched off the piece with the slow-match held in the left hand. As the missile left the gun, each leaped lightly upon it, and was borne through the air with the speed of lightning. In a few moments they met, just over the center of the valley. Each lifted his hat, and made the other a grave salute, at the same instant springing off his own ball and alighting upon that of his adversary, which swiftly bore him back to the place whence he started. Hawthorne returned without mishap; but General Quattlebum had not paid sufficient attention to his center of gravity: he fell from a vast height to the bottom of the valley, and his mighty carcass dammed up a river which flowed through it, so that before he could extricate himself the valley became a lake, which is known as Lake Quattlebum to this day.

The young auditors of such a story required no Superman comic strip. Amusing, too, were their father's special presents: a china donkey wearing a tall gray hat, a marble Bacchus holding a mug in one hand and patting a fat paunch with the other, and similar objects designed to delight a humorous fancy. Other occasions for amusement in the family circle were the nicknames he gave people: Dr. Drysdale, the family physician, he renamed "Dr. Dryasdust"; Mrs. Squarey, a neighbor, became "Mrs. Roundey"; and the children he regularly called "the Old People." Hawthorne understood, and liked to stimulate, the young imagination.

Christmas was more emphasized in England than in New England, and the Hawthornes enjoyed the festal air of the season. "I waked before light," Mrs. Hawthorne wrote her father of their first Christmas morning in England, "and thought I heard some ineffable music. I thought of the song of the angels on that blessed morn; but while listening, through a sudden opening in the air, or breeze blowing towards us, I found it was not the angels, but the bells of Liverpool." Mummers sang carols at the gate, and Mrs. Hawthorne read aloud to the children Milton's "Hymn of the Nativity." Ticknor's gift of a barrel of apples from New England added substantially to the health and happiness of the first Christmas. The second Christmas found the Hawthornes still in Rock Park; it was then that Hawthorne wrote in his journal, "I think I have been happier, this Christmas, than ever before—by our own fireside, and with my wife and children about me. More content to enjoy what I have; less anxious for anything beyond it, in this life." Throughout the years abroad the Hawthornes found the key to happiness in what Hawthorne aptly called "the home we carry in ourselves."

One of the earliest guests at Rock Park was Henry Bright, whom Longfellow had introduced to Hawthorne in America and whom Hawthorne, after his return from abroad, said he liked better than any other person he met in England. Only twenty-three at the beginning of their acquaintance, and a graduate of Trinity College, Cambridge, Bright was associated with his father in a firm engaged in commerce with South America and Australia; but he had literary interests too and wrote frequent reviews for the *Westminster* and other journals. Hawthorne paid him a graceful and sincere compliment in *Our Old Home*, where he said of Bright's friendly visits,

He used to come and sit or stand by my fireside, talking vivaciously and eloquently with me about literature and life, his own national characteristics and mine, with such kindly endurance of the many rough republicanisms wherewith I assailed him, and such frank and amiable assertion of all sorts of English prejudices and mistakes, that I understood his countrymen infinitely the better for him and was almost prepared to love the intensest Englishman of them all, for his sake.

Largely through Bright's efforts the Hawthornes were by degrees drawn a little into Liverpool "society." There were invitations to Sandheys, the residence of the Brights, and to Norris

Green, the residence of the Heywoods, who were relatives of the Brights. Though "a dainty lady of fashion" (as Mrs. Hawthorne admiringly described her), Mrs. Heywood took an active interest in reforming the Liverpool slums, and her husband donated £7,000 a year to charity. The dinners given by the Brights, Heywoods, Hollands, and other Liverpool magnates were very elaborate, and Hawthorne and his wife attended a sufficient number of them. Hawthorne drew the line, however, at Mrs. Heywood's fancy dress ball, offering his excuses to the lady in an amusing note, though Sophia would gladly have gone. Sophia, indeed, was more susceptible to the attractions of splendid social entertainments than her husband, and though not given to finery (not at all "tonish" she said of herself), she animatedly described appointments and costumes in letters to her relatives in Boston. Her own costume on one occasion seems "tonish" enough from the following description sent to her sister's children:

I had on a sky-blue glacé silk, with three flounces, which were embroidered with white floss, making a very silvery shine. The dress had low neck and short sleeves; but I wore a jacket of starred *blonde* with flowing sleeves; and had round me also a shawl of Madeira lace, which, though very airy, fleecy, and cloud-looking, is warm and soft. My headdress was pearl, in the shape of bunches of grapes and leaves, mingled with blue ribbon, with a wreath of pearl-traced leaves round my hair, which was rolled in coronet fashion.

Hawthorne was less amenable to fashion. With a stubbornness reminiscent of Sam Sewall's refusal to wear a wig, he objected to the current fashion in gentlemen's neckdress.

Mr. Hawthorne curses the hour [Sophia wrote her father] when white muslin cravats became the *sine qua non* of a gentleman's full dress. I believe he would even rather wear a sword and cocked hat, for he declares a white muslin cravat the last abomination, the chief enormity of fashion, and that all the natural feelings of a man cry out against it; and that it is alike abhorrent to taste and to sentiment. To all this I reply that he looks a great deal handsomer with white about his throat than with a stiff old black satin stock, which always to me looks like the stocks, and that it is habit only which makes him prefer it.

Whether attired in fashion or out of fashion, Hawthorne (often unaccompanied by his wife, whose health was variable) went, and went again, to dinners given by wealthy merchants and landowners. He enjoyed himself greatly at Mr. Aiken's dinner, where he drank whiskey with the sons of Burns and heard them sing their father's poems. Their eyes glowed, he particularly recorded, when they came to the line, "The rank is but the guinea's stamp." Less enjoyable was the entertainment at Mr. Bramley-Moore's, for Samuel Warren, a popular writer of the day, made a fulsome speech in Hawthorne's honor and the host, while circulating his wines rather too briskly, alluded to their cost. Not altogether enjoyable either was the visit to Smithell's Hall at Bolton le Moors, for although Hawthorne was fascinated by the house, several centuries old, and its legend of the "bloody footstep," he resented the discourtesy and bad taste of his hostess, Mrs. Peter Ainsworth. She told a story intended to illustrate the mistakes which Americans made in the use of the English language, the butt of her joke being no less an American than George Bancroft.* "It is very queer," Hawthorne sharply remarked in his journal, "this resolute quizzing of our manners, when we are really and truly much better figures, and with much more capacity of polish, for drawing-room or dining-room than the English themselves are. John Bull is a rough animal, and incapable of high-polish, and his female is well adapted to him." Matthew Arnold later sympathized with Hawthorne's discomfort. "Hawthorne was a sensitive man," Arnold wrote, "so situated in England that he was perpetually in contact with the British Philistine, and the British Philistine is a trying personage."

After two years at Rock Park, which were pleasant enough de-

---

* Bancroft was reported by Mrs. Ainsworth as having remarked that in America his wife had been in *delicate* health, but after living in England she had become quite *indelicate*. If correctly reported, Bancroft probably intended a joke of his own.

spite irritations caused by the consulate and the British Philistines, the Hawthornes led an unsettled life during the remaining two years in England. In the autumn of 1855 it was decided that Mrs. Hawthorne's health could not stand another English winter. Arrangements were therefore made for her to take the two girls (Una was now eleven, Rose four) to spend the winter with the J. L. O'Sullivans in Portugal, where O'Sullivan was Minister, and for Hawthorne and Julian (now nine) to live during their absence at Mrs. Blodgett's boardinghouse in Liverpool. Husband and wife viewed the separation—the first of appreciable length in their married life of thirteen years—with sorrow, but the situation seemed to call for heroic measures. On September 5 the Hawthornes had their first view of London, and after about a month there they moved on reluctantly to Southampton, where they found the steamer *Madrid* bound for Portugal. On board at sailing time, Hawthorne commended his unescorted wife and daughters to the captain's especial care. "And then," Hawthorne recorded in the journal,

we thought it best to cut short the parting scene. . . . My wife behaved heroically, Una was cheerful, and Rosebud seemed only anxious to get off. Poor Fanny, our nurse, was altogether cast down, and shed tears, either from regret at leaving her native land, or dread of sickness, or general despondency. We bade one another farewell, and leaving them on the deck of the vessel, Julian and I returned to the hotel.

On the journey by train back to Liverpool that evening Hawthorne saw the fragment of a rainbow among the clouds and took comfort in the thought of a prosperous voyage for his loved ones when he remembered the old sea adage, "A rainbow at night is the sailor's delight."

Father and son were soon comfortably settled at Mrs. Blodgett's. The first night they went forth in the rain to witness the celebration of the victorious conclusion of the Crimean War. Flags were waving, cap pistols were being fired in the crowded streets, and huge illuminated letters—V and A, and V and N, for Victoria,

Albert, and Napoleon, the ally of the English—shone forth in the darkness. So engrossed were they that they stayed out well beyond Julian's regular bedtime. "I wonder," Hawthorne remarked in the notebook, "what his mother would have said. But the old boy must now begin to see life, and to feel it."

At Mrs. Blodgett's there was an abundance of good food and agreeable society. The boardinghouse was a favorite resort of American sea captains, and Hawthorne liked to sit with them in the smoking room in the evening and listen to their talk of voyages, unruly mates and crews, equinoctial gales, and the relative merits of different ships and their commanders. One captain who avoided Mrs. Blodgett's gave as the reason that the conversation made him seasick, "and indeed," Hawthorne observed, "the smell of tar and bilge-water is somewhat strongly perceptible in it." "And yet," he added, "these men are alive, and talk of real matters, and matters which they know." The conversation frequently turned on points of American superiority over England. "It would do John Bull good," Hawthorne declared, "to come and sit at our table, and adjourn with us to our smoking-room, but he would be apt to go away a little crest-fallen."

Meanwhile Mrs. Hawthorne and her daughters were cordially received by the O'Sullivans in Lisbon. In the warmer climate her health improved appreciably, and as a member of the household of the American Minister she saw something of the waning splendor of the Portuguese capital and its royalty. She attended the ballet and the opera, and described the performances vividly in letters to Julian. The climax of her social season in Portugal was her presentation to the young King and his father, the Regent. Like any good American, she "did not find it at all embarrassing to be in private audience with two Kings," she said, "though quite unused to a royal *tête-à-tête*."

But despite the invigorating talk of sea captains in Liverpool and the brilliant glimpses of theater and court in Lisbon, the winter of 1855–56 was a long and tedious one for Hawthorne and his wife. "I have suffered woefully from low spirits for sometime past," Hawthorne wrote frankly in his journal in January, 1856:

My desolate, bachelor condition, I suppose, is the cause. Really, I have no pleasure in anything; and I feel my tread to be heavier and my physical movement more sluggish than in happier times; a weight is always upon me. My appetite is not good. I sleep ill, lying awake late at night to think sad thoughts, and to imagine sombre things, and awakening before light with the same thoughts and fancies still in my mind. My heart sinks always as I ascend the stairs to my office, from a dim augury of ill news that I may perhaps hear—of black-sealed letters—or some such horrors. Nothing gives me any joy. I have learned what the bitterness of exile is, in these days; and I never should have known it but for the absence of my wife.

He poured out his misery and love in letters to Sophia:

One thing, dearest, I have been most thoroughly taught by this separation—that is, the absolute necessity of expression. I must tell thee I love thee. I must be told that thou lovest me. It must be said in words and symbolized with caresses; or else, at last, imprisoned Love will go frantic, and tear all to pieces the heart that holds it. . . . Oh, my love, it is a desperate thing that I cannot embrace thee this very instant. Dost thou ever feel, at one and the same moment, the impossibility of doing without me, and also the impossibility of having me? . . . Thou *never* again shalt go away anywhere without me. My two arms shall be thy tropics, and my breast thy equator; and from henceforth forever I will keep thee a great deal too warm, so that thou shalt cry out—"Do let me breathe the cool outward air for a moment!" But I will not! . . . Oh, dearest, dearest, interminably and infinitely dearest—I don't know how to end that ejaculation. The use of kisses and caresses is, that they supersede language, and express what there are no words for. I need them at this moment—need to give them, and to receive them. . . . Oh, my wife, I do want thee so intolerably. Nothing else is real, except the bond between thee and me. The people around me are but shadows. I am myself but a shadow, till thou takest me in thy arms, and convertest me into substance. Till thou comest back, I do but walk in a dream.

Sophia's letters in reply are no longer extant, but that they were in kind goes without saying. In a note written not long before sailing —one of the comparatively few of her letters to Hawthorne which have survived—she had expressed her resignation to the unavoidable separation:

because thou art the soul of my life I do not look forward with delight to a winter in Lisbon. . . . I once thought that no power on earth should ever induce me to live without thee, and especially that an ocean should never roll between us. But I am overpowered by necessity, and since my life is of importance to thee, I will not dare to neglect any means of preserving it. . . . Farewell, dearest, wisest, best. Thy dove.

In March, 1856, Francis Bennoch—London merchant and amateur of letters gratefully referred to by Hawthorne in *Our Old Home* as the man to whom he owed most in England—persuaded Hawthorne to come to London for a three weeks' visit. Under Bennoch's enthusiastic sponsorship Hawthorne gave himself freely to a strenuous round of excursions and social entertainments. "They have found me out, these London people," he wrote his wife, "and I believe I should have engagements for every day, and two or three a day, if I staid here through the season. They thicken upon me, the longer I remain."

At Bennoch's house, where the host "warmed his guests," as Hawthorne put it, "like a household fire by the influence of his broad, ruddy, kindly face and glowing eyes and hospitable demeanor," Hawthorne met Mrs. Newton Crosland, a littérateur who was—he recorded—"a vast admirer of *The Scarlet Letter* and especially the character of Hester." (Mrs. Crosland later remembered Hawthorne as "a stalwart man, in mid-prime, whose blue eyes had a peculiarly soft expression.") Next came an excursion to Aldershot Camp, at Farnborough, where Bennoch and Hawthorne sat up till four o'clock in the morning fraternizing with the officers of the North Cork Rifles. From Aldershot the friendly pair—gaining momentum all the while—went to Albury to visit Martin Tupper (author of the best-selling *Proverbial Phi-*

losophy), whom Hawthorne regarded as "an absurd little man" until he learned of a secret tragedy in his life. Back in London, Hawthorne had dinner at the Milton Club where he was "toasted and roasted and done entirely brown," and a late supper the same evening at the house of Eneas Sweetland Dallas, an editorial writer for the London *Times*. After listening to talk about that great newspaper and asking questions about its management and policy, Hawthorne decided that it did not quite deserve its prestige, for its articles were "certainly not written in so high a moral vein as might be wished." The next evening he had dinner at the Reform Club with Charles Mackay, journalist and song writer, and Douglas Jerrold, playwright and contributor to *Punch*. On this occasion Hawthorne introduced the subject of Thoreau, saying that the most interesting incident of Thoreau's life in the woods was that after a while the birds ceased to be afraid of him and would perch upon his shoulder. In response to their expressions of interest, Hawthorne promised to send his companions copies of *A Week* and *Walden*. Other events of this crowded time were another supper party at Dallas', where Hawthorne met Miss Isabella Dallas Glyn, "hot and wearied," he observed, from her performance of Cleopatra, and Charles Reade (who later told Fields that Hawthorne had "an eye like a violet with a soul in it"); a visit to the Samuel Carter Halls at Woking; dinner—and a speech—at the lord mayor's Mansion House where he saw the beautiful Jewess who was to serve as a model for Miriam in *The Marble Faun;* dinner in the refectory of the House of Commons, where he caught a glimpse of Disraeli, "sallow," he thought, and "unwholesome looking"; dinner at the house of Henry Stevens, the famous bibliographer and collector from Vermont, who showed Hawthorne Dr. Johnson's autograph in Dryden's translation of Virgil, a large collection of Bibles of all dates, and some original manuscripts by Burns and Franklin. The London excursion, Hawthorne summed up, was "rich in incident and character," and he meticulously and fully preserved the richness in his notebook. He prized this record of his immersion in active life at the center of things—

the completest he had ever experienced—and read his "London journal" to the Brights, with a good deal of satisfaction, upon his return to Liverpool.

The three weeks in London enlivened his spirits considerably, thereby helping him to bear the remaining weeks of separation. After an absence of eight months Mrs. Hawthorne and the daughters landed at Southampton on June 9, 1856. The meeting is not recorded, but the fullness of feeling is abundantly conveyed in Hawthorne's brief entry, "I cannot write today." To say the words which perhaps failed him at the moment, he put into his wife's hands Coventry Patmore's "The Angel in the House."

Though interrupted by periodical trips to the office in Liverpool, the summer of 1856 was pleasantly spent in Bennoch's house at Black Heath, while the owners traveled on the continent. From this London suburb Hawthorne—either with or without his family—frequently "railed" to London. On one occasion he had high breakfast at the house of Richard Monkton Milnes, where he met Macaulay, the Brownings, and the mother of Florence Nightingale. (He enjoyed particularly his conversation with Mrs. Browning: "She is of that quickly appreciative and responsive order of women," he said, "with whom I can talk more freely than with any men.") On another he called on Delia Bacon, thus beginning a friendly service which culminated in his financing, with considerable loss, the publication of her book on Shakespeare.* Sophia accompanied him to a party given by the S. C. Halls in their London apartment, where he and Jenny Lind were, he supposed, "the lions of the evening." But he preferred to remain at Black Heath on the warm, sunny days "loitering slowly through *Dombey and Son*, intermingled with much talk, and broken in upon often by the children with their sports." Bennoch's house and garden were

* Although Miss Bacon (unbalanced, or shortly to become so) was offended by Hawthorne's refusal to endorse in his preface to her volume her view of the origin of Shakespeare's plays, he persisted in his good offices both because he thought the book contained some valuable insights despite its erroneous conclusions and because he was glad (for reasons of chivalry and patriotism) to be of service to a fellow countrywoman and New Englander. Miss Bacon had previously applied without success to Emerson for aid in getting her work published.

very homelike. When the sun passed off the lawn he played at bowls with the children. If Sophia's health had been a little more rugged he thought he should be "as happy as the English summer day is long."

After several days in early September at Oxford, where they were chaperoned by the indefatigable Bennoch and lavishly entertained by an ex-mayor of the town, the Hawthornes moved on to Southport, located about twenty miles north of Liverpool on the coast of the Irish Sea. The climate proving favorable to Mrs. Hawthorne's health, the family remained at Southport until the next July, and Hawthorne commuted daily to the consulate, leaving regularly on the eleven o'clock train and returning with equal regularity on the five o'clock. Their lodgings consisted of three chambers and a parlor in a tall stone house styled Brunswick Terrace, the rent being 10s. 6d. for each bed and 12s. 6d. for the parlor. The English system of lodginghouses, Hawthorne thought, had its good points but it afforded no relief from domestic cares, for the tenants must supply their own meals. The faithful Fanny Wrigley, however, relieved Mrs. Hawthorne of most of the household drudgery. Their rooms faced a vast expanse of sandy beach. At low tide the beach was exposed for a great distance seaward, and at high tide one could wade almost an equal distance from the shore. Bathers splashed in the shallow water. As he walked with his family over the dreary and wind-swept sands, Hawthorne mused that the body of Lycidas could have been washed ashore there.

The uneventful life at Southport was enlivened in November by a visit from Herman Melville, on his way to Turkey and the Holy Land, who stayed from Tuesday till Thursday. On the intervening day the two friends took a long walk, and (Hawthorne's notebook continues with the most understanding passage ever written about Melville)

sat down in a hollow among the sand hills (sheltering ourselves from the high, cool wind) and smoked a cigar. Melville, as he always does, began to reason of Providence and futurity, and of everything that lies beyond human ken, and informed me that he had "pretty much made up his mind to be annihilated"; but still he does not seem to rest in that anticipation; and, I think, will never rest until he gets hold of a definite belief. It is strange how he persists—and has persisted ever since I knew him, and probably long before—in wandering to-and-fro over these deserts, as dismal and monotonous as the sand hills amid which we were sitting. He can neither believe, nor be comfortable in his unbelief; and he is too honest and courageous not to try to do one or the other. If he were a religious man, he would be one of the most truly religious and reverential; he has a very high and noble nature, and is better worth immortality than most of us.

Melville's record of the visit was brief but cordial: "At Southport. An agreeable day. Took a long walk by the sea. Sands & grass. Wild and desolate. A strong wind. Good talk. In the evening, Stout & Fox & Geese. Julian grown into a fine lad; Una taller than her mother. Mrs. Hawthorne not in good health. Mr. Hawthorne stayed home for me." On Friday Henry Bright showed Melville the sights of Liverpool, while the latter perhaps recalled the Redburn days of his youth, and on Saturday Hawthorne and Melville visited the city of Chester. Upon their return to Liverpool, they parted at a street corner in the rainy evening. Melville seemed to Hawthorne "much overshadowed" since he had last seen him at the Wayside in 1852, but he hoped that he would "brighten" in the course of his journey. They did not meet again.

After about ten months at Southport the Hawthornes took lodgings at Old Trafford in July, 1857, and continued there for two months, the object being to see the great Arts Exhibition then on display in near-by Manchester. The rent for their modest quarters in ordinary times, Hawthorne supposed, would have been £25 per year, but since an influx of visitors had greatly increased the demand, the price was £6 10s. per week. A constant stream of cabs and omnibuses passed in front of the house, carrying passengers to and from the exhibition.

Hawthorne went repeatedly to the exhibition and conscientiously took advantage of this first opportunity of his life for the systematic study of painting. After several visits he reported esthetic progress, saying that he actually began "to receive some pleasure from looking at pictures." He especially enjoyed Hogarth's paintings: "nothing truer to English life and character was ever painted," he said, than "The March to Finchley." Murillo's "Good Shepherd" he thought "the loveliest picture" he had ever seen. He particularly liked also the Dutch masters, feeling perhaps a kinship between their art and his own. "They must have laid down their brushes with perfect satisfaction," he remarked, "knowing that each one of their million touches had been necessary to the effect, and that there was not one too little or too much. These Dutchmen get at the soul of common things, and so make them types and interpreters of the spiritual world." But an inherited Puritan strictness often cropped up to prevent his free enjoyment of the fine arts. "I am weary of naked goddesses," he declared, "who never had any real life and warmth in the painter's imagination—or, if so, it was the impure warmth of the unchaste women who sat or sprawled for them."

Hawthorne's art study was interestingly interrupted one afternoon when Alexander Ireland, editor of the Manchester *Examiner* and friend of Emerson, pointed out Tennyson in the crowd of spectators. Knowing how much his wife would like to see Tennyson, Hawthorne hastily summoned her from another part of the building and together they gazed at "the one poet" of their day (as Hawthorne called him) while he moved rapidly from picture to picture. Tennyson was accompanied by his young son, and as the two left the hall, the boy following his father at some distance, Mrs. Hawthorne (so she wrote her sister Elizabeth) "seized the darling with gold hair, and kissed him to my heart's content; and he smiled and seemed well pleased. And I was well pleased to have had in my arms Tennyson's child." Hawthorne would have been glad to know Tennyson, glad indeed, he said, "to smoke a cigar with him." But Ireland offered no introduction, being himself not personally acquainted with the "Poet Laureate" (how "English," Hawthorne thought, that Ireland "should designate him by this fantastic dignity, instead of by his name"), and Hawthorne was not the man to introduce himself to a famous stranger in a public place, least of all to Tennyson, in whose aspect he detected "a morbid painfulness, a something not to be meddled with." As for Sophia's "raid" (as she quite properly called it), Tennyson himself had not witnessed the incident and it could well remain anonymous.

After two months at Old Trafford the Hawthornes struck camp again, in September, 1857, and took lodgings at Lansdowne Circus, Leamington. Two months later they moved from Leamington to Great Russell Street, London, whence after another interval of two months, in January, 1858, they left England for the continent. While at Leamington the Hawthornes acquired a governess for the children in the person of Miss Ada Shepard, a pleasant and efficient young graduate of Antioch College, of which Horace Mann was president. Hawthorne enjoyed Leamington and the country round about it; he did not know a place where he would rather live, he said, than "this new village of mid-most Old England." In London (in addition to the usual tireless sight-seeing) he continued his art education at Marlborough House and the National Gallery; met Coventry Patmore, whose "Angel in the House" was, he said, "a poem for happy married people to read together, and understand by the light of their own past and present life"; listened skeptically while Dr. James John Garth Wilkinson, called in to prescribe for the children's measles, told of spiritualistic phenomena; and sympathized deeply with Bennoch, who had recently suffered financial reverses. Almost his last thought before leaving England was of his friend's misfortune. He suggested hopefully that he might recoup his fortunes in America, while privately doubting the wisdom of such a venture, for it would be a mistake to transplant a man like Bennoch, he feared, "from this warm, cheerful, juicy English life into our drier and less genial sphere."

One of the chief reasons for coming abroad was to see England, and during the four years there Hawthorne did as thorough a job of sight-seeing as was consistent with the performance of his official duties. His conscience did not allow him to neglect either the consulate or his travels. On idle days (they were comparatively few) such as those spent at Black Heath, he was troubled, he said, by a "weight or sting in my conscience for not spending this fine weather in making expeditions to see a thousand interesting objects." From this standpoint the winter at Southport seemed to him "a blank." Long a sympathetic student of English history and literature, he took a lively interest in England's historical and literary scenes. He managed to visit most of them—many he went back to again and again—and described them richly and lovingly in his notebook. The travels began near Liverpool and the radius was gradually extended.

During the first year, when consular affairs seemed especially urgent, he contented himself with brief excursions to near-by places—to Bebbington, Eastham, Chester, Wales, and the Isle of Man. He reveled in the antiquity and the sense of the past. The church at Bebbington was "old, old, old—looking just the same as it did in Bloody Mary's days; just as it did in Cromwell's time." The Old Yew of Eastham, still standing, had figured in history for six hundred years. On the Isle of Man he noted a runic monument which dwarfed even the Yew of Eastham in antiquity. Everywhere he experienced the pleasure of having things "answer to" his "trans-Atlantic fancies."

The first extended tour, participated in by the entire family and not undertaken until the summer of 1855, was quite naturally to the Shakespeare country. Hawthorne felt no emotion in Shakespeare's house, he wrote in the journal, "nor any quickening of the imagination. It is agreeable enough to reflect that I have seen it; and I think I can form, now, a more sensible and vivid idea of Shakespeare as a flesh-and-blood man; but I am not quite sure that this latter effect is altogether desirable." More stimulating to the imagination were Charlecote Park where he saw domesticated deer, one of whose ancestors Shakespeare may have described in *As You Like It*, and Leicester's Hospital in Warwick, which was to figure prominently in *Dr. Grimshawe's Secret*. If Stratford and its environs were a conventional first choice, the next—Lichfield and Uttoxeter, in memory of Dr. Johnson—was a more personal and compelling one. Leaving his family at Leamington, Hawthorne went to Lichfield and Uttoxeter on what he called "one of the few purely sentimental pilgrimages" of his life. He thought the statue of Dr. Johnson in Lichfield "touching and effective" and at Dr. Johnson's birthplace he set his foot on the worn steps and laid his hand on the wall of the house, "because Johnson's hand and foot might have been in those same places." At Uttoxeter he attempted to identify the spot where Dr. Johnson had stood in the rain as penance for disobeying his father. The penance was a dramatic incident which especially appealed to Hawthorne, and he told it and retold it in his writings—first in *Biographical Stories for Children* and later in "Uttoxeter" and *Our Old Home*. Both as man and artist Hawthorne felt a closer affinity to Dr. Johnson and the other great Augustans than to either Shakespeare or the romantics.

With little if any slackening of interest, the entire family set out for the Lake Country in July, 1855. At Swan Inn, Newby Bridge, near the foot of Lake Windermere, the genial landlord, Thomas White, loaded the table at breakfast and supper with trout, cold beef, ham, toast, and muffins and provided three fine courses for dinner and excellent wine. For a four days' stay the charge for the party of six (five Hawthornes and Fanny Wrigley, the nurse) was £8 5s. Hawthorne lingered long over Furness Abbey and studied its historical reconstruction in Thomas West's *Antiquities of Furness*. From Newby Bridge they went by steamboat to the head of Windermere and thence by carriage to Rydal and Grasmere. Rydal Lake was disappointing to both Hawthorne and his wife because of its smallness, judged by American standards, but Sophia thought that it received dignity from the surrounding hills and that (as she wrote her sister Elizabeth) "it was irreverent in Mr. Hawthorne to say he 'could carry it all away in a porringer.'" The house of Wordsworth (who had died five years before) was entirely satisfying—"so delightfully situated" (Hawthorne wrote in his notebook), "so secluded, so hedged about with shrubbery and adorned with flowers, so ivy-grown on one side, so beautified with many years of the personal care of him who lived in it and loved it, that it seemed the very place for a poet's residence." At Keswick it was rewarding to walk about the grounds of what had been Southey's residence and peep through the windows into the library, though Southey himself, Hawthorne thought, "was not a picturesque man, nor one whose personal character takes a strong hold of the imagination." The mountain and lake scenery of this region was perhaps more interesting than its literary associations. The mountains particularly seemed to Hawthorne more picturesque, on the whole, than those of New England because "they have great variety of shape, rising into peaks, falling in abrupt precipices, stretching along in zig-zag outlines." "I shall always be glad of this tour," he said upon its conclusion, "and shall wonder the more at England, which comprehends so much, such a rich variety, within its little bounds. If England were all the world, it still would have been worth while for the Creator to have made it."

In September, 1855, the whole family visited Shrewsbury, where Hawthorne remembered Falstaff's "long hour" and Farquhar's *Recruiting Officer* and found pleasant walking in the old streets: "There are passages," he wrote in the journal, "opening under archways, and winding up between high edifices, very tempting to the explorer, and generally leading to some court, or some queer old range of buildings, or piece of architecture, which it would be the greatest pity to miss seeing." After Shrewsbury the Hawthornes moved on to London and remained there for a month of indefatigable sight-seeing. Hawthorne liked best of all to wander through the streets, often getting lost only to find himself unexpectedly among things which he had always read and dreamed about. What interested him most in his saunterings, he said, was "the London of the writers of the Queen Anne Age— whatever Pope, the Spectator, DeFoe, and Johnson and Goldsmith have mentioned." His investigations, however, were not specialized but comprehensive. St. Paul's and the Abbey, both of which he visited again and again and liked about equally well; the Zoological Gardens, which Julian enjoyed more than his father; the Crystal Palace, "a gigantic toy for the English people to play with"; the Tower, where he noted among many other fascinating items the room in which Sir Walter Raleigh wrote his *History of the World;* Greenwich Hospital, whose sailor inmates England loved for Nelson's sake; Rotherhithe, long familiar from *Gulliver's Travels;* the British Museum, whose contents so overwhelmed him that he was tempted for the moment to wish that the whole past might be swept away; the Houses of Parliament, which suffered by comparison with the Abbey because the architect (he appropriated Emerson's phrase for it) had not "builded better than he knew"—these and many other famous places were the subjects of study and description.

In May, 1856, Hawthorne went to the Scottish Highlands and luxuriated in the scenes long associated with the poems and novels of Sir Walter Scott, though in some instances the places seemed less impressive in reality than in Scott's descriptions. In June— accompanied by his wife, who had just returned from Portugal— he visited Salisbury. Here he despaired of ever describing cathedrals adequately, yet, more than anything else he had seen in England, they "filled out" his ideal. He felt the spell particularly of the Salisbury Close: "I never beheld anything so cozy, so indicative of domestic comfort for whole centuries together—houses so fit to live in, or to die in, and where it would be so pleasant to lead a young maiden wife beneath the antique portal, and dwell with her, till husband and wife were patriarchal—as those delectable old houses." But speaking more practically as a man, and American, of the nineteenth century, he continued: "These are places, however, in which mankind makes no progress; the rushing tumult of human life here subsides into a deep, quiet pool, with perhaps a gentle circular eddy, but no onward movement. The same identical thought, I suppose, goes round, in a slow whirl, from one generation to another, as I have seen a withered leaf do, in the pool of a brook."

In the spring and early summer of 1857, accompanied by his wife and one or more of the children, Hawthorne toured extensively again: to Newstead Abbey, Peterborough, Lincoln, and Boston (where a memorial window was about to be dedicated to John Cotton, famous minister of both Bostons); to Dumfries and the other places redolent of Burns; and—this being Hawthorne's second visit—to Abbotsford, Edinburgh, and the country of Rob Roy. In the autumn of 1857 many scenes were revisited—notably Warwick and Leicester's Hospital and the famous things of London. When places were revisited they were redescribed as faithfully as if they had not been described before.

While viewing England thus extensively—and only a small fraction of his effort in this kind has been told here—Hawthorne was of two minds, which might be called the historical and the contemporary, or perhaps the English and the American.

As a descendant of Englishmen and a creative writer whose imagination had been nourished by English history and literature, Hawthorne felt a powerful hereditary attraction to "our old home" and its storied and poetical associations. One of his best statements of this attraction is found in the account of Redclyffe's feeling for England in *Dr. Grimshawe's Secret:*

He began to feel the deep yearning which a sensitive American—his mind full of English thoughts, his imagination of English poetry, his heart of English character and sentiment—cannot fail to be influenced by,—the yearning of the blood within his veins for that from which it has been estranged; the half-fanciful regret that he should ever have been separated from these woods, these fields, these natural features of scenery, to which his nature was moulded, from the men who are still so like himself, from these habits of life and thought which (though he may not have known them for two centuries) he still perceives to have remained in some mysterious way latent in the depths of his character, and soon to be reassumed, not as a foreigner would do it, but like habits native to him, and only suspended for a season.

As a New England Puritan and an American democrat, on the other hand, Hawthorne often disapproved of English institutions and often resented the English condescension. While appreciating to the full the great cathedrals as architectural monuments, he condemned the institution which they housed as "musty." "The spirit of my Puritan ancestors was mighty in me," he wrote at York on Easter Sunday, "and I did not wonder at their being out of patience with all this mummery." While admiring the beautiful estates of the nobility and admitting that many noblemen led noble lives, he was shocked by the great social and economic inequalities which were evident on every side. In Liverpool he saw poverty and squalor the like of which was still unknown in his own country. The social inequalities were even more distressing to him than the economic. He drew a dramatic contrast between two marriage services witnessed in Manchester Cathedral: one—an aristocratic wedding—participated in by a bishop and several canons and brightened by the chiming of bells and the adornments of wealth and fashion; the other—the saddest sight he ever looked upon, he said—a ceremony in which a single clergyman married six pairs of paupers in such a way, Hawthorne remarked, that "he came dangerously near making every man and woman the husband or wife of every other." England, he felt, would one day be compelled to face the question of social and economic inequality. England, too, would one day have to take a fairer view of America and Americans. The English press and English people generally, Hawthorne found to his discomfort, habitually disparaged American manners and achievements. "The time will come, sooner or later," he said to Ticknor prophetically, "when John Bull will look to us for his salvation." "An Englishman in adversity," he grimly observed during the Crimean War, "is a very respectable character; he does not lose his dignity, but merely comes to a proper conceit of himself."

During his stay in England Hawthorne's American patriotism became more emphasized. He kept in touch with his friends in America and with events there. He was often homesick for the hill at the Wayside and for his publisher's place of business, affectionately known as "the Old Corner." He constantly urged his friends to come to England, offering good reasons why they should: Ticknor and Fields, to visit their English authors; Pike, to take the vice-consulship at Manchester; Longfellow, to receive the libations of his English admirers. The arrival of American newspapers, sent regularly by Ticknor, was always an event worthy of record in his journal. Though the events which they reported gave cause for serious apprehension Hawthorne remained faithful to Pierce and to the views on slavery which he had expressed in the campaign biography. When Elizabeth Peabody, hoping to make a convert, sent him a tract on abolition, he returned it with the comment, "Like every other Abolitionist, you look at matters with an awful squint, which distorts everything within your line of vision; and it is queer, though natural, that you think everybody squints, except yourself." Mrs. Hawthorne loyally supported her husband's views, writing sharply to her sister: "No one can ever convince me that the Cabinet and President are not as conscientious, as upright, as patriotic, as Christian, as those who condemn them. . . . Your letters would be far more appropriate to a slaveholder than to me." Despite the darkening cloud of irrepressible conflict Hawthorne believed that America would pull through. "We shall grow and flourish," he wrote Ticknor in June, 1856, "in spite of the devil. . . . I keep a steadfast faith in the destinies of my country, and will not be staggered, whatever happens."

Hawthorne had hoped to write, while in England, a romance with an English setting. The materials in his notebook, which he kept so faithfully, "were intended," he said, "for the side-scenes and backgrounds and exterior adornment of a work of fiction." In January, 1855, he spoke of "the germ of a new Romance" in his mind, which would be "all the better for ripening slowly." In April of the same year he outlined the story tentatively as follows:

In my Romance, the original emigrant to America may have carried away with him a family secret, whereby it was in his power (had he so chosen) to have brought about the ruin of the family. This secret he transmits to his American progeny, by whom it is inherited throughout all the intervening generations. At last, the hero of the Romance comes to England, and finds that by means of this secret, he still has it in his power to procure the downfall of the family. It would be something similar to the story of Meleager, whose fate depended on the firebrand that his mother had snatched out of the flames.

In May Hawthorne wrote hopefully to Longfellow of the work in prospect:

Don't you think that the autumn may be the golden age both of the intellect and imagination? *You* certainly grow richer and deeper at every step of your advance in life. I shall be glad to think that I, too, may improve—that, for instance, there may be something ruddier, warmer, and more genial, in my latter fruitage. It is good for the moral nature of an American to live in England, among a more simple and natural people than ourselves. Ale is an excellent moral nutriment; so is English mutton; and perhaps the effect of both will be visible in my next Romance.

So great, however, were the distractions of his official duties and of sight-seeing that the "English Romance" had to be put aside. In February, 1857, he felt "some symptoms" of being "a literary man again"; in November he thought that if he could be "perfectly quiet for a few months, something would result." But the necessary repose was lacking, and the projected work was deferred until after he should be settled in Italy.

His pen, nevertheless, was not idle during the English years: his English journal consists of more than 300,000 words. First published in its entirety in 1941, it has a strong claim to the rank of one of its author's major works. No other American writer has described England so vividly and completely or has comparatively weighed with so much care and insight the English and American cultures. *The English Notebooks*, therefore, affords much more than material for Hawthorne's biography. At once a great exploratory document in the history of Anglo-American relations and a fascinating pictorial record of the vanished Victorian world, Hawthorne's journal alone is an ample literary justification of the four years spent in England.

Hawthorne resigned his office as of August 31, 1857, but he had to await the tardy arrival of his successor, Beverly Tucker of Virginia, the appointee of Buchanan, who had succeeded Pierce in the presidency. He had also to wind up his accounts with the government, a transaction made more difficult by the illness of Wilding, his efficient clerk. Casting up his personal and official accounts, he was content with the result. The consulate had not been as profitable as he had hoped for a congressional act passed about the middle of his term had reduced the consular emoluments—unjustly, Hawthorne thought, because the law retroactively violated the conditions on which current appointments had been accepted. But despite the reduction and the heavy expense of taking his family about England, he had made a good deal more money than he could have made by writing. He had been able to pay back the sum which Hillard and other friends had given him at the time of his removal from the Salem Custom House. He had also been able to help Bridge and O'Sullivan out of financial difficulties. The accumulated savings from his office amounted to about $30,000, and he felt that the income from this money, which had been faithfully invested by Ticknor, could be depended upon to provide the necessities for his family. Some luxuries he thought could be purchased with the royalties from the books which he had already written and would still write. In a letter to Ticknor in 1857 he summed up his financial situation in both retrospect and prospect:

The Consulate has not proved quite what I expected, in point of profit; but still, as my books have been selling profitably during these past four years, I have acquired from all sources what I may call a moderate competence. During my further stay in Europe, I shall probably spend more than my income; but after my return, I shall be able to live at less expense, and, by writing one or two more books, shall make up for over-expenditures. It is a vast relief to me, to feel that my wife and children will be left in comfortable circumstances, in case of my death. I may say, in this respect, "the bitterness of death is past."

In the autumn of 1857 the Hawthornes were eager to be off to the continent. After the business of the consulate had been finally wound up they were detained still further when the children came down with the measles, and it was not until the beginning of January that all things were in readiness for their departure. When ex-Consul Hawthorne called at the American Legation in London to arrange for passports, he felt a new sense of personal freedom and of the inalienable dignity of American citizenship as well:

The very moment I rang at Mr. Dallas's door [he wrote in his notebook], it swung open, and the porter ushered me with great courtesy into the waiting-room; not that he knew me, or anything about me, except that I was probably an American citizen. This is the deference which an American servant of the public finds it expedient to show to his sovereigns. Thank Heaven, I am a sovereign again, and no longer a servant; and really it is very queer, how I look down upon our Ambassadors, and dignitaries of all sorts, not excepting the President himself.

The Hawthornes and Miss Ada Shepard, the new governess, were up before daylight on January 5, 1858, getting ready for the journey to Paris and thence to Italy. Their belongings filled a dozen trunks and half a dozen carpetbags. While they were riding on the train from London to Folkestone the snow began to fall, and it seemed to Hawthorne as if they had outstayed their English welcome; yet they had been in England so long, he mused, that it seemed "a cold and shivery thing to go anywhere else." The voyage to Boulogne was rough and the weather bleak and cold, but Hawthorne remained on deck long enough to note the receding white cliffs of Albion.

CHAPTER IX

ITALY, 1858–1859 *

O N the channel passage two members of the Hawthorne party—little Rose and Miss Ada Shepard—were seasick. Hawthorne himself never suffered from seasickness; but being a little apprehensive of this particular voyage he fortified himself with a glass of brandy-and-water and found the two hours' passage the most enjoyable part of the day.

The train journey from Boulogne to Paris was bleak and cold. There were foot warmers in the car but the cold crept in nevertheless. Viewed imperfectly through holes scratched in the frost on the car windows, the French countryside appeared to resemble New England in winter: broad, bare, brown fields, with streaks of snow at the foot of ridges and along fences or in the furrows of ploughed soil. Hawthorne's impression of France would always be, he declared, that of "an Arctic region."

At Amiens there was botheration from the railway officials, whose intentions were good but whose speech was unintelligible to Hawthorne. If they had spoken slowly and distinctly, he would have understood them well enough, for he was familiar with the written language and the rules for its pronunciation. But their rapid speech was to him "a mere string of gabble." Fortunately Ada Shepard, who had concentrated in the modern languages at Antioch College and was preparing herself for a professorship there, came to his aid. The ensuing conversation gave to Hawthorne, he said, "a new conception as to the value of speech."

Miss Shepard was sympathetically amused. "It is very funny," she wrote Clay Badger, her fiancé, in America,† "to see Mr.

* In the present chapter I am greatly indebted to Norman Holmes Pearson's edition (soon to be published) of Hawthorne's *French and Italian Notebooks*.
† Ada Shepard's letters (all of them unpublished) have been made available through the courtesy of Norman Holmes Pearson.

Hawthorne among these French officials. A band of them comes upon him pouring forth their rapid speech, until he is quite bewildered, and turns to me with a despairing expression, or assaults them himself in English." In response to a customs official's question "Avez-vous quelque chose a déclarer?" Hawthorne (Miss Shepard reported later from Marseilles) "held out his carpet-bags, saying 'Do you want to examine them?'" Miss Shepard performed the office of interpreter faithfully and efficiently throughout the Hawthornes' journeys on the continent. It was an important service (over and above that of governess, which she also performed to complete satisfaction), and the Hawthornes were fully appreciative. "As they cannot afford to have a courier," she told Clay, "I do not know what would become of them and their baggage if they were left to themselves."

The frigid weather continued in Paris, where the Hawthornes stayed at the Hôtel du Louvre. Hawthorne's discomfort was increased by an acute cold, which was accompanied by a persistent bleeding of the nose. "Thus my blood," he remarked jocosely, "must be reckoned among the rivers of human gore which have been shed in Paris." Despite these handicaps he journeyed forth bravely with his family to see the Louvre, Notre Dame, and the other famous places, and filled fifty closely written pages of his journal with descriptions and reactions.

The splendor of Paris [he wrote] takes me altogether by surprise; such stately edifices, prolonging themselves in unwearying magnificence and beauty. . . . The light stone, or stucco, wholly untarnished by smoke and soot, puts London to the blush, if a blush could be seen through its dingy face. . . . I never knew what a palace was till I had a glimpse of the Louvre and the Tuilleries. . . . The life of the scene, too, is infinitely more picturesque than London, with its monotonous throng of smug faces and black coats; whereas, here, you see soldiers and priests; policemen in cocked hats; Zouaves, with turbans, long mantles, and bronzed, half-Moorish faces; and a great many people whom you perceive to be outside of your experience.

But notwithstanding the splendor and the picturesqueness, Hawthorne soon tired of Paris. Its life seemed too artificial: "Nothing," he said, "really thrives here; man and vegetables have but an artificial life, like flowers stuck in a little mould, but never taking root." Moreover, after London, Paris seemed an alien world. The blood tie, which he had felt profoundly in England, was lacking. France did "grand and beautiful things," but he felt no sympathy with the French people. "Their eyes do not win me," he said, "nor do their glances melt and mingle with mine."

After paying their bill at the Hôtel du Louvre (it was 450 francs for a week's lodging and breakfast), the Hawthorne group—now augmented by Miss Maria Mitchell, an astronomer from Nantucket—left Paris on January 12, 1858, and proceeded to Rome via Marseilles and Civitavecchia. From the window of the railway carriage, in the late afternoon, Hawthorne saw, for the first time since leaving America, a crimson and orange sunset, and when the sky grew dark, bright stars ("brighter than stars ever were in England"), some of which Miss Mitchell identified for the instruction of the children. At Marseilles he was impressed chiefly by the nastiness and indecency:

The water closet of the hotel [he wrote], though it is in a nook hard by the salle-à-manger, is a place of horrors. All over the town, people consult their necessities without a scruple, no matter what be the sex of the passer-by. The cabinets provided by public authority are scarcely so decent, as regards concealment, as none at all. Private enterprise seeks to accommodate the necessitous; and on the quai I saw "Cabinets d'aisance" advertised, with a painting of the particular commodity offered to public patronage.

Beyond the quay was the Mediterranean, which he now saw for the first time, "blue as heaven, and bright with sunshine." He had never looked at a finer sea view, but he staunchly refused to concede that the waters along the New England coast were less beautiful than these, "were they twenty times the Mediterranean."

From Marseilles to Civitavecchia (the port of Rome) the Hawthornes traveled by a leisurely steamer which stopped for an entire day at Genoa and for another at Leghorn. Hawthorne was still uncomfortable with a cold and fever, but at Genoa he marveled at the brilliant splendor of the Cathedral of San Lorenzo (a splendor which the English cathedrals must have had, he thought, before the Reformation) and at Leghorn he loyally visited the tomb of Smollett.

The journey from Civitavecchia to Rome—a distance of about forty miles—was an exciting adventure. Since there was no railroad it was necessary to hire a carriage (*vettura*). Hawthorne bargained with the driver (*vetturino*) to transport the party, with their mountain of luggage, in a vettura drawn by four horses, for the sum of three napoleons. The vetturino promised to accomplish the journey in eight hours but the collapse of one of the horses extended the time to almost ten. Leaving Civitavecchia in the late afternoon, the party was soon traveling in darkness along a road which was said to be infested with bandits. Only a few days before, a Catholic bishop from Nova Scotia had been robbed somewhere on this very route. And indeed, "there was not a single mile of the dreary and desolate tract of country over which we passed," Hawthorne recorded, "where we might not have been robbed and murdered with impunity." Fully aware of the danger of their situation and perhaps even exaggerating it, Hawthorne attempted to cheer his companions by lighthearted conversation. Miss Shepard had never heard him talk so much before. "He was very witty," she told Clay Badger; "I wish I had room to write some of the funny things he said." Like Desdemona he beguiled the thing he was by seeming otherwise. At midnight (of January 20) the group finally reached Rome, where Hawthorne, in his eagerness to get his charges safely to bed at Spillman's Hotel, gave the customs officer a substantial bribe.

Before leaving America the Hawthornes had intended to spend a year in Italy, and the intention was never questioned during their stay in England. It seems likely that this part of their plan for going abroad was owing more to Mrs. Hawthorne than to Haw-

thorne himself, for from early youth Sophia had longed for Italy
—and for Rome especially—with a romantic longing. To her, as
to so many others in the nineteenth century, Rome was the home
of the arts, the cradle of western civilization, and (as Byron happily put it) "the city of the soul." "Oh why not live in Rome!" she
had exclaimed to her sister Elizabeth in 1832, and had shed tears of
despair when she reflected upon her far separation from "painting,
statuary, mosaics, bas-reliefs, frescoes, colonnades, porticos, foun-
tains, gardens," and other beautiful Italian objects. The arrival in
Rome, then, was primarily the realization of Mrs. Hawthorne's
long-cherished dream. She was not disappointed:

I am in Rome, Rome, *Rome!* [she announced to the same sister]. I
have stood in the Forum and beneath the Arch of Titus, at the end of
the Sacra Via. I have wandered about the Coliseum, the stupendous
grandeur of which equals my dream and hope. I have seen the sun
kindling the open courts of the Temple of Peace. . . . I have climbed
the Capitolini and stood before the Capitol, by the side of the eques-
trian statue of Marcus Aurelius. . . . I have been into the Pantheon,
whose sublime portico quietly rises out of the region of criticism into
its own sphere—a fit entrance to the temple of all the gods. . . . I
have been to St. Peter's.

The passage reflects the mood and style of "Childe Harold's Pilgrimage." In her notebooks Mrs. Hawthorne praised Byron's
poem for its "inspired utterances," its "perfect truthfulness of figure." "We could never have appreciated Byron's genius," she said,
"if we had not come to Italy."

Hawthorne's interest in Italy was not appreciably heightened
by Byron, who was not one of his particular favorites. But he was
glad to go to Italy for several reasons. He was, like all good husbands, happy to please his wife. He welcomed the opportunity of
continuing his own education in the fine arts after his good beginning at the Manchester Exhibition. Then, too, he enjoyed roam-
ing about the world. If the continental countries touched him less
deeply than the "old home," if his mind was less stored with Italian
lore than with English, he nevertheless felt the normal educated

interest in the European past. And finally, as he told his friend Horatio Bridge, to spend a year in Italy was quite a practical and convenient thing to do: "I can live economically in Italy," he said, "and can pursue my literary avocations as well there as elsewhere." The remark suggests no great ardor for "the city of the soul," but, in the event, Rome was to exert an extraordinary attraction upon him.

The travelers found the weather in Rome, as well as in Paris, extremely cold. Julian's earliest recollection of Rome was of sliding on the ice surrounding a fountain near St. Peter's. His father slid too, but somewhat grimly. Even Mrs. Hawthorne's ardor was cooled by the frigid temperature: it was impossible, she confessed, for an icicle to glow with emotion. Their lodgings—a suite of ten rooms at 37 Via Porta Pinciana (whose monthly rental was $100) —could not be heated adequately. The fireplaces were large enough but their effective utilization would have required, Hawthorne thought, the great logs of a New England forest. His discomfort aggravated by a feverish cold, he wrapped himself in his greatcoat and endured his misery as best he could. It was an unfortunate introduction to Rome, and the first records in his journal reflect his private malaise. "Old Rome," he wrote on February 3, "does seem to lie here like a dead and mostly decayed corpse, retaining here and there a trace of the noble shape it was, but with a sort of fungous growth upon it, and no life but of the worms that creep in and out."

On February 7 he complained that he could not get into the current of his journal and that he had not yet begun the sightseeing of Rome. But he was already doing better than he admitted, for on that day he filled ten pages with descriptions of things recently seen. With the moderation of the weather and the improvement of his health, his responses became more cordial. On February 11 the family visited the Carnival (which was to be a prominent feature of *The Marble Faun*)—Mrs. Hawthorne, Julian, Rose, and Hawthorne riding up and down the Corso in a carriage and exchanging confetti with the crowd, while Una, Ada Shepard, and Miss Mitchell looked on from a balcony. Hawthorne professed not to enjoy himself greatly; with Anglo-Saxon predilection he preferred the Greenwich Fair. But Una, Julian, and Rose, he observed, had a good time, and he himself, a year later, was to find the Roman Carnival more enjoyable.

Hawthorne's mood soon improved and his interest in Rome steadily grew. But whether in the right mood or not, sight-seeing and "journalizing," while he was abroad, were a matter of conscience with him; there was always the feeling that an opportunity —long deferred and expensively purchased—should not be lost. And if his conscience or strength should fail, Sophia was ever ready to screw his courage to the sticking place. For a woman so often ill or verging on actual illness, she was amazingly tireless. Her "receptivity" (Hawthorne observed on one occasion when he refused to see any more pictures till another day) was "unlimited and forever fresh." While sight-seeing, Mrs. Hawthorne often sat down to make a quick pencil sketch of an interesting object, unperturbed if spectators gathered around her and commented on her work. It was not an uncommon occurrence in Italy for several of the Hawthorne party to be sketching simultaneously —Mrs. Hawthorne, Miss Shepard, Una, and even Julian and Rose —though only Mrs. Hawthorne's drawings have been preserved for posterity.*

After the day's sight-seeing and sketching, after tea and the children's bedtime, Hawthorne and his wife and Ada Shepard sat down at the large living room table to write. There was "a profound quiet," Ada reported, "broken only by the busy, active scratches" of their pens. Hawthorne, of course, was writing his journal. During the first four months in Rome he filled about 250 closely written pages; his entire Italian journal (covering a period of sixteen months) contains nearly 200,000 words. Mrs. Hawthorne was also busy with a journal, for which her husband expressed great admiration: "Mrs. Hawthorne," he wrote to Tick-

* See the reproductions in Julian Hawthorne's *Hawthorne and His Circle,* p. 300.

nor, "altogether excels me as a writer of travels. Her descriptions are the most perfect pictures that ever were put on paper; it is a pity they cannot be published; but neither she nor I would like to see her name on your list of female authors." Neither Hawthorne's nor his wife's journal was published during his lifetime, but after his death Mrs. Hawthorne first brought out selections from his writings in this kind, and then (reluctantly, because of her husband's often expressed aversion to female authorship) selections from her own. Her reasons for acting contrary to her husband's scruples were the importunity of friends, the need of money, and the chance that her writing might be of use in the world. "If these notes," she said in her preface, "will aid anyone in the least to enjoy, as I have enjoyed, the illustrious works of the Great Masters in Architecture, Sculpture, and Painting, I shall be well repaid for the pain it has cost me to appear before the public." Where professional authorship was concerned, Hawthorne was an old-fashioned husband (he for God only, she for God in him); Sophia was sufficiently old-fashioned, too, in her marital attitude, but pride of authorship seconded by financial need caused her to violate, in this sole instance, a canonical injunction.

While Hawthorne and his wife worked at their journals, Ada Shepard wrote copious letters to her beloved Clay Badger. Much in her letters concerned the Hawthornes—her admiration of Hawthorne and his wife, her love for the children, her happiness as a member of the family. "This," she said, "is the happiest home-circle I have ever seen." "Mrs. Hawthorne read to us for some time after tea, in the New Testament," she wrote on one occasion, "and I enjoyed it very much. Her three beautiful children gathered around her and listened with delight, while Mr. Hawthorne and I sat by the fire and heard and saw with almost equal pleasure." After an acquaintance of a few months, she declared, "I love Mr. Hawthorne very much, and do not understand why people believe him cold. He is certainly extremely reserved, but he is noble and true and good, and is full of kindly feeling. . . . I admire him exceedingly, and do not feel in the least afraid of him as I had imagined I should be." "His nature," she added, "is like thine in many respects, dearest Clay,"—which was, under the circumstances, perhaps the highest compliment she could pay Hawthorne. Mrs. Hawthorne, she wrote, was "not beautiful"—"most people would call her particularly plain. She has not a single pretty feature, and her form is far from beautiful. Yet, with all Mr. Hawthorne's yearnings for perfection and beauty everywhere, his heart seems entirely satisfied in her. Nay, I think he is ten times the man he might have been without her. . . . She is able to sympathize with him in his highest aspirations and is his companion in every mood." Mrs. Hawthorne, moreover, was "amiable," "extraordinarily delicate and true in her perceptions," and always kind, calling Ada her "eldest daughter." Ada, indeed, could find but one fault— something remarkable in one woman's judgment of another— namely, "an undue carefulness about money affairs and a fear of being cheated" by tradespeople. She had noticed the same trait in Mrs. Horace Mann (Mrs. Hawthorne's sister) and in Una. In a later letter, however, Ada was almost sorry she had mentioned the fault, for Mrs. Hawthorne was "a very noble woman." On their part, the Hawthornes had nothing but praise for the amiable, intelligent young graduate of Mr. Mann's college at Yellow Springs. The commendation which Ada valued most was Hawthorne's remark to Miss Mitchell, who passed it on to Ada, "She is unspoiled." The compliment was doubtless deserved. A young woman of twenty-one who could act as interpreter and companion to the family, teach reading, spelling, writing, composition, Latin, Greek, German, French, Italian, arithmetic, algebra, geometry, geography, and chronology to the Hawthorne children and other children who joined her little school from time to time, and in all of these things give general satisfaction, maintaining the while a modest deportment and even temper, must have been a paragon of learning, amiability, and good sense.

"I never knew anyone," Miss Shepard wrote Clay Badger, "whom all Americans seemed so to delight to honor as Mr. Hawthorne." The observation was prompted by the hospitable reception given Hawthorne and his family by several American artists who, in 1858–59, were cultivating their art in Rome. Hawthorne soon found himself on a cordial footing with them; he liked to study their personalities (as he liked to study "picturesque" personalities wherever he found them) and the work that was going forward in their studios. The American art colony included William Wetmore Story, whose statue of Cleopatra Hawthorne celebrated in *The Marble Faun;* Cephas Giovanni Thompson, who had painted Hawthorne's portrait in Boston in 1850, and of whom Hawthorne wrote after a visit to his studio in Rome in 1858, "I do not think there is a better painter living, among Americans at least, and not one so earnest, faithful, and religious in his worship of art"; Thomas Crawford, whose monumental figure of Washington on horseback Hawthorne thought "a very foolish and illogical piece of work"; and, among still others, two young women who interested Hawthorne—Maria Louisa Lander of Salem, who made a bust of Hawthorne, and Harriet Hosmer of Watertown, Massachusetts, who was a protégée of the English sculptor, John Gibson.

Hawthorne was interested not only in the productions of Miss Lander and Miss Hosmer but in their modes of life; before Henry James, he studied with relish and insight the case of the American young woman abroad. He was a little repelled by Miss Hosmer's mannish attire, while admiring her independence:

She had on petticoats, I think; but I did not look so low, my attention being chiefly drawn to a sort of man's sack of purple or plum-colored broadcloth, into the side-pockets of which her hands were thrust as she came forward to greet us. She withdrew one hand, however, and presented it cordially to my wife (whom she already knew) and to myself without waiting for an introduction. She had on a male shirt, collar, and cravat, with a brooch of Etruscan gold; and on her head was a picturesque little cap of black velvet. . . . There never was anything so jaunty as her movement and action; she was indeed very queer, but she seemed to be her actual self, and nothing affected or made up; so that, for my part, I give her full leave to wear what may suit her best, and to behave as her inner woman prompts.

On another occasion he noticed chiefly the mannishness, "the upper half of her person as usual," he remarked, "having quite as much the aspect of male juvenility as of young womanhood." Miss Lander was more to his liking; her costume was less eccentric. Her personality and general situation seemed to him to have "very available points," as indeed they proved to be when he set about, a little later, the creation of Hilda in *The Marble Faun*. He described Miss Lander as

a young woman, living in almost perfect independence, thousands of miles from her New England home, going fearlessly about these mysterious streets, by night as well as by day, with no household ties, no rule or law but that within her; yet acting with quietness and simplicity and keeping, after all, within a homely line of right. Miss Lander has become strongly attached to Rome, and says that, when she dreams of home, it is merely of paying a short visit, and coming back before her trunk is unpacked.

These "points" are applicable to Hilda, and were also found—except perhaps the "quietness and simplicity"—in Miss Hosmer. Hawthorne's approval of this unconventional type in *The Marble Faun* was credited by at least one historian with having lured many American girls to Rome.*

Hawthorne attempted to explain the fascination which Rome exerted not only upon the American young woman who wanted to be an artist but upon artists generally. Their residence in Rome was not a necessity, for "there is clay elsewhere," he said, "and marble enough, and heads to model; and ideas may be made sensible objects at home as well as here." The explanation was to be found, he thought, in "the peculiar mode of life, and its freedom from the enthralments of Society." Then, too, a community of interests has its advantages, for "though," he observed, "the artists care little about one another's works, yet they keep one another warm by the presence of so many of them." It was this warming environment produced by kindred workers which Hawthorne himself had felt the lack of in his early life.

* See E. D. R. Bianciardi's *At Home in Italy* (quoted by Pearson).

He cultivated the artistic fraternity with more than ordinary interest. He was a frequent visitor at the studios. He enjoyed the talk about art, some of which he used in the chapter "An Aesthetic Company" in *The Marble Faun*. He relished, also, the gossip. One piece of gossip, with Hawthorne's reflections thereon, has become famous. Joseph Mozier, a sculptor from Vermont, held the Hawthornes spellbound one evening with talk about Margaret Fuller:

Mr. Mozier says that Ossoli's family [Hawthorne wrote in his journal], though technically noble, is really of no rank whatever; the elder brother, with the title of marquis, being at this very time a working brick layer, and the sisters walking the streets without bonnets—that is, being in the station of peasant girls, in the female populace of Rome. Ossoli himself, to the best of his belief, was Margaret's servant, or had something to do with the care of her apartments. He was the handsomest man whom Mr. Mozier ever saw, but entirely ignorant even of his own language, scarcely able to read at all, destitute of manners; in short, half an idiot, and without any pretensions to be a gentleman. At Margaret's request, Mr. Mozier had taken him into his studio, with a view to ascertain whether he was capable of instruction in sculpture; but after four months' labor, Ossoli produced a thing intended to be a copy of a human foot; but the big toe was on the wrong side. He could not possibly have had the least appreciation of Margaret, and the wonder is, what attraction she found in this boor, this man without the intellectual spark—she that had always shown such a cruel and bitter scorn of intellectual delinquency. As from her towards him, I do not understand what feeling there could have been, except it were purely sensual; as from him towards her, there could hardly have been even this, for she had not the charm of womanhood. But she was a woman anxious to try all things, and fill up her experience in all directions; she had a strong and coarse nature, too, which she had done her utmost to refine, with infinite pains, but which of course could only be superficially changed. The solution of the riddle lies in this direction; nor does one's conscience revolt at the idea of thus solving it; for—at least, this is my own experience—Margaret has not left, in the hearts and minds of those who knew her, any deep witness of her integrity and purity. She was a great humbug; of course with much talent, and much moral ideality, or else she could not have been so great a humbug. But she had stuck herself full of borrowed qualities, which she chose to provide herself with, but which had no root in her.

Mr. Mozier added that Margaret had quite lost all power of literary production before she left Rome, though occasionally the charm and power of her conversation would reappear. To his certain knowledge, she had no important manuscripts with her when she sailed (she having shown him all she had, with a view to his securing their publication in America) and the History of the Roman Revolution, about which there was so much lamentation in the belief that it had been lost with her, never had existence. Thus there appears to have been a total collapse in poor Margaret, morally and intellectually; and tragic as her catastrophe was, Providence was, after all, kind in putting her, and her clownish husband, and their child, on board that fated ship. There never was such a tragedy as her whole story; the sadder and sterner, because so much of the ridiculous was mixed up with it, and because she could bear anything better than to be ridiculous. It was such an awful joke, that she should have resolved—in all sincerity no doubt—to make herself the greatest, wisest, best woman of the age; and, to that end, she set to work on her strange, heavy, unpliable, and, in many respects, defective and evil nature, and adorned it with a mosaic of admirable qualities, such as she chose to possess; putting in here a splendid talent, and there a moral excellence, and polishing each separate piece, and the whole together, till it seemed to shine afar and dazzle all who saw it. She took credit to herself for having been her own Redeemer, if not her own Creator; and, indeed, she was far more a work of art than any of Mr. Mozier's statues. But she was not working on inanimate substance, like marble or clay; there was something within her that she could not possibly come at, to re-create it and refine it; and, by and by, this rude old potency bestirred itself, and undid all her labor in the twinkling of an eye. On the whole, I do not know but I like her the better for it—the better, because she proved herself a very woman, after all, and fell as the weakest of her sisters might.

It would be difficult to find a better parable of Calvinism in the literature of New England, while Hawthorne's concluding emphasis upon our common humanity is a point sometimes missed by students of the old orthodoxy. Zenobia (in *The Blithedale Ro-*

mance) was perhaps suggested in part by Margaret Fuller, but the view of Margaret in the passage just quoted is broadly representative of Hawthorne's view of human nature generally, and the difficulty of transforming it by an artificial culture. Sometimes thought merely malicious, the passage actually moves beyond the personal to the philosophical.

Hawthorne continued to busy himself in Rome with the study of the fine arts, though with no intention of sticking himself full of borrowed qualities. His was not the attitude of the culture seeker for culture's sake. Indeed, there is a suggestion of the American "Innocents" of a generation later in his expression of "doubt whether we do not bamboozle ourselves in the greater part of the admiration which we learn to bestow" upon famous works of art. He often complained, moreover, of weariness. But he continued to apply himself, seriously and hopefully, to the task before him, and was able, from time to time, honestly to report esthetic growth. "I am sensible that a process is going on," he wrote after about five months in Italy, "that puts me in a state to see pictures with less toil, and more pleasure, and makes me more fastidious, yet more sensible of beauty where I saw none before."

He delighted in the Dutch masters, "who painted such brass pots that you can see your face in them, and such earthen jugs that they will surely hold water." He repeatedly went to see Guido's Beatrice Cenci, which he called "the most profoundly wrought picture in the world." (Hilda, likewise, in *The Marble Faun*, would "sit down before the picture of Beatrice day after day, and let it sink into her heart.") Among works of sculpture the Venus di Medici (in Florence) perhaps interested him most. "The Venus is one of the things," he declared, "the charm of which does not diminish on better acquaintance. . . . I do not, and cannot think of her as a senseless image, but as a being that lives to gladden the world, incapable of decay and death; as young and fair today as she was three thousand years ago, and still to be young and fair as long as a beautiful thought shall require physical embodiment."

Despite the Keatsean joyousness in his reaction to the Venus di Medici, Hawthorne's approach to sculpture and painting was in general less esthetic than moral. In this respect he was like Emerson, who said of the Apollo Belvedere that he could see that the god did not drink port wine. In Hawthorne, as in Emerson, one may call the attitude Puritan. Quite understandably, Hawthorne disapproved of sensuality in figures which purported to represent religious devotion. "Titian's Magdalen," he wrote,

is very coarse and sensual, with only an impudent assumption of penitence and religious sentiment, scarcely so deep as the eyelids; but it is a splendid picture, nevertheless, with those naked, life-like arms, and the hands that press the rich locks about her, and so carefully let those two voluptuous breasts be seen. She a penitent! She would shake off all pretense to it, as easily as she would shake aside that clustering hair and offer her nude front to the next comer.

"Titian," he concluded, "must have been a very good-for-nothing old man."

He objected also to nudity in modern sculpture—an objection which was partly a question of realism, as the objection to Titian's picture was partly a question of consistency and sincerity. After visiting E. S. Bartholomew's studio, where he saw another female figure in process of being sculptured, he declared impatiently, "I do not altogether see the necessity of ever sculpturing another nakedness. Man is no longer a naked animal; his clothes are as natural to him as his skin, and sculpture has no more right to undress him than to flay him." He argued with Mrs. Anna B. Jameson, a popular historian of art, for the desirability of using the costume of the day in modern sculpture, contending that as the function of the art is to "idealize the man of the day to himself," sculpture must accomplish this end while clothing men and women in whatever costume they wear. When Mrs. Jameson mentioned buttons and breeches as insuperable difficulties, Hawthorne roundly declared that if such difficulties could not be overcome the art ought to perish. His position in this instance seems to have been dictated less by moral scruple than by common sense.

Of profounder interest than the art of Italy was its religion. Like all good New Englanders, to be sure, Hawthorne had inherited the dissidence of dissent and the protestantism of the Protestant religion. He was either indifferent or averse to much of the ecclesiastical hierarchy and ceremony. Roman priests appeared to him "pampered, sensual, with red and bloated cheeks, and carnal eyes." He could heartily wish they were better men, more worthy of their high office. The Pope did not greatly interest him, for though on one occasion in St. Peter's Pio Nono's proximity impressed him "kindly and favorably," on another occasion (Easter Sunday of 1858) he grew weary of the prolonged ceremonial and did not remain to witness the papal benediction bestowed from the balcony of the church.

The Roman Catholic religion, nevertheless, had "many admirable points." It seemed to him "a faith which marvellously adapts itself to every human need." An important, perhaps the chief, means of adaptation was the confessional, for the special appreciation of which Hawthorne's long preoccupation with the psychology of guilt was an excellent preparation. Indeed, the office of the confessional was not a new or alien concept to Hawthorne: while writing *The Scarlet Letter*, he once told James Russell Lowell, it had been part of his plan to make Dimmesdale confess himself to a Catholic priest. Such a device would have been "psychologically admirable," Lowell thought. And so it would; but Hawthorne in *The Scarlet Letter* was a historian as well as a psychologist, and the historian would probably have some difficulty in finding a Catholic priest in the Boston of 1650.

In St. Peter's Hawthorne saw a range of confessionals, where penitents speaking various languages—Italian, French, German, Spanish, Polish, and English—might confess their sins. "What an institution that is!" he exclaimed in his journal: "Man needs it so, that it seems as if God must have ordained it." This and other notebook passages describing the confessional were utilized in *The Marble Faun* in that great and moving chapter entitled "The World's Cathedral." Troubled by the knowledge of the murder committed by her friends, Donatello and Miriam, Hilda "flung herself down in the penitent's place; and, tremulously, passionately, with sobs, tears, and the turbulent overflow of emotion too long repressed, she poured out the dark story which had infused its poison into her innocent life." And after this had been accomplished, Hawthorne continued in the novel, "Ah, what a relief! When the hysteric gasp, the strife between words and sobs, had subsided, what a torture had passed away from her soul!" Neither Hawthorne nor his wife was in danger of becoming a Roman Catholic, but it is not entirely accidental or unconnected with family influences that his younger daughter Rose (who was eight years of age in 1859) later became a convert and was for many years, as Mother Alphonsa, a revered sister of mercy.

Hawthorne was interested, too, though somewhat incidentally, in the priest's role in this drama of the confessional. There may have been a personal reason for his interest, for according to Mrs. Hawthorne many readers of *The Scarlet Letter* inflicted their confessions upon its author. While standing near the confessionals in St. Peter's on one occasion, Hawthorne saw a priest come suddenly out of one of them, "looking weary and moist with perspiration." "It must be very tedious," he reflected, "to listen, day after day, to the minute and commonplace iniquities of the multitude of penitents; and it cannot be often that these are redeemed by the treasure-trove of a great sin." Hawthorne could look at both sides of the process—the priest's as well as the penitent's—and though deeply impressed by what he saw, he did not think it necessary for that reason to surrender either his objectivity or his sense of humor.

After four months in Rome the Hawthornes set out for Florence, on May 24, 1858, partly to escape the malarial air of Rome in the summer and partly to enlarge their knowledge of Italy. The journey was a picturesque one by vettura, the contract being that the vetturino should supply meals and lodging en route as well as transportation in return for the sum of 95 scudi and 5 crowns. The carriage was drawn by three horses; in the mountainous regions two horses were added, and on one especially steep ascent a pair of oxen. Hawthorne and Julian often walked up the hills both to relieve the straining team and to stretch their legs. The travelers were on the road eight days, stopping to see the sights at Terni, Borghetto, Foligno, Perugia, Passignano, Arezzo, and Incisa. Upon arriving in Florence they engaged the lower *piano* of the Casa del Bello at $50 a month, arrangements having been made for them in advance by Hiram Powers, the American sculptor. Looking back upon the journey from Rome to Florence, Hawthorne thought it had been "one of the brightest and most uncareful interludes" of his life.

In addition to the art and architecture the Hawthornes, while in Florence, enjoyed the society of the Powers and the Brownings. Hawthorne visited Powers' studio, where he saw the Fisher Boy and Proserpine. In the course of their talk about art he asked Powers if he could model a blush, and was unconvinced by the sculptor's affirmative answer. He was more impressed by Powers' objections to the face of the Venus di Medici, and was almost persuaded, though unwillingly, that the face of Proserpine was truer to nature. Hawthorne found Powers' talk about art, and a variety of other subjects as well, "fresh, original, and full of bone and muscle." He had never before felt an impulse to write down so much of a man's conversation as of Hiram Powers'.

On the evening of June 8, 1858, Mrs. Hawthorne, Ada Shepard, and Hawthorne went to the Casa Guidi to see the Brownings, of whom—especially of Mrs. Browning and the boy Pennini—Hawthorne drew remarkable portraits in his journal:

I never saw such a boy as this before [he wrote of Pennini]; so slender, fragile, and sprite-like, not as if he were actually in ill-health, but as if he had little or nothing to do with human flesh and blood. His face is very pretty and most intelligent, and exceedingly like his mother's, whose constitutional lack of stamina I suppose he inherits. He is nine years old, and seems at once less childlike and less manly than would befit that age. I should not quite like to be the father of such a boy, and should fear to stake so much interest and affection on him as he cannot fail to inspire. I wonder what is to become of him;—whether he will ever grow to be a man;—whether it is desirable that he should. His parents ought to turn their whole attention to making him gross and earthly, and giving him a thicker scabbard to sheath his spirit in.

Mrs. Browning, Hawthorne continued, was

a pale little woman, scarcely embodied at all; at any rate, only substantial enough to put forth her slender fingers to be grasped, and to speak with a shrill, yet sweet, tenuity of voice. Really, I do not see how Mr. Browning can suppose that he has an earthly wife, any more than an earthly child; both are of the elfin breed, and will flit away from him some day, when he least thinks of it. She is a good and kind fairy, however, and sweetly disposed towards the human race, although only remotely akin to it. It is wonderful to see how small she is; how diminutive, and peaked, as it were, her face, without being ugly; how pale her cheek; how bright and dark her eyes. There is not such another figure in this world; and her black ringlets cluster down into her neck and make her face look the whiter for their sable profusion. I could not form any judgment about her age; it may range anywhere within the limits of human life, or elfin-life. When I met her in London, at Mr. Milnes's breakfast-table, she did not impress me so strangely; for the morning light is more prosaic than the dim illumination of their great, tapestried drawing-room; and besides, sitting next to her, she did not then have occasion to raise her voice in speaking, and I was not sensible what a slender pipe she has. It is as if a grasshopper should speak. It is marvellous to me how so extraordinary, so acute, so sensitive a creature, can impress us as she does with the certainty of her benevolence. It seems to me there were a million chances to one that she would have been a miracle of acidity and bitterness.

The Hawthornes saw the Brownings not only at the Casa Guidi but also at their own Casa del Bello and at the villa of Miss Isabella Blagden, who was a hospitable hostess and a lifelong friend of the Brownings. It was at Miss Blagden's villa that, the talk turning to the popular subject of spiritualism, the exciting discovery was made that Ada Shepard was a medium. Without understanding what she did, or entirely believing in it, Ada wrote out messages from Mrs. Hawthorne's mother (recently deceased) which Mrs. Hawthorne found beautiful and consoling. Mrs. Browning also believed in these and other spiritualistic phenomena, while Browning and Hawthorne professed absolute skepticism.

It was a busy, pleasant social life which the Hawthornes led in Florence in the summer of 1858; Miss Shepard noted that they "went out" much more than she had seen them do before.

After spending June and July at the Casa del Bello in Florence the Hawthornes, for August and September, hired from an impoverished Italian nobleman (at the rate of 28 scudi a month) the Villa Montauto, which was situated in the hills within walking distance from the city. Here they found the most picturesque of their many domiciles. The villa was so extensive that each member of the family could have had a suite of rooms for his own use. Hawthorne established himself on the ground floor where he occupied, according to his own description, "a dressing-room, a large vaulted saloon, and a square writing-closet, about five paces across, the walls and ceilings of the two latter being ornamented with angels and cherubs aloft, in fresco, and with temples, pillars, statues, vases, broken columns, peacocks, parrots, vines, sunflowers (all in fresco) below." Una's chamber had a vaulted ceiling with intersecting arches, and adjoining it were a great salon, which Miss Shepard used as a schoolroom, and a little oratory adorned with sacred prints, crucifixes, and a life-size skull, accurately carved out of gray alabaster. An even more interesting feature of the premises was an old square tower, later—like so many items in the Italian journal—to be transferred bodily to *The Marble Faun*. "Machicolated and battlemented, with two or three iron-grated windows up and down its height besides smaller apertures through the stone work," this old tower doubtless went back to the Middle Ages. "Many a cross-bowman," Hawthorne surmised, "had shot his shafts from those windows and loopholes, and from the vantage-height of those gray battlements." Evenings, the family liked to climb to the top of the tower to see the sunset. And after the others had gone down Hawthorne liked to stay on in the growing dusk, looking out over the tiled roofs and towers of Florence toward the misty Apennines while he meditatively smoked a cigar. Hawthorne enjoyed the Villa Montauto "immensely," he told Fields. The sun was warm, the air dry. For the first time since leaving his hilltop at the Wayside, he could lie at full length on the ground without fear of catching cold. ("Moist England," he observed, "would punish a man soundly for taking such liberties with her bosom.") Julian Hawthorne, in retrospect, believed the Florentine summer to have been the happiest period of his father's life. But the allotted time drew rapidly to a close. On October 1, after sad parting glances at Florence and its environs, the Hawthornes took the train to Siena, and after twelve days of sightseeing there they set out for Rome by vettura, a mode of travel which again proved enjoyable. Hawthorne recorded an extraordinary eulogy of their vetturino, Constantino Bacci:

Constantino took us to good hotels and feasted us with the best; he was kind to us all, and especially to little Rosebud, who used to run by his side, with her small hand in his great brown one; he was cheerful in his deportment, and expressed his good spirits by the smack of his whip, which is the barometer of a vetturino's inward weather; he drove admirably, and would rumble up to the door of an albergo, and stop to a hair's breadth just where it was most convenient for us to alight; he would hire postillions and horses, where other vetturini would take nothing better than sluggish oxen, to help us up the hilly roads, so that sometimes we had a team of seven; he did all that we could possibly require of him, and was content, and more, with a buonmano of five scudi, in addition to the stipulated price [70 scudi]. Finally, I think the tears had risen almost to his eyelids when we parted with him.

Constantino Bacci appreciably raised Hawthorne's estimate of the Italian character.

On a bright mid-October morning the party drew near Rome along the Appian Way. Their return evoked a kind of home-feeling, and the Eternal City exercised its spell as it had not done before. "Rome certainly does draw into itself my heart," Hawthorne felt at the time—a little extravagantly perhaps—"as I think even London or even little Concord itself, or old sleepy Salem, never did." Quarters at 68 Piazza Poli had already been arranged for, and the plan was to live there six months and then, in April, 1859, to return to America. The brightest days, however, were soon followed by the darkest, and plans and prospects alike were dashed by the most tragic experience of Hawthorne's life—the prolonged and nearly fatal illness of his fourteen-year-old daughter, Una.

On November 2, 1858, Hawthorne recorded in his journal that Una was ill of the Roman fever. He traced the contagion to her having sat down to sketch in the Coliseum. The attack did not seem especially severe, yet it was accompanied by a delirium which made "the poor child talk in rhythmical measure," he said, "like a tragic heroine—as if the fever lifted her feet off the earth." On November 4 Ada Shepard reported to Clay Badger that Una was out of danger, and on November 8 that she was rapidly recovering, but on December 11 that she had had another attack. Indeed, for six months the terrible fever would advance, recede, and advance again. (It receded long enough in March, 1859, to permit the family, including Una, to attend the Roman Carnival for a second season.) To make matters worse, Mrs. Hawthorne had a prolonged illness in December, Miss Shepard in January, and Hawthorne in February. It was the first time since boyhood, Miss Shepard learned, that he had been obliged to lie in bed or see a physician. She seemed justified in concluding that "Rome is a very unfavorable place for residence, as far as health is concerned."

Una's most serious illness was in early April. Dr. Franco, the attending physician, seemed to have little hope of her recovery. In his diary of April 8 Hawthorne wrote "God help us!" from the depths of his despair. Mrs. Hawthorne was "perfectly strong and calm . . . wonderfully calm and strong . . . as brave and strong a spirit," Ada testified, "as I always knew she must be." Hawthorne wondered what would happen to his wife when she lost hope, but she did not lose hope.

During Una's crisis, which lasted about two weeks, many friends were helpful and solicitous. Mrs. Browning brought a broth. Mrs. Story sat up with Una, thereby allowing Mrs. Hawthorne to get a little sleep. Carriages were constantly driving to the door with inquiries. On one day in particular, Mrs. Hawthorne recalled in a letter to her sister Elizabeth, "there seemed a cloud of good spirits in the drawing-room, Mrs. Ward, Mrs. Browning, Mrs. Story, all standing and waiting. Magnificent flowers were always coming. . . . The American Minister constantly called. Mr. Aubrey de Vere came. Everyone who had seen Una in society came to ask." To the mother the anxious time could be, at least in retrospect, a time of social triumph, too.

Meanwhile Hawthorne walked and talked with Franklin Pierce, who had recently been retired from the presidency, and had arrived in Rome, as it happened, in the nick of time to help his friend through this trying period. To Pierce Mrs. Hawthorne thought she almost owed her husband's life, and Hawthorne himself said that, never having had before a trouble that went to his "very vitals," he fully appreciated for the first time "what comfort there might be in the nearby sympathy of a friend." Pierce really did him good, he thought, and he would "always love him the better for the recollection of these dark days." They talked about poor Una, and then of politics, a subject of interest to Hawthorne as well as to Pierce; and Pierce showed Hawthorne a letter, signed by all the members of his Cabinet, in which they had expressed at the close of his administration "their feelings of respect and attachment." A better topic could not have been hit upon for diverting Hawthorne's mind from his present trouble.

Una's illness required the postponement of their departure from Rome, which had been planned for April, 1859. But by May Dr. Franco declared the patient well enough to travel, and the Hawthornes were eager to leave the city which they had found so full of pestilence. On May 25 they set out once more with their mountain of luggage. Hawthorne's farewell to Rome was one of mixed feelings. Although, as he said, he had been "very miserable there, and languid with the effects of the atmosphere," he confessed "a love" for Rome; no place, he felt, had ever taken "so strong a hold" of his being. Early on the morning of their departure he took a last walk to the Pincian, and the Borghese Grounds and St. Peter's, and thought they had "never looked so beautiful, nor the sky so bright and blue."

The return itinerary included Civitavecchia (reached by the new railroad, now crowded with refugees from the Austrian War), Leghorn, Genoa, Marseilles; Avignon, where a week's sight-seeing was accomplished, Hawthorne flagging somewhat, Mrs. Hawthorne proving still unweariable; and Geneva, where the conscientious travelers spent several days exploring Lake Geneva and the Castle of Chillon. They continued to be afflicted with misfortunes, even among the Alps. Mrs. Hawthorne sprained her ankle, Julian had a cold, Una's strength appeared precarious, and Mont Blanc refused to show itself from behind heavy clouds. There was some consolation, perhaps, in the unusually convenient and efficient manner in which the railroad transported the party to Paris and on to Havre. Hawthorne felt inclined to exclaim "Long live Louis Napoleon!" but checked himself with the thought that a tourist "generally profits by all that is worst for the inhabitants of the country." Even the palatial edifices with which Napoleon had adorned Paris, he reflected, "were better for a stranger to look at than for the Emperor's own people to pay for." Hawthorne's understanding of a democratic economy obviously exceeded that of some American travelers in Italy and Germany in the 1930's.

At Havre, on June 22, Miss Shepard set sail for America after having been for nearly two years a member of the Hawthornes' household. Her experience had been a beneficial one and extremely pleasant—except for one distressing episode. During Una's illness in Rome Dr. Franco, a married man, had made love to her. She had repelled his advances stoutly but he had persisted day after day. After a while she had begun to feel a kind of sympathy for him. She had wondered if, while attending her during her own illness, he had given her a potion, or if she were being hypnotized by his snaky eyes. But like the Lady in *Comus*, she had been able to resist successfully to the end through the power of chastity. She had not told the Hawthornes, not wishing—especially when Dr. Franco was their chief reliance—to destroy their confidence in Una's physician. Now, as she boarded the *Vanderbilt* for New York, she could count herself at last safe from Dr. Franco's evil fascination. Upon reaching America she lost no time in marrying Clay Badger.

From Havre the Hawthornes (never to be the wiser concerning Ada and Dr. Franco) journeyed to Southampton, and thence to Mrs. Coxes's boardinghouse, 6 Golden Square, London, which had been engaged for them by their always faithful friend, Francis Bennoch. In London they enjoyed seeing old friends and meeting new ones. Henry Chorley, the *Athenaeum* critic, called. Hawthorne went to a dinner given by Sir Francis Moon, and made one more after-dinner speech. Hawthorne and his wife soon found themselves in abundant social request. Their plan was to sail for America in August, but James T. Fields, now in London with his charming new wife, came forward with a proposition which Hawthorne could not afford to refuse or defer. Through Fields' good offices the London publishers Smith and Elder had agreed to pay £600 for a new romance by Nathaniel Hawthorne. Inasmuch as Hawthorne had written while in Italy the first draft of a new romance, he now decided to settle down in England and put it in shape for publication as soon as possible. He had expected to rewrite his book after returning to the Wayside, but it now appeared advantageous to cooperate closely with Smith and Elder and to make certain of the English copyright. Perhaps, too, he was glad of an excuse to stay a while longer in England, which seemed more than ever an "old home" after his travels in alien lands.

There was no doubt, at any rate, that he wanted and needed the £600. The $30,000 accumulated at the consulate had shrunk appreciably. The cost of maintenance and travel for a large household had been great. During 1859 Hawthorne listed in his pocket diary disbursements totaling £730. The amount spent in 1858 must have been at least as much. One investment, a loan of $10,000 to J. L. O'Sullivan on real estate in New York City, appeared insecure (and eventually, according to Julian Hawthorne, was a total loss). Moreover, there were outside demands, many people supposing the ex-consul of Liverpool richer than he was. "Mr. Hawthorne," Sophia wrote Elizabeth Peabody, "has relations and personal friends who look to him with great desire." She expressed disappointment (in February, 1860) "at the small result of the four years' toil at the Consulate" and regret that she could not give financial aid to Miss Peabody, who apparently expected it, and to their impoverished brother, Nathaniel. The financial pressure was increased still more by the prospect of making some necessary additions to the Wayside. One thing was certain: Hawthorne would have to supplement his dwindling reserves by a fresh income from his pen.

Italy had not proved as favorable to creative writing as he had hoped. There had been, for one thing, the constant demand of sight-seeing and the necessary record thereof, and for another, the languorous effect of the Italian climate. Hawthorne nevertheless had done some writing at Rome in the spring of 1858, at Florence in the summer, and again at Rome in the fall and winter of 1858–59.

Having brought from England the germ of an English romance, Hawthorne wrote a rough draft of the story in April–May, 1858. He put it aside, however (the sketch was never reworked and was posthumously published as *The Ancestral Footstep*), after he had become interested in the Faun of Praxiteles. On April 22, 1858, he wrote in his journal:

It seems to me that a story, with all sorts of fun and pathos in it, might be contrived on the idea of the faun's species having become intermingled with the human race. . . . The tail might have disappeared by dint of constant intermarriage with ordinary mortals; but the pretty, hairy ears should occasionally reappear in members of the family; and the moral instincts and intellectual characteristics of the faun might be most picturesquely brought out, without detriment to the human interest of the story.

And on April 30 he wrote, "The idea keeps recurring to me of writing a little Romance about the Faun of Praxiteles." When he settled down to writing at Florence in the summer, therefore, he did not rework the English romance but sketched out the romance of the faun instead. On July 27 he was busy with the new story, and having completed a first sketch by September 1, he postponed further work until after his return to Rome. He wrote to Fields September 3, "I have planned two romances, one or both of which I could have ready for the press in a few months, if I were either in England or America." Established in Rome once more, he set to work on the expansion of the sketch made at Florence and, despite all distractions, wrote almost daily, his pocket diary recording the completion of the rough draft on January 30, 1859. It was this rough draft which Hawthorne decided, the following July, to stay in England long enough to rewrite.

Because the social life of London proved too diverting for serious literary labor, the Hawthornes went to Redcar on the Yorkshire coast. Here, almost within hearing of the surf of the German Ocean, Hawthorne began "in great earnest" (his pocket diary records) the third and final draft of *The Marble Faun*. His writing schedule is impressive. Between July 26, the beginning date, and November 8, when he finished the last of the 508 manuscript pages, he wrote daily (usually from nine to three, sometimes longer) with the exception of only seven days including Sundays. Three days were lost in early October when the Hawthornes moved to the milder climate of Leamington; two days were taken off when Henry Bright came to Leamington for a week-end visit, and one day, likewise, when George Hillard of Boston dropped in to renew an old friendship.

During the process of writing and even after the work was completed, Hawthorne's mood was uneven. He had his ups and downs. According to his pocket diary he "made slow and poor progress" on July 28, and on the 29th he "scribbled fitfully with many idle pauses and no good result." On the 30th he wrote "tolerably well" and on August 1 "with middling success." He got on "a little more satisfactorily than heretofore" on August 4, and on the 6th, while making "no great progress," he was becoming "more interested." The growing interest thereafter is reflected in the frequent extension of the writing time to half-past three, and the occasional addition of "an hour after dinner." The tide ebbed, however, on August 14, when "discouraged and depressed," he "tried to write, but could make out nothing." On September 10 he gave his wife the finished portion (which he estimated as more than half) to read, being certain no doubt of her praise and its buoyant effect.

On October 17 Hawthorne sent to Smith and Elder by express the manuscript as far as page 429. The remaining 79 pages were forwarded on November 9, the day after their completion. Mrs. Hawthorne reported to Miss Peabody that her husband was "very well, and in very good spirits, despite all his hard toil of so many months," but that "as usual" he thought the book "good for nothing." "But I am used to such opinions," she continued, "and understand why he feels depressed. . . . The true judgment of the work was his *first* idea of it, when it seemed to him worth the doing." Hawthorne vacillated in his opinion of the romance as indeed he had vacillated in his opinions of his earlier books. To Fields he wrote, on October 10, that he "admired it exceedingly at intervals" but was "liable to cold fits" during which he thought it "the most infernal nonsense." On November 17 he told Fields in a confident mood that it was "much the best" thing he had ever done. In the following April he took the considered view, in a letter to Ticknor, that if he had ever written anything well it ought to be this romance, for he had "never thought or felt more deeply, or taken more pains." But like even more famous authors —like Dante, whose book kept him lean for many years—he confessed to being "worn down" from the writing; he thought it was "not wholesome" for him to write at all.

Hawthorne was busy with proofs during December and January (1859–60), and the book was published in London on February 28 as *Transformation* (though Hawthorne disapproved of the title) and in Boston a few days later as *The Marble Faun*. Author and publisher were pleased with the book's reception in both England and America. Chorley reviewed it for the *Athenaeum*, Bright for the *Examiner*, Lowell and Whipple for the *Atlantic*. Unless possibly to Irving, the London *Times* had never been so complimentary to an American author. John Lothrop Motley (from whose balcony the Hawthornes had witnessed their second Carnival in Rome) wrote an appreciative letter which gave Hawthorne much pleasure. By the middle of April *Transformation* was in its third edition, and *The Marble Faun* was doing equally well. Fields wrote in May from London, "On all hands among the best people I hear golden opinions. . . . Your Boston publishers hold up their heads higher than ever now. You can't imagine what lots of attention I get in London from the fact that I am one of the boys who published for you in America."

There had been, however, one persistent objection in the critical reception of the book—namely, that the author had not told with sufficient explicitness what actually happened in the story—and this objection Hawthorne good-naturedly took cognizance of in a short epilogue written in March and appended to the second edition. The epilogue, though, stubbornly refrained from telling very much. Hawthorne would not compromise his view of what a "romance" legitimately was. *The Marble Faun* was not intended for literal-minded readers. For all those who ask such questions as whether the Faun actually had furry ears, he declared quite frankly in the epilogue, "the book is a failure." The English seemed to him much less imaginative, where his kind of fiction was concerned, than Americans. "These beer-sodden beefeaters," he said to Motley, "do not know how to read a Romance."

The Marble Faun being well launched, it was now time once more to think of going home. There were moments when the thought gave him a certain apprehension. Possibly he would not be satisfied with a settled abode after so much moving from place to place. Then, too, the controversy over slavery (for Hawthorne continued to read the American papers religiously throughout his residence abroad) seemed to be approaching the explosive point, and it was not pleasant to think of finding his native land, upon his return, torn by civil strife. He must have wondered also if his extended absence had produced an estrangement of the kind which so many of his stories warn against. "Americans," he said to Hillard, "are liable to get out of sorts with their native land by being long away from it." In October, 1859, he told Ticknor that he had "out-lived all feeling of home-sickness."

But the last statement was untrue, as Hawthorne himself discovered when the time of departure drew near. On April 19, 1860 (significantly the anniversary of Concord and Lexington, when the embattled farmers fired the shot heard round the world), he wrote to Ticknor, "All my homesickness has fallen on me at once, and even Julian is scarcely more impatient than myself." He became excited, about this time, over a prize fight between an Englishman and an American and regretted that the match was terminated without a decision, especially since he thought that the American, John Heenan, had had an excellent chance of winning. During the remaining weeks in England a strong undercurrent of home-feeling swept away all desire to remain abroad. He warned Motley against the "treason" of expatriation. The American praise of *The Marble Faun* sounded like a "welcome home." He looked forward eagerly to seeing his friends again in Concord and Cambridge and at the old "corner" in Boston where Ticknor and Fields received their authors. In short, whatever complaints about America Hawthorne might indulge himself in, few writers have been stauncher patriots than he. "Although Mr. Hawthorne takes a great deal of comfort in abusing America occasionally himself," Miss Ada Shepard once aptly observed, "he does not allow others to do it unrebuked in his presence."

In the spring of 1860 the Hawthornes removed from Leamington to Bath for the sake of Mrs. Hawthorne's health. During the winter she had had a serious attack of bronchitis, and Hawthorne would have despaired of her life but for his knowledge of her remarkable recuperative powers. Although her health improved at Bath she was still unequal to social demands, and Hawthorne met some of these unaccompanied by his wife. For several days in May he was the guest of the Motleys in London, where he found himself much sought after. "Thou wouldst be stricken dumb," he wrote Sophia, "to see how quietly I accept a whole string of invitations, and, what is more, perform my engagements without a murmur." As on former occasions of the kind, he thought that the stir of London life did him "a wonderful deal of good." An event worthy of record in his notebook was a dinner at Lord Dufferin's where he met, among others, the Honorable Caroline Norton, once a famous beauty and still charming, Hawthorne thought, though well past fifty. Another notable experience was a journey with Henry Bright to Cambridge University, where this best of English friends received an honorary M.A. Before saying farewell to Bright, Hawthorne gave him as a personal memento the manuscript of *Transformation*.

The Liverpool sailing was set for June 16 and nothing intervened to compel a postponement. By June 10 the Hawthornes were guests, once more and for the last time, at Mrs. Blodgett's hospitable boardinghouse. Here they were joined on the 15th by James and Annie Fields, who were completing a year's honeymoon abroad. Early the next morning the Hawthornes, accompanied by the Fields, boarded the red-funneled steamer lying in the Mersey and to their delight were welcomed by Captain Leitch, who had brought them over nearly seven years before. As the boat slipped down the Mersey, Hawthorne leaned against the rail while the familiar dingy wharves and smoky sky of Liverpool gradually faded from his view.

CHAPTER X

THE WAYSIDE ONCE MORE, 1860–1864

THE twelve days' voyage home on the *Europa* was extremely pleasant. The sea was calm, the twilights long, the nights luminous with moonlight. Hawthorne told Fields that he would like "to sail on and on forever, and never touch the shore again." Mrs. Hawthorne and Mrs. Fields struck up a lively friendship, having "delicious talks" (Annie Fields recorded in her diary) in the evening. During the day Mrs. Fields was busy with a volume of Ruskin's *Modern Painters*, and the other members of the party did a good deal of reading also, fearing to tire one another with too much conversation. Fields alone was seasick, and Hawthorne prescribed such odd remedies as pies made of Mother Carey's chickens and a dose of salts distilled from the tears of Niobe. "The divine spirit of humor was upon him," Fields said.

After landing at Boston on the morning of June 28, 1860, the Hawthornes proceeded in the heat and glaring sunshine to Concord, where they found the Wayside very much the same as when they had left it.* After England the June countryside seemed parched, and after the spacious quarters occupied in Rome and Florence the Wayside seemed cramped.

The Hawthornes were welcomed home by old friends. Thoreau called and found Hawthorne unaltered except that he was very brown from his sea voyage. Emerson gave a little evening party, at which the guests—the others being Alcott, Thoreau, Frank Sanborn, and W. M. Hunt, the artist—were regaled with strawberries and cream. Alcott offered to assist Hawthorne in landscaping his grounds, and Ellery Channing strongly recom-

* From 1853 to 1859 the house had been occupied by Mrs. Hawthorne's brother, Nathaniel Peabody, and afterward by her sister, Mrs. Horace Mann, whose husband had died in the summer of 1859.

mended Sanborn's school, recently established, for the children. Meanwhile, the Hawthorne family soon found themselves on the old terms of sociability with the Emersons and Alcotts; the Emerson house in particular became almost a second home to Una and Julian, who were of an age with Edith and Edward Emerson. Outside of Concord a more imposing welcome was extended to Hawthorne at a dinner in Boston given by Ticknor and Fields. Hawthorne enjoyed especially on this occasion his talk with Lowell, whom he was glad to thank for his perceptive review of *The Marble Faun.* Lowell was much gratified by Hawthorne's appreciation, and observed that he looked no older, despite a moustache acquired in Italy, and that he was "easier in society than formerly." The dinner was a pleasant affair, though one guest—Franklin Pierce—seemed to Lowell out of place in such a company.

Notwithstanding the welcome home, which was both cordial and official, the Hawthornes were unable to settle down comfortably at the Wayside until the house should be enlarged, and the process of revamping, as always, proved more protracted and more costly than they had foreseen. Hawthorne expected to spend about $500 on improvements, but before he had finished the cost had mounted to well over $2,000. Changes included a three-story addition running up behind the old house, second-story rooms over the kitchen and the old study, a new entrance, marble mantels, and other expensive items. Hawthorne's new study was in the tower, which was the top story of the addition and from which he could look out over the Concord hills and meadows. He told Longfellow that he climbed into his study through a trap door upon which his chair rested while he was writing.

Carpenters, painters, and paperers were busy, in their desultory way, through the fall, winter, and spring of 1860–61. On May 16, 1861, Hawthorne reported to Ticknor that the house was at last finished and painted and really made "a very pretty appearance." On the inside, meanwhile, a good deal of redecorating and refurnishing was going on under the direction of Mrs. Hawthorne, who had always shown a talent for artistic design. The calcimining and papering of walls and the making of chintz covers for chairs and sofas continued well into 1862. Hawthorne was disturbed perhaps less by the confusion than by the expense. "What will be the use of having a house," he said to Ticknor, "if it costs me all my means of living in it? . . . It is folly for a mortal man to do anything more than pitch a tent." But despite unavoidable worries, he was reasonably satisfied with what had been done. While confessing that from the architectural standpoint the renovated Wayside was "the absurdest anomaly," he told Bridge that the total result was "a pretty and convenient house enough, no larger than necessary for my family and an occasional friend, and no finer than a modest position in life demands."

By degrees the family became adjusted to a busy, happy routine. Julian was preparing for Harvard at Sanborn's coeducational school in Concord. Rose entered a girls' school near by. Although Una's health was still uncertain (she had suffered a recurrence of the Roman fever in the summer of 1860 and had been restored, her parents thought, by electrical treatments), in 1861 she was studying privately with George Bradford—a friend of Hawthorne's since Brook Farm days—reciting twice a week in Italian, Latin, arithmetic, and botany. She and Julian joined freely in the social activities of Concord's young people. There were delightful picnics for Sanborn's scholars and their friends at Flint Pond, whither the picnickers rode in carriages and wagons. There were dances and masquerades at the town hall. One masquerade—in March, 1862—caused a flurry of domestic activity, for Una's gown and Julian's disguise as the Earl of Leicester cost Mrs. Hawthorne much effort; she was "limp," she told Annie Fields, after the masquerade. But mothers are never permanently weary in welldoing, and in June the Hawthornes gave a dance at the Wayside for forty young people. The house was decorated with a profusion of roses sent by Mrs. Emerson and Ephraim Bull, the Concord horticulturist. Hawthorne looked in on the dancers—"like a grand Olympian descended to a Paradise of children," his wife thought—and shook hands with the guests as they departed.

When a rosy-cheeked girl expressed timidity at approaching the Olympian, her escort, Judge Hoar's son, reassured her with "It is proper and he is not a bear."

The Hawthorne household was not only sociable but neighborly and public spirited as well. Mrs. Hawthorne, to be sure, was the directing genius in altruistic efforts. In February, 1863, she was tireless in assisting the Alcotts during the illness of Louisa, who had had a nervous breakdown while nursing soldiers in the Union Hospital at Georgetown. During the following winter all hands at the Wayside (except Hawthorne) were busy preparing art objects to be sold at a great Concord Fair, for the benefit of Negro orphans. Una and Rose painted vases; Julian executed an "illumination" of Tennyson's "Ring Out, Wild Bells," and Mrs. Hawthorne made a book of the rhyme of Gaffer Grey, putting the text into German letter and illustrating it from old prints and from ideas of her own. The objects contributed by the four brought a total of $100 at the fair: such was their artistic merit, and such also the philanthropic spirit of the good people of Concord.

Of these and other activities at the Wayside Mrs. Hawthorne wrote full accounts to Annie Fields, with whom she enjoyed a friendly intimacy. Indeed, after their return from abroad, the Hawthornes were more closely associated with the Fields than with any other family. Fields and his wife (affectionately referred to in the Hawthorne circle as "Heartsease" and "Mrs. Meadows") were often guests at the Wayside, where a visit, Annie thought, was worth twenty elsewhere. In summer weather Fields liked to climb with Hawthorne the wooded hill back of the house, or saunter to the Old Manse, rich in memories to the author of the *Mosses*, or lie in the tall grass by the river, or talk about Hawthorne's contributions—those already done and those promised— to the *Atlantic Monthly*, of which Fields had become editor in 1861. More often the Hawthornes—individually and collectively —were guests at the Fields' house at 37 Charles Street, Boston. Julian made himself at home there, sometimes walking the eighteen miles from Concord; Mrs. Hawthorne and the girls enjoyed gala entertainments there when a celebrity was present and the theater or a concert was thrown in for good measure—though she sometimes expressed anxiety lest their dresses might not be fine enough for the occasion. Hawthorne preferred quieter visits, going less often than asked and avoiding, as much as possible, special occasions. Mrs. Fields' drawing room overlooking the bay was, he said in 1864, one of his "choicest ideal places."

Another attraction in Boston after his return from abroad was the Saturday Club, which had been organized in 1856 and which met at the Parker House for dinner and conversation at 3 P.M. on the last Saturday of each month. Hawthorne had been elected to. membership in 1859. The roster of the club in 1861 included, among others, Agassiz, Emerson, Lowell, Motley, Whipple, Holmes, Prescott, Whittier, Norton, S. G. Howe, and Longfellow. Although Hawthorne did not attend the meetings religiously, he was often present. On these occasions he usually contrived to sit next to Longfellow, with whom he always felt perfectly at ease and with whose tragic misfortune (his wife was burned to death in 1861) he deeply sympathized. He could not "reconcile this calamity," he told Fields, to his "sense of fitness," for "there ought to have been no deep sorrow in the life of a man like him." In 1862 Hawthorne took it upon himself, in a letter to the club's secretary, Horatio Woodman, to recommend Fields for membership. He advocated Fields' desirability as "a genial and kindly nature, in which the intellect (though quite sufficiently) is not most prominently developed." The danger in the club, he said, was that its membership should be made up too exclusively of "clashing intellects" and Fields would perform an office similar to that of Longfellow, whose "harmonizing temper," rather than his "mind," made "the charm of his society." Over and above the regular dinners of the Saturday Club there were special ones, some of which Hawthorne came from Concord to attend. One instance was Fields' dinner for Anthony Trollope in September, 1861. Hawthorne was doubtless glad to see the author of *The*

Warden and *Barchester Towers*, which he had read in England and admiringly described as "solid and substantial, written on the strength of beef and through the inspiration of ale." Trollope seems to have liked Hawthorne at this one and only meeting, for Fields wrote a few days after the dinner, "Trollope fell in love with you . . . and swears you are the handsomest Yankee that ever walked the planet."

Not only Boston but more distant places attracted Hawthorne during his last years, for despite a strong home-feeling he frequently felt the need for a change of scene. This was especially so in summer, when the inland air of Concord was often close and oppressive, and he remembered the invigoration he had many times experienced on the seacoasts of England and New England. Now that he was irrevocably settled in Concord, he was inclined to regret that he had not chosen the seaside as the place of his permanent abode. But the ocean was not far away, and brief excursions there were still easily possible.

"Wilted with the hot weather" (he told Fields) and "dying for a salt breath," Hawthorne—accompanied by Julian, who was also impatient to get to the sea—went to West Beach, Beverley, in July, 1861, for a two weeks' stay. They had lodgings at a farmhouse, where the entertainment was simple and inexpensive, and spent the days at the beach or in the adjacent pine woods. Hawthorne liked the location so much, he wrote his wife, that if he had seen sooner "these noble woods of white pine and these rocks and beaches" he might have built his "tower" there rather than in Concord. Elizabeth Hawthorne, who lived near by, joined her brother and nephew in berrypicking rambles. Elizabeth was a person (Julian said later) with "a cold, clear, dispassionate common-sense, softened by a touch of humor such as few women possess"; she was also a great admirer of her brother's books. Hawthorne urged her to pay a return visit to the Wayside (which she did the following month, when she delighted Rose with the skill with which she knitted socks for the soldiers). The vacation at Beverley was pleasant and beneficial enough, but Hawthorne soon wearied of separation even though his wife urged him to stay longer for his own good. After a fortnight he expressed in a letter to Rose the "conclusion that when a person has a comfortable home of his own, and a good little Bab [Rose] of his own, and a good great Onion [Una], and a best mamma, he had better stay with them than roam abroad."

But Hawthorne continued to roam nevertheless. Although he was far from accepting Emerson's rarefied, unhuman view of personal relations that

> When each the other shall avoid
> Shall each by each be most enjoyed,

he found that journeys away from home conveyed various benefits, not the least being a renewed appreciation of home itself. When Concord got muggy again in August, 1862, Hawthorne, again accompanied by Julian, journeyed by steamboat from Boston to Hallowell, Maine, by train from Hallowell to Bangor, and by stagecoach (an all-night ride over rough roads) from Bangor to West Gouldsborough on the Maine Coast. Here again they enjoyed the rustic fare of a farmhouse. During the day they swam in the bay, or rowed, or fished for flounders, or ate a picnic chowder on the beach, or sat in the shadow of a rock, looking out over the water, while Hawthorne smoked a cigar. In the evenings Hawthorne talked politics with their host, a farmer, who (Julian observed in a diary kept at the time, which obviously reflected his father's opinions) was not an abolitionist but a sensible fellow who could hear and understand two sides of a question. The fact that he ate with his knife did not lower his guests' estimate of his intelligence. Hawthorne once more found himself at home among native New England types—the farmer, the country lawyer, the village editor, the lumberman (a Colonel Burnham, now on furlough from McClellan's army)—and he wrote about them in his notebook with the same interest, discernment, and nice attention to detail which characterize the Maine and North Adams journals of 1837–38. The people of Maine, he concluded, were "very much ruder of aspect than those of Massachusetts, but quite as intelligent, and as comprehensive of the affairs of the time." Two weeks of this varied enjoyment were about enough for the time being; moreover, as Hawthorne told his wife, they were compelled to return because of the disrepair of Julian's breeches—"what with bushes, briers, swamps, rocks, beach, mud, sea-water, and various hard usage and mischances."

At home at the Wayside, Hawthorne was scarcely less sociable than with his vacation acquaintances. Young William Dean Howells found him hospitable and inclined to talk freely. While they sat together on a log on the hilltop, Hawthorne asked about the West, which (Howells reported) he "seemed to fancy much more purely American" than the eastern states. Howells was delighted with the note of introduction which Hawthorne gave him to Emerson, "I find this young man worthy," and concluded the account of his visit by saying that he "entirely liked Hawthorne." So did Miss Gail Hamilton, another contributor to the *Atlantic*, after a visit of several days in 1863. "He is a glorious man," she wrote, "a very ideal man in his personal appearance, with an infinite forehead, his gray, dry, long hair thrown back from it in all directions, deep lamps of eyes glowing out from under their heavy arches, black eyebrows and moustache, a florid healthy face—a pure, sensitive, reticent, individual man, whom it is enough to have seen, to have looked at, to have been in the same house with. He talks little, but he talks extremely well." Hawthorne in return enjoyed Miss Hamilton, despite his fancied antipathy to women writers. "We found Gail Hamilton," he told Fields, "a most comfortable and desirable guest to have in the house. My wife likes her hugely, and for my part, I had no idea that there was such a sensible woman of letters in the world. She is just as healthy-minded as if she had never touched a pen. I am glad she had a pleasant time, and hope she will come back."

Among many others who came to the Wayside for varying lengths of time during Hawthorne's last years and met with unfailing cordiality were Franklin Pierce (whose name Hawthorne turned into the anagram "Princelie Frank"), W. D. Ticknor (whose generous gifts of cigars, wine, and hard cider were not necessary to secure a welcome), and the old friends of Salem, William B. Pike, now Collector of the Salem Port, and Zachariah Burchmore, whose chronic poverty Hawthorne attempted to relieve by a gift of $50.

Despite all such unfeigned cordiality Hawthorne gained the reputation, in some quarters, of aloofness. Emerson regretted his failure "to conquer a friendship," attributing it to Hawthorne's "unwillingness and caprice." Alcott complained of Hawthorne's "dodging about amongst the trees on his hilltop as if he feared his neighbor's eyes would catch him." And Mrs. Harriet Beecher Stowe accused Mrs. Hawthorne of doing "picket-duty" when Brigadier General Francis C. Barlow and Mrs. Julia Ward Howe announced their intention of making a call. One needs to be reminded, for the sake of a true perspective, that Hawthorne was a writer by profession, not a receptionist, and that he liked the people he liked. He could be amused by Alcott on occasion, but a little of Alcott went a long way, as the following good-natured verses, written to divert his children, suggest:

> There dwelt a Sage at Apple-Slump,
> Whose dinner never made him plump;
> Give him carrots, potatoes, squash, parsnips, and peas,
> And some boiled macaroni, without any cheese,
> And a plate of raw apples, to hold on his knees,
> And a glass of sweet cider, to wash down all these,—
> And he'd prate of the Spirit as long as you'd please,—
> This airy Sage of Apple-Slump.

If to Hawthorne Alcott was a bore (and even to Emerson he was tedious, albeit an archangel), Emerson himself was not entirely congenial, either temperamentally or philosophically. Rose Hawthorne perhaps expressed her father's feeling when she spoke of "caviling at Emerson's perpetual smile" because "he ought to wait for something to smile at." And as for the general public—among whom Mrs. Stowe, Mrs. Howe, and General Barlow may not improperly be included—Hawthorne could personally greet them or not, as he pleased. Alcott said that Hawthorne spent most of his time in his tower with book and pen and the solace of the weed—which is perhaps just what every good practicing writer ought to do.

For settled, orderly natures, accomplishment usually requires routine, which in Hawthorne's case consisted of writing in the morning, walking in the afternoon, and reading in the evening. Not the least pleasant of the three parts of the day was the evening reading, which Hawthorne still often did aloud, to the continued delight of his family. A particularly notable course of reading, covered in 1861, comprised the Waverley Novels and Lockhart's *Life of Scott*, the pleasure being enhanced by the gifts of Ticknor and Fields' new edition of Scott, dedicated to Washington Irving, and of Lockhart, dedicated to Hawthorne himself. Of the experience Julian later wrote that it was "something to remember":

All the characters [Julian said] seemed to live and move visibly before us. The expression of Hawthorne's face changed, as he read, in harmony with the speech or the passage. It was very pleasant to see him sitting with a book; he would settle himself comfortably in his chair, and hold the book open in his left hand, his fingers clasping it over the top; and as he read, there was a constantly recurrent forward movement of his head, which seemed somehow to give distinctness and significance to the sentences and paragraphs, and indicated the constant living *rapport* between him and the author.

Besides Scott and Lockhart, the reading during the last years at the Wayside included F. G. Tuckerman's *Poems*, Elizabeth Drew Stoddard's *The Morgesons*, Donald Grant Mitchell's *My Farm of Edgewood*, Gail Hamilton's *Country Living and Country Thinking*, Rebecca Harding Davis' *Margaret Howth*, Harriet Prescott Spofford's *The Amber Gods*, Longfellow's *Tales of the Wayside Inn*, and other contemporary American books. Mrs. Hawthorne wrote Annie Fields that her husband and Julian thought Miss Hamilton "the only good lady-author in America" and that the reading of her book was constantly interrupted by exclamations of "How admirable!" The works of Mrs. Davis and Mrs. Spofford (representatives of the new realism) were objected to by Mrs. Hawthorne—and perhaps by Hawthorne also—because of their "bad style," "crudeness," and "bald passion." To Tuckerman and Mitchell Hawthorne wrote friendly notes of appreciation and to Longfellow, he said with deep sincerity, "I take vast satisfaction in your poetry, and take very little in most other men's, except it be the grand old strains that have been sounding all through my life. Nothing can be better done than these tales of yours, one and all." In the "Prelude" to his book Longfellow had made a graceful allusion to Hawthorne, who now went on to express his pleasure in the compliment: "It gratified me much to find my own name shining in your verse—even as if I had been gazing up at the moon, and detected my own features in its profile." There was no frigate like a book unless it was Ticknor's cider, with which—after the stint of reading had been done, and the children got off to bed—Hawthorne and Sophia made themselves jolly. He told the good donor that he had never drunk any cider that he liked so well and that his wife shared his high opinion.

Not long after his return from Europe Hawthorne resumed the business of writing, partly from the artist's inner compulsion, and partly from the conviction that he could not afford, financially, to be idle. Fields was eager for contributions to the *Atlantic* and the voluminous English journal seemed to afford the most readily available material for such a purpose. Hawthorne, therefore, set about recasting certain portions of the journal in the form of sketches of English scenery, life, and manners. Beginning with "The Haunts of Burns," which appeared in the *Atlantic* for October, 1860, he continued at a deliberate but accelerated pace with "Near Oxford" (October, 1861), "Pilgrimage to Old Boston" (January, 1862), "Leamington Spa" (October, 1862), "About Warwick" (December, 1862), "Recollections of a Gifted Woman" * (January, 1863), "A London Suburb" † (March,

---

* The "gifted woman" was Delia Bacon.
† Blackheath, where Bennoch lived.

1863), "Up the Thames" (May, 1863), "Outside Glimpses of English Poverty" (July, 1863), and "Civic Banquets" (August, 1863). The sketches were a great success, and editor Fields clamored for more and still more.

In September, 1862, Fields wrote enthusiastically:

I wish to tell you how greatly admired your paper on Leamington is; how everybody swears it is one of your or anybody's best; how I am stopped in the street to laugh with friends over your fat dowager; how the papers all praise the article and ask for more of the same sort. You must send me a paper for my December number and my January issue also. I can't get on without them, and I beg you will on receipt of this let me know the subjects of both articles. Hereof fail not!

He enclosed a check for $100, the sum paid for each of the articles up to this time. In December Fields stepped up the praise and the pay, writing:

We have never printed an article in the "Atlantic" that has been more applauded than "About Warwick." That absolutely perfect paper is hailed with delight all over the land. Curtis had his cup of coffee with us today and he joined the chorus with enthusiasm. Lowell and Longfellow chanted high praises to me last night, and Holmes swears you are the Prince of English writers. He holds his own plume straight into the air as you know, but he knocks under to you. . . . In future you must receive $100 for all articles of ten pages or less, and for all over ten pages $10 per page additional. This last paper ["Recollections of a Gifted Woman"] occupies 15 pages, so I gave Mrs. Hawthorne $150 today. You must tell me if this is satisfactory.

It was more than satisfactory, for, as Hawthorne replied, he had been "satisfied before." He had never made any money to speak of from his writings until he joined up with Fields. It was gratifying now to know, he said, that his work was "worth its price." "My literary success," he continued with grateful candor, "whatever it has been or may be, is the result of my connection with you. Somehow or other, you smote the rock of public sympathy on my behalf; and a stream gushed forth in sufficient quantity to quench my thirst, though not to drown me." The stream consisted of money as well as praise. A writer with a family to support requires something more than a success of esteem. The new rate for articles put Hawthorne near the top of the *Atlantic* scale. At about the same time, Fields was paying Bayard Taylor $60 for an article and Longfellow, the most popular of all the New England writers, $100 for two sonnets.

In addition to the ten English sketches, Hawthorne contributed to the *Atlantic*, for July, 1862, an article on the progress of the war. In March–April of that year, accompanied by the faithful Ticknor, he had spent a month in Washington as the guest of Horatio Bridge, now Chief of the Naval Bureau of Provisions and Clothing, with the rank of commodore. Like visitors in Washington during other wars, he was not hopeful of the outcome: "Things and men," he told Fields, "look better at a distance than close at hand." He had had, nevertheless, a thoroughly enjoyable time. He had sat for his portrait to Emanuel Leutze, then engaged in ornamenting the Capitol building, and Leutze had enlivened the sittings with first-rate cigars and champagne. He had visited Fortress Monroe, inspected the *Monitor*, and seen the battered *Cumberland* which, though defeated, had refused to surrender to the *Merrimac*. Hawthorne had been moved by the sight of the three masts sticking up out of the water, with a tattered bit of the American flag fluttering from the top of one of them—more moved, in fact, than he had thought he could be by a spectacle of this kind. He had traveled also, through deep mud, to Manassas and Harper's Ferry, and seen some Confederate prisoners, whom he had liked, and some refugee Negro slaves, known as "contrabands," whom he had pitied. And not the least interesting experience of the Washington visit had been a call at the White House in company with a Massachusetts delegation, which had presented to the President an ivory-handled whip (of obvious symbolism) made in the Massachusetts State Prison.

The *Atlantic* article ("Chiefly About War Matters") based upon these experiences did not make good war propaganda, for its tone was objective, critical, and humorous. Fields, nevertheless, was willing to print it if Hawthorne would omit the passage on Lincoln, which read in part as follows:

By and by there was a little stir on the staircase and in the passage-way, and in lounged a tall, loose-jointed figure, of an exaggerated Yankee port and demeanor, whom (as being about the homeliest man I ever saw, yet by no means repulsive or disagreeable) it was impossible not to recognize as Uncle Abe. . . . There is no describing his lengthy awkwardness, nor the uncouthness of his movement; and yet it seemed as if I had been in the habit of seeing him daily, and had shaken hands with him a thousand times in some village street; so true was he to the aspect of the pattern American, though with a certain extravagance which, possibly, I exaggerated still further by the delighted eagerness with which I took it in. If put to guess his calling and livelihood, I should have taken him for a country schoolmaster as soon as anything. He was dressed in a rusty black frock-coat and pantaloons, unbrushed, and worn so faithfully that the suit had adapted itself to the curves and angularities of his figure, and had grown to be an outer skin of the man. He had shabby slippers on his feet. His hair was black, still unmixed with gray, stiff, somewhat bushy, and had apparently been acquainted with neither brush nor comb that morning. . . . His complexion is dark and sallow . . . he has thick black eyebrows and an impending brow; his nose is large, and the lines about his mouth are very strongly defined.

The whole physiognomy is as coarse a one as you would meet anywhere in the length and breadth of the States; but, withal, it is redeemed, illuminated, softened, and brightened by a kindly though serious look out of his eyes, and an expression of homely sagacity, that seems weighted with rich results of village experience. A great deal of native sense; no bookish cultivation, no refinement; honest at heart, and thoroughly so, and yet, in some sort, sly,—at least, endowed with a sort of tact and wisdom that are akin to craft, and would impel him, I think, to take an antagonist in the flank, rather than to make a bull-run at him right in front. But, on the whole, I liked this sallow, queer, sagacious visage, with the homely human sympathies that warmed it; and, for my small share in the matter, would as lief have Uncle Abe for a ruler as any man whom it would have been practicable to put in his place. . . . We retired out of the presence in high good-humor, only regretting that we could not have seen the President sit down and fold up his legs (which is said to be a most extraordinary spectacle) or have heard him tell one of those delectable stories for which he is so celebrated.

Hawthorne consented, though reluctantly, to the omission of the passage, and the article appeared without it. "What a terrible thing it is," he complained to Fields, "to try to let off a little bit of truth into this miserable humbug of a world! Upon my honor, the omitted part seems to me to have a historical value." Fields had the good judgment to restore the Lincoln passage, though not until after the death of both author and subject.*

Meanwhile, Hawthorne was busy also with a work of fiction. In February, 1861, he told Fields that he was spending two or three hours daily in his "sky-parlor," that his efforts had produced no very important results thus far, but that perhaps he would have a "new Romance" ready by the time New England should become a separate nation. In May he said that the war interfered with his literary labor and that there would probably be no demand for romances for a long while, even if he should succeed in writing one. In November he promised the romance to Fields for serial publication in the *Atlantic*, though he feared the "harping on one string . . . from month to month . . . would tire the reader out." The story would be "pretty long," he said, and would certainly not be ready in early 1862—in fact he didn't know precisely when it would be ready. In February, 1862, he told Bridge that each week found him a little more advanced toward the completion of the new work but that he was "not very well, being mentally and physically languid."

For several reasons Hawthorne continued unable, during 1862–63, to bring his new fiction to satisfactory completion: the production of the English sketches, the distractions of the war, his failing energy. In August, 1863, Fields—with the best of intentions—applied additional pressure: he would pay $200 for each monthly installment of the romance in the magazine. Needing the money,

* See Fields' *Yesterdays with Authors*, 1871.

Hawthorne made a renewed attempt despite a "preternatural reluctance" and consented to an announcement that the work would
appear serially in 1864. But his efforts were unavailing. In January,
1864, he told Fields that his mind had "lost, for the present, its
temper and fine edge," and in February, that he would never finish
the announced work. It was a humiliating and pathetic confession
to make, but Hawthorne held on to his sense of humor: Say to
your *Atlantic* readers, he suggested, that "Mr. Hawthorne's brain
is addled at last."

Actually (as the posthumous publications were to show) Hawthorne had written a large amount of manuscript and had not one
but two romances—*Septimius Felton*, which exists in two ver-
sions, and *Dr. Grimshawe's Secret*—almost ready for publication.
There were, besides, the long sketch known as *The Ancestral
Footstep*, which he had done in Italy, and three chapters of *The
Dolliver Romance*, upon which he was last engaged. *The Ancestral Footstep* and *Dr. Grimshawe's Secret* have as their theme a
young American's refusal of an English inheritance—a refusal
prompted by a fresh realization of the democratic opportunities
of his native country. The fragmentary *Dolliver Romance* and the
full-length *Septimius Felton* develop the idea of an elixir of life
which would produce a deathless man. In the latter story, the elixir
is rejected because earthly immortality, it is argued, would disrupt
the natural order of things; in the former, the author apparently
had in mind for old Dr. Dolliver a gradual rejuvenation. Since
Thoreau had told Hawthorne of a former resident of the Wayside
who had believed he would live forever, Hawthorne planned to
write a sketch of Thoreau (who had died in 1862) as a preface to
his romance on the elixir of life. It is therefore doubly regrettable
that he did not complete such a work to his exacting satisfaction,
for he had a truer appreciation of Thoreau than most of Thoreau's
contemporaries. If Hawthorne had written his essay, the course
of Thoreau's reputation in the nineteenth century might have
been more prosperous.

On September 18, 1863, Ticknor and Fields brought out in

book form under the title *Our Old Home* Hawthorne's English sketches—the ten which had appeared in the *Atlantic* and two others, "Consular Experiences' and "Lichfield and Uttoxeter." The book sold well—promptly going into a second edition— thanks partly to a double success of scandal. The English objected strenuously to Hawthorne's description of the English dowager of fifty:

She has [he had written in part] an awful ponderosity of frame, not pulpy, like the looser development of our few fat women, but massive with solid beef and streaky tallow; so that (though struggling manfully against the idea) you inevitably think of her as made up of steaks and sirloins. When she walks, her advance is elephantine. When she sits down, it is on a great round space of her Maker's footstool, where she looks as if nothing could ever move her.

And added to the protests in England against such sacrilege was an even greater storm of objection in America to the book's dedication to Franklin Pierce, whose Southern sympathies had made him unpopular in the North and particularly among New England abolitionists.

Pierce was one of a considerable number of Northern Democrats known as "Copperheads." Throughout the Civil War he publicly advocated the immediate cessation of hostilities and a return to the *status quo ante bellum.* On July 4, 1863, he delivered in Concord, New Hampshire, his home town, a speech in which he declared that "aggression by arms" was not "a suitable or possible remedy for existing evils" and that "the great objects" for which the Constitution had been formed could be achieved "through peaceful agencies alone." It so happened that Hawthorne was visiting his friend at the time and sat on the platform during the delivery of a speech which the next day's newspapers called "treasonable." Another coincidence—even more dramatic—underscored in the popular mind Hawthorne's connection with the "treason" of Pierce. On the day of the publication of *Our Old Home,* the New York *Evening Post* and other leading newspapers in the North printed a letter from Pierce to Jefferson Davis, written in 1860, in which Pierce had said:

Without discussing the question of right, of abstract power to secede, I have never believed that actual disruption of the Union can occur without blood; and if through the madness of Northern abolitionists that dire calamity must come, the fighting will not be along Mason and Dixon's line merely. It will be within our own borders, in our own streets. . . . Those who defy law and scout constitutional obligations will, if we ever reach the arbitrament of arms, find occupation enough at home.

Northern propagandists promptly denounced Pierce as a traitor and charged that the secession of the Southern states had been brought about through the collusion of Pierce and other Northern Democrats. It was an unlucky hour for the appearance of *Our Old Home* and its dedicatory letter asserting the author's confidence in Pierce's "loyalty."

Many readers supposed that Hawthorne had merely stultified himself in testifying to the loyalty of an obvious traitor. But such readers were incapable of distinguishing between loyalty to the Northern side of the war and loyalty to the Union of States established by the founding fathers. It was the latter which Hawthorne asserted and admired—a faithfulness, he said, to "the grand idea of an irrevocable Union," which Pierce had learned in childhood from his "brave father" and had maintained throughout his public life. Many readers erred also in supposing that Hawthorne agreed with Pierce and the Copperheads in their attitude toward the war itself. But such was not the case. Although he did not set forth his own views in the dedicatory letter, he made clear his position—and it was a sensible, realistic position to take in 1862–63—in letters to Elizabeth Peabody, Horatio Bridge, and Henry Bright in England. He had always thought, he said, that the war should have been avoided, but after it had once started he had "longed for military success as much as any man or woman of the North." Military victory, though, would hardly suffice to bring about the restoration of the Union, for "if we pummel the South ever so hard," he said, "they will love us none the better for it." The North ought to prosecute the war rather, he thought, in order to dictate the boundary line and reclaim the border states. "Maryland, Virginia, Kentucky, and Missouri," he argued, were "fully capable of being made free soil"; he would "fight to the death" for their reclamation and "let the rest go." Owning an affection for the old Union but unable to see the feasibility of its restoration, he consoled himself with the sorrowful thought that "heaven was heaven still, as Milton sings, after Lucifer and a third part of the angels had seceded from its golden palaces."

Hawthorne, then, was not in political agreement with Pierce in 1863, and he intended the dedication only as a testimonial of friendship. The testimonial was appropriate enough in view of the fact that without the Liverpool consulship, which Pierce had given him, he would never have seen England or written *Our Old Home*. Despite the appropriateness Fields had made a strenuous effort to dissuade the author, foreseeing unpleasant complications. Whereupon Hawthorne had sent to his politic publisher the following declaration:

I find that it would be a piece of poltroonery in me to withdraw either the dedication or the dedicatory letter. My long and intimate personal relations with Pierce render the dedication altogether proper, especially as regards this book, which would have had no existence without his kindness; and if he is so exceedingly unpopular that his name is enough to sink the volume, there is so much the more need that an old friend should stand by him. I cannot, merely on account of pecuniary profit or literary reputation, go back from what I have deliberately felt and thought it right to do; and if I were to tear out the dedication, I should never look at the volume again without remorse and shame. As for the literary public, it must accept my book precisely as I think fit to give it, or let it alone. . . . If the public of the North see fit to ostracize me for this, I can only say that I would gladly sacrifice a thousand or two of dollars rather than retain the good-will of such a herd of dolts and mean-spirited scoundrels.

Ironically enough, as often happens, and as author and publisher in this instance did not foresee, the dedication increased the sale of the book by giving it more advertising than it would otherwise have had. But the world of Concord, Cambridge, and Boston bristled with censure, of which Hawthorne could not have been unaware even though much of it was more or less private. Emerson deprecated, in his journal, Hawthorne's "perverse politics and unfortunate friendship for that paltry Franklin Pierce," and neatly excised from his own copy of *Our Old Home* the offending dedication. Lowell, in a letter to Miss Norton, snobbishly ridiculed Pierce, whom he had just met in Hawthorne's company, as the true original of Elijah Pogram in Dickens' *Martin Chuzzlewit*. Charles Eliot Norton wrote G. W. Curtis that he was "half annoyed, half amused at Hawthorne . . . His dedication to F. Pierce reads like the bitterest of satires; and in that I have my satisfaction. The public will laugh." Mrs. Harriet Beecher Stowe—always righteous and recently rich from the sale of *Uncle Tom's Cabin* (which Fields renamed *Uncle Thomas' Mansion*)—castigated author and publisher alike in the following communication to the publisher: "Do tell me if our friend Hawthorne praises that arch traitor Pierce in his preface and your loyal firm publishes it. I never read the preface and have not yet seen the book but they say so here and I can scarcely believe it of you—if I can of him. I regret that I went to see him last summer. What! Patronize such a traitor to our faces! I can scarce believe it." Elizabeth Peabody and Mary Mann were relieved at least to this extent—that Hawthorne, they ventured to believe, would never again mention the name of Franklin Pierce to *them*. Such was the hysteria of war that, outside of Hawthorne's immediate family, probably only a few persons in New England understood or appreciated what he had done. One of these, it is gratifying to know, was Annie Fields, who wrote in her diary that Hawthorne was motivated by "friendship of the purest," that "such adherence was indeed noble," that the dedication was "a beautiful incident in his life." Mrs. Fields also noted that Hawthorne "loved old friends in a way not often seen."

Hawthorne's health had been gradually declining ever since his return from Europe. Mrs. Hawthorne thought that he, as well as Una, had had the Roman fever in Rome, or something akin to it, and that he was suffering from its aftermath and the effects of the distress caused by Una's illness. She thought, too, that he lived in constant fear lest Una's illness would again recur—it had already recurred once since their return home. "When he looks," Mrs. Hawthorne wrote to Fields in December, 1862, "at his Rose of Sharon—so firm and strong now—I think he feels uncertain that she still lives and blooms, so deeply scored into his soul was the expectation of her death."

Anxiety breeds anxiety, and Hawthorne's great worry concerning Una's health multiplied itself in other worries which weighed upon him oppressively. The war was a cause of unhappiness, and the distrustful attitude of friends and neighbors toward his position on war issues undoubtedly contributed to his anxious state of mind. He was often unable to write because of his worries; and he worried all the more because of his inability to write, especially since he needed to increase his income, and Fields was offering always bigger payments for anything from his pen. The Liverpool savings were melting away; the house had cost four times what he had expected it to cost, and there were still many things that needed to be done around the place; the children were requiring more money as they grew older (Julian entered Harvard in 1863); the war was producing inflationary prices, no one could foresee the end, perhaps the whole book business would go to smash, yet the only recourse seemed to be a renewed effort at the writing desk. He thought that he would feel better if he lived by the sea instead of in Concord, which was muggy in summer and Transcendental the year round. He thought that if he could revisit England he would feel better. If unchecked, such a spiral of anxiety could result only in breakdown.

By the autumn of 1863 Hawthorne was a sick man. Try as he might, he could not regain the old buoyance and vigor. There were days in the winter of 1863–64 when he could write. But the good days became less frequent, and the days when he was apathetic and depressed more and more prevailed. Fields strove manfully to cheer him up, and Longfellow proposed to Fields a little dinner for Hawthorne in Boston, the diners (he suggested) to consist of "two sad authors and two jolly publishers—nobody else." It was an affecting meeting of old and congenial friends. To Longfellow, Hawthorne "looked gray and grand" but "with something very pathetic about him."

In December, 1863, Hawthorne went to Boston, despite his indisposition, to be present at the funeral of Mrs. Franklin Pierce, and finding his friend overwhelmed with sadness, he accompanied Pierce after the funeral to his home in Concord, New Hampshire. On his return he stopped overnight at the Fields' where his spirits seemed to brighten. Sitting with Annie Fields in the drawing room while the afternoon twilight deepened over Charles Street and the bay beyond, he talked freely, and with touches of his old humor, about a variety of subjects. He recalled his happy boyhood in Maine and the college years at Bowdoin. He laughed at something in Boswell and declared Boswell one of the most remarkable men who ever lived. He said that he had been compelled to tell Alcott why it was impossible for neighbors to live upon amicable terms with Mrs. Alcott and that Alcott had acknowledged the truth of all he had said for, indeed, who should know it better? He wondered "why the good old custom of coming together to get drunk had gone out." "He was intensely witty," Mrs. Fields wrote in concluding her diary record of Hawthorne's talk, "but his wit is of so ethereal a texture that the fine essence has vanished."

The improvement shown at the Fields' was of short duration. Although Hawthorne had "no positive malady," his wife wrote Mrs. Fields, and was "only negative," she felt, in March, 1864, that he was "indeed very indisposed" and that it was "imperative for him to change the air and scene." A leisurely journey in a southward direction seemed the best therapy. Accordingly, Hawthorne and the devoted Ticknor went to New York in late March with the intention of taking a boat to Havana; but prolonged stormy

weather prevented the voyage, and the two journeyed on to Philadelphia instead. Here, at the Continental Hotel, Ticknor con-
tracted pneumonia and after a few days' illness died on April 10,
despite the efforts of an allopathic physician who, Hawthorne
told Fields, "belabored with pills and powders, and then proceeded
to cup, and poultice, and blister, according to the ancient rule of
that tribe of savages."

The death of Ticknor was naturally a great shock to Hawthorne. Besides the loss of a dear friend he felt the grim irony in the
reversal of roles, a reversal by which the strong man was laid low
and the invalid was required, if only for the nonce, to be heroically strong. Mrs. Hawthorne described to Mrs. Fields his exhausted and unnerved condition when he reached the Wayside:

As soon as I saw his face I was frightened . . . so haggard, so white,
so deeply scored with pain and fatigue was the face, so much more
ill he looked than I ever saw him before. He had walked from the station because he saw no carriage there, and his brow was streaming
with a perfect rain—so great had been the effort to walk so far. Oh
Annie!—Well, he needed much to get home to me, where he could
fling off all care of himself and give a little way to his feelings—pent
up and kept back for so long—especially since his watch and ward of
most excellent, kind Mr. Ticknor. It relieved him somewhat to break
down as he spoke of that scene and of Howard Ticknor. . . . But he
was so weak and weary he could not sit up much, and lay on the couch
nearly all the time in a kind of uneasy somnolency, not wishing to be
read to even, not able to attend or fix his thoughts at all

The Saturday Club was having a special dinner on April 23 to
celebrate the tercentenary of Shakespeare's birth, and Emerson
called at the Wayside to offer to escort Hawthorne to Boston for
the occasion but found him too feeble to go; he could as easily
build London, Mrs. Hawthorne told Annie Fields, as go to the
Shakespeare dinner. He became weaker daily. After breakfast he
had to lie down for a long while. Mrs. Hawthorne would not let
him go up and down stairs unattended. She made him laugh
weakly with something from Thackeray, she wrote Annie, "but a

smile looks strange on a face that once shone like a thousand suns with smiles. The light . . . has gone all out of his eyes entirely. An infinite weariness films them quite." She wished he were in Cuba or some other island of the Gulf Stream, for the cold wind "ruined him." She was completely at a loss to know what took away his strength. His steps were uncertain, his eyes were uncertain, he had an "infinite restlessness," his look was "distressed and harassed," his pulse, she thought, was irregular.

Despite Hawthorne's condition another journey seemed to offer the only hope of recovery—this time an excursion with Pierce, by private carriage, into the New Hampshire hills. On May 7 Hawthorne wrote Pierce (his last letter) that he hoped to revive rapidly when once they were on the road, and on May 11 he met Pierce in Boston. Mrs. Hawthorne had high hopes of the tonic value of the journey. "I think the serene jog trot," she wrote Mrs. Fields,

into country places, by trout streams and old farm houses, away from care and news, will be very restorative. The boy-associations with the General will refresh him. They will fish and muse and rest and saunter upon horses' feet and be in the air all the time in fine weather. . . . General Pierce has been a most tender constant nurse for many years and knows how to take care. And his love for Mr. Hawthorne is the strongest passion of his soul, now his wife is departed. . . . I should be afraid to have him go away without me, if I did not trust to the tender watchfulness of General Pierce.

Hawthorne had refused to see a physician, partly because of his distrust of medical science generally, and more especially in his present illness because of his horror of the medical treatment which he had seen administered to Ticknor. Without his foreknowledge, however, his wife contrived, with the help of Fields, to arrange a brief, informal interview in Boston with Dr. Holmes. His condition, Holmes wrote later, was very unfavorable. There were persistent local symptoms, the doctor discovered, referred especially to the stomach—boring pain, distension, indigestion. There were also a marked loss of weight and an obvious depression of spirits. The genial Holmes confined his treatment to words of encouragement and the prescription of a sedative and cordial.

On May 12 Hawthorne and Pierce traveled by train to Concord, New Hampshire, where they were delayed by rainy weather. On the 16th they began their carriage journey and continued northward at a leisurely pace, stopping at Franklin, Laconia, and Centre Harbor, and reaching Plymouth, New Hampshire, on the evening of the 18th. Between three and four o'clock on the morning of the 19th Pierce went into Hawthorne's room and discovered that he was dead. Pierce believed that the seat of the disease was the brain or spine, or both, for on the last day of their journey Hawthorne had been almost unable to walk or use his hands. Dr. Holmes said that there had been nothing in Hawthorne's appearance eight days before to suggest that he would die so soon. He surmised that Hawthorne had died by fainting, "the gentlest," he said, "of all modes of release." He lacked a month and a half of completing his sixtieth year.

On May 23, which was an unusually beautiful day, Hawthorne was buried in the Sleepy Hollow Cemetery at Concord. Longfellow, Lowell, Holmes, Whipple, Alcott, Hillard, Fields, and Emerson were among the pallbearers, and Franklin Pierce accompanied Mrs. Hawthorne and the children. A large number of people gathered in the church and in the cemetery. The manuscript of *The Dolliver Romance* lay on the casket. In the church the Rev. James Freeman Clarke, who had officiated at the marriage of Hawthorne and Sophia twenty-two years before, said (Emerson recorded in his journal) that Hawthorne had done more justice than any other writer to the shades of life, had shown a sympathy with the evil in man's nature, and like Jesus, was the friend of sinners.

Sophia was sustained by a mystical religious faith. Her husband's funeral became for her "a festival of Life." "Do not fear for me dark hours," she wrote to Mrs. Fields. "There is nothing dark for me henceforth. . . . I have no more to ask but that I may be able to comfort all who mourn as I am comforted. . . . God has

turned for me the silver lining and for me the darkest cloud has
broken into ten thousand singing birds."

Appropriate, often felicitous, tributes were paid by friends.
Longfellow, to whom Mrs. Hawthorne gave as a memento of a
long friendship her husband's copy of Goldsmith, wrote the famous poem which concludes with the lines,

> Ah! who shall lift that wand of magic power
> And the lost clew regain?
> The unfinished window in Aladdin's tower
> Unfinished must remain!

Holmes said in the *Atlantic* that Hawthorne's works would "keep
his name in remembrance as long as the language in which he
shaped his deep imaginations is spoken by human lips." Henry
Bright said in a memorial article in the London *Examiner* that "the
better Hawthorne was known, the stronger in every case the love
and admiration grew." To Lowell, Hawthorne was "the rarest
creative imagination of the century, the rarest in some ideal respects since Shakespeare." There were a few dissenting opinions,
expressed either publicly or privately, but these did not pass un-
challenged. Lowell rebuked Emerson for his low estimate of Hawthorne's writings, "silencing" him, Mrs. Fields said, with a sharp
speech. Fields loyally refused to publish in the *Atlantic* an article
by G. W. Curtis * which objected to Hawthorne's politics. The
more notable of later tributes by personal friends were Fields'
reminiscences in *Yesterdays with Authors*, Mrs. Fields' short biography, and Horatio Bridge's *Personal Recollections of Nathaniel
Hawthorne*.

Hawthorne's family continued to live at the Wayside for four
years. During this time Mrs. Hawthorne experienced serious financial difficulties. War and postwar prices continued to rise, and the
income from the estate (which was appraised at $26,000 and of
which George Hillard was appointed executor) was insufficient
for her family's requirements, although Franklin Pierce contrib-

---

* Curtis' article appeared in the *North American Review*, October, 1864.

uted generously toward Julian's expenses at Harvard. Partly because of financial need and partly because of the encouragement of Fields and his wife, she put aside her scruples against publishing her husband's notebooks. Twelve installments—for which Fields paid $1,200—appeared in the *Atlantic Monthly* in 1866. Her editions of the notebooks were published as *Passages from the American Note-Books* (1868), *Passages from the English Note-Books* (1870), and *Passages from the French and Italian Note-Books* (1871). In her editing, Mrs. Hawthorne—sometimes with, but more often without, the collaboration of Fields *—took great liberties with the original manuscripts.† She strove by omission and revision to give to the text the form which she thought Hawthorne himself would have given to it had he prepared the manuscripts for publication.

In October, 1868, Mrs. Hawthorne and the children left the Wayside and went to Dresden, Germany, to live. One reason was probably the hope of living more cheaply in Europe. Then too, Europe and its storied associations doubtless attracted her and her daughters now more strongly than ever before. And perhaps still another reason for her going abroad to live was her estrangement from Fields who, she had come (with very questionable justice) to believe, had defrauded her and her husband of their rightful income.‡ Owing to the continental wars she moved in 1870 to London, where she died in February, 1871. Una, never robust, stayed in London, engaging in Anglican social service, and died there, unmarried, in 1877. The other two children lived for many years: Julian, a moderately successful writer of novels and miscellaneous books, died in 1934; Rose, after a brief, unhappy marriage to George Parsons Lathrop, entered the Catholic Church, and as Mother Alphonsa presided over homes for cancer patients

---

* For details, see my article, "Editing Hawthorne's Notebooks," listed in the biographical sources, p. 268.

† For details, see the introductions to my editions of *The American Notebooks* and *The English Notebooks*, listed in the biographical sources, p. 267.

‡ For details see my article, "Mrs. Hawthorne's Quarrel with James T. Fields," listed in the biographical sources, p. 268.

in New York City and in Hawthorne, New York, where she died in 1926.

To an extraordinary degree the memory of Hawthorne was vitally, vibrantly present to his widow and children. They affectionately reread his books and pored over the posthumous manuscripts. Una—aided by Robert Browning—transcribed *Septimius Felton,* published in 1872. Rose published in 1897 her *Memories of Hawthorne,* which consisted of family letters and devoted commentary on them. Julian never tired of studying and writing about his father's life and works. His many contributions to the subject include an edition of *Doctor Grimshawe's Secret* (1882); a two-volume biography, *Nathaniel Hawthorne and His Wife* (1884); and *Hawthorne and His Circle* (1903). Mrs. Hawthorne gave the years of her widowhood to editing her husband's notebooks. Her hours "sang," she told Fields, as she labored over the manuscripts: "all the heavenly springtime" of her married life came back to her, she said, in Hawthorne's "cadences, so rich and delicate." For to her and to her children he was still the fountain light of all their day, the master light of all their seeing.

CHAPTER XI

THE COLLECTED WORKS

TWELVE years after Hawthorne's death his publishers brought out a collected edition of his works, and ten other collected editions appeared before the turn of the century. His volumes took their place on the library shelves as a compact embodiment of a lifetime's work, beside sets of Scott, who had been his boyhood delight, beside sets of Swift and Johnson like those he had given to the Athenean Society at Bowdoin, and sets of Irving and Cooper, his countrymen, whose company he had joined and whose rank he had surpassed. Hawthorne became, and has continued to be, a classic figure in literature, to be read, to be studied, to be cherished.

Hawthorne was a serious-minded writer whose works, taken together, constitute in the highest sense a criticism of life. The characters and settings are there as he experienced them through observation; the configurations and tensions came organically from his sympathy and understanding. He probed to the deepest realities of the mind and spirit, and his meanings possess a certain timelessness which carried with it a prophetic sense of the ages to follow.

His perception carried him back to the roots of the Puritan tradition and from them forward again. His favorite writers in English literature were the sage and serious Spenser; Milton, who took as his great theme the justification of the ways of God to man; and Bunyan, "moulded," Hawthorne said, "of homeliest clay, but instinct with celestial fire." Though a great favorite of his boyhood, Scott, he thought, lacked significance for the modern world: "The world nowadays," he observed, "requires a more earnest purpose, a deeper moral, and a closer and homelier truth than he was qualified to supply it with." The Puritan virtues—absent from Scott and present in Spenser, Milton, and Bunyan—

Hawthorne found also in large measure in the early writers of New England. From them came the figures and the moods which were to characterize the world of his fiction.

A descendant of the Puritans, Hawthorne was drawn to them by ancestral ties: "Strong traits of their nature," he declared, "have intertwined themselves with mine." He was drawn to them, too, by his patriotic and democratic sympathies, for the English Puritans had struck a blow for freedom in the regicide of Charles; and the New England Puritans had struck blows even more decisive (like those celebrated in "Endicott and the Red Cross" and "The Gray Champion") which had their logical culmination, Hawthorne thought, in the American Revolution. He was drawn to them, again, by his perception of certain basic truths in their doctrine.

The attraction did not blind him to their faults and limitations. Hawthorne repeatedly castigates them for their bigotry, intolerance, and cruelty. In "The Maypole of Merry Mount," Endicott is an "immitigable zealot," the Puritans are "most dismal wretches." In a scene of memorable horror in "The Gentle Boy," Puritan children—"a brood of baby fiends" who have caught the contagion of their parents' hatred—brutally attack and all but kill poor Ilbrahim, the Quaker child. Of the five women who gather close to the platform where Hester Prynne, the adulteress, stands in the public gaze, only one takes a charitable view of her case.

With a historian's perspective, he could fairly judge the persecutors and the persecuted as well. If forced to choose between the rival parties at Merry Mount, Hawthorne would go with Endicott, for life must not be spent in wanton revelry; but the sympathetic characters are the Lord and Lady of the May, who, though they renounce the vanities of the revelers, may be supposed to bring to the Puritan community a graciousness and innocent mirth. In "The Gentle Boy" Hawthorne approves neither of the Puritans, the bloody persecutors, nor of the Quakers, those unbridled fanatics who disturbed the peace of the community and seemed even to invite the scourge and dungeon. Aside from Ilbrahim, the pathetic victim of the tale, the most sympathetic character is Dorothy Pearson, the kindly Puritan who gives Ilbrahim a home. She represents, the author says, "rational piety."

Before he could approve of Puritanism it would have to undergo a good deal of modification in the direction of tolerance, charity, and common sense, but despite the reservations, his leaning was to the Puritan view of life. This leaning was doubtless made more pronounced by the fashionable liberalism of Hawthorne's own time. What is the nature of man? Is he not innately good, entirely free, and infinitely perfectible, a god *in posse* who is soon to be, if he is not already quite, a god *in esse?* To questions like these, Hawthorne dissented. Both his grounding in the Puritan tradition and his sense of hard fact, his realism, compelled him to give answers contrary to those of Channing and Emerson. Hawthorne set himself against nineteenth-century progressivism, not because its utopian aims were not desirable but because (as he said of John Brown) it "preposterously miscalculated the possibilities." Too often it ignored, he thought, the fallible, sinful nature of man, the life-and-death struggle between good and evil in human society and in the private breast, the inexorable influence of earlier modes and habits which form a predestinating chain of causality. The triumph of virtue and the good life would not be as easy as many people seemed to think. The evidence of history and of contemporary society appeared incompatible with the sudden metamorphosis of mankind.

He was concerned with "the truth of the human heart" (as he put it in his preface to *The House of the Seven Gables*) rather than with theology. But some of the tenets of the Puritans seemed in many ways to square with human experience. Evil is a reality in the world; the depravity of the unregenerate man is no myth. There seems to be in human affairs a kind of predestination, which Hawthorne calls (depending on whether its manifestation is malignant or benevolent) now Fate, now Providence. If Hawthorne's emphasis is upon sin more than salvation, the reason in part may have been that the optimism of his age seemed to him to need tempering more than encouraging. "Human destinies look ominous," he said in *The Blithedale Romance*, "without some perceptible intermixture of the sable or the gray."

Unitarians and Transcendentalists, and scientists too, Hawthorne thought, painted too bright a picture; they underestimated the human difficulties and the element of struggle. Guido's picture showing the triumph of the Archangel Michael over Lucifer was an unsatisfactory symbol of human life because it did not show the dust and heat of combat. Miriam's criticism in *The Marble Faun* reflects the author's own view:

"Is it thus that virtue looks the moment after its death-struggle with evil? No, no; I could have told Guido better. A full third of the Archangel's feathers should have been torn from his wings; the rest all ruffled, till they looked like Satan's own! His sword should be streaming with blood, and perhaps broken half-way to the hilt; his armor crushed, his robes rent, his breast gory; a bleeding gash on his brow, cutting right across the stern scowl of battle! He should press his foot hard down upon the old serpent, as if his very soul depended upon it, feeling him squirm mightily, and doubting whether the fight were half over yet, and how the victory might turn! . . . The battle never was such child's play as Guido's dapper Archangel seems to have found it."

Hawthorne agreed with the proposition of Thomas Shepard, New England minister of the seventeenth century, that "every easy way to heaven is a false way," and demonstrated his agreement in a pungently satirical allegory, "The Celestial Railroad." The story is an adaptation from Bunyan's *Pilgrim's Progress*, with modern improvements. Instead of going to the Celestial City on foot like Bunyan's pilgrim, Hawthorne's characters ride comfortably on the railroad train. Burdens are no longer carried on the back but checked in the baggage car. A bridge spans the Slough of Despond, a tunnel cuts through the Hill Difficulty, modern gas lamps illuminate the Valley of the Shadow of Death. But the train stops short of the Celestial City owing to a limitation of franchise. Bunyan's way, Hawthorne thought, was still the best. The railroad in Hawthorne's story becomes a symbol of those contrivances—whether philosophical systems or mechanical inventions—which promise an easy and ready way to perfection.

If the reformers in religion—the Unitarians and Transcendentalists—could not change the nature of man by asserting his goodness, could not do away with the Slough of Despond by filling it with "books of morality, volumes of French philosophy and German rationalism, tracts, sermons, and essays of modern clergymen, extracts from Plato, Confucius, and various Hindoo sages" (to quote from "The Celestial Railroad"), neither could the social reformers achieve their ends by such simple expedients as they proposed. It seemed to Hawthorne pure naïveté to believe otherwise. The reformers themselves scarcely knew what they were up against. Hollingsworth, in *The Blithedale Romance,* undertook the reformation of criminals through an appeal to their higher instincts. Coverdale remarked that Hollingsworth "ought to have commenced his investigation of the subject by perpetrating some huge sin in his proper person, and examining the condition of his higher instincts afterwards." Such hardheaded comment did not meet with general approval in mid-nineteenth century America, where a nominal political equality, science and evolutionism, improved machinery, flattering views of human nature, and reform movements of various kinds seemed about to produce an earthly paradise.

Hawthorne opposed his own skepticism to the faith in reform. He foresaw that prohibitory statutes (like the Maine liquor law) would not prevent the consumption of alcohol. He foresaw, too, that the emancipation of the Negro—though regarded by abolitionists like Whittier as a final and complete solution—would not solve the tangled, deep-seated problem of race relations.

Legislative fiat is not enough where the nature of man is intricately concerned. In the allegorical story, "Earth's Holocaust," the reformers, who have been given a free hand, toss into the fire all sorts of embodiments of evil, real or alleged: aristocratic emblems, hogsheads of liquor, boxes of tea, coffee, and tobacco,

weapons and munitions of war, even marriage certificates, titles
to property, and the sacred books of religion. While the onlookers
are jubilant over the prospect of a new day, "a dark-complexioned
personage," who may be taken as the devil's advocate, calls attention to a fatal omission: the human heart itself. "And unless they
hit upon some method of purifying that foul cavern," he continues, "forth from it will reissue all the shapes of wrong and misery—the same old shapes or worse ones—which they have taken
such a vast deal of trouble to consume to ashes. I have stood by this
livelong night and laughed in my sleeve at the whole business. Oh,
take my word for it, it will be the old world yet!" The author's
epilogue goes on to reinforce the moral of the parable:

How sad a truth, if true it were, that man's agelong endeavor for
perfection had served only to render him the mockery of the evil
principle, from the fatal circumstance of an error at the very root of
the matter! The heart, the heart,—there was that little yet boundless
sphere wherein existed the original wrong of which the crime and
misery of this outward world were merely types. Purify that inward
sphere, and the many shapes of evil that haunt the outward, and which
now seem almost our only realities, will turn to shadowy phantoms
and vanish of their own accord; but if we go no deeper than the intellect, and strive, with merely that feeble instrument, to discern and
rectify what is wrong, our whole accomplishment will be a dream.

Hawthorne may have remembered the following sentences from
Jonathan Edwards' treatise on the "Religious Affections" (or sentences like them in many another New England divine): "Without a change of nature, men's practice will not be thoroughly
changed. . . . As long as corrupt nature is not mortified, but the
principle left whole in a man, it is a vain thing to expect that it
should not govern. But if the old nature be indeed mortified, and a
new and heavenly nature infused, then may it well be expected
that men will walk in newness of life." Hawthorne and Edwards,
then, were agreed that regeneration must come from within; that
it was an affair of the heart, the religious affections, and not of the
intellect merely; that the inward sphere must be purified.

Hawthorne's characters show many moral gradations of the heart, ranging from almost white to almost black, with subtle shadings of gray in between. The impurities of the inward sphere take on many forms, but their root cause is selfishness and pride.

In "Ethan Brand" Hawthorne defined "the unpardonable sin" as "the sin of an intellect that triumphed over the sense of brotherhood with man and reverence for God, and sacrificed everything to its own mighty claims." By assiduous self-cultivation, Brand attained academic pre-eminence as a scientific philosopher, but "Where was the heart?" Hawthorne asks:

That, indeed, had withered—had contracted--had hardened—had perished! It had ceased to partake of the universal throb. He had lost his hold of the magnetic chain of humanity. He was no longer a brother-man, opening the chambers or the dungeons of our common nature by the key of holy sympathy, which gave him a right to share in all its secrets; he was now a cold observer, looking on mankind as the subject of his experiment, and at length converting man and woman to be his puppets. . . . Thus Ethan Brand became a fiend. He began to be so from the moment that his moral nature had ceased to keep the pace of improvement with his intellect.

Brand was an experimental psychologist who had used a young girl as the subject of an experiment and had "wasted, absorbed, and perhaps annihilated her soul in the process."

Hawthorne more than once warns of the dangers of an exclusively scientific attitude toward life. Such an attitude, he thought, was apt to result in the dehumanizing of the experimenter and the sacrifice of helpless victims. Dr. Cacaphodel, a medical scientist (in "The Great Carbuncle"), "had wilted and dried himself into a mummy" and "had drained his body of all its richest blood." Dr. Rappaccini, a botanist and physiologist (in "Rappaccini's Daughter"), is "as true a man of science as ever distilled his own heart in an alembic," but he is also a heartless monster who "cares infinitely more for science than for mankind. His patients are interesting to him only as subjects for some new experiment. He would sacrifice human life, his own among the rest, or whatever else was dearest to him, for the sake of adding so much as a grain of mustard seed to the great heap of his accumulated knowledge." The description is a true one, for he sacrifices his daughter in an experiment to determine the effect of poisonous plants on the human body. Aylmer, another experimenter (in "The Birthmark"), kills his wife, though unintentionally, in an attempt to produce flawless beauty. He is full of the pride of scientific achievement, "confident in his science." The frontiers of science seemed to offer limitless possibilities; Alymer confidently believed that the scientist "would ascend from one step of powerful intelligence to another, until he should lay his hand on the secret of creative force and perhaps make new worlds for himself." His love for science triumphs over his love for his wife, and his grief at the end of the story, one must believe, is not so much over the death of Georgiana as the failure of the experiment. Throughout the story Aylmer has sought to justify his course by regarding it as the noble pursuit of perfection, and his dying wife selflessly tells him the same: "You have aimed loftily," she says, "you have done nobly." But such is not the author's meaning; Aylmer tragically missed "a profounder wisdom."

Hawthorne, one must infer from these examples, did not share the unqualified enthusiasm of his century for the onward march of science, for it could not have been unintentional with him that his blackest villains, like Chillingworth in *The Scarlet Letter*, are men of scientific training. He could scarcely have joined in Whitman's ejaculation, "Hurrah for positive science!" or have sympathized with Emerson's wish, expressed in his old age, for leisure to "run to the college or the scientific school which offered the best lectures on Geology, Chemistry, Minerals, and Botany," for "how could leisure or labor be better employed?" That, at any rate, the moral nature of the world has long since ceased to keep the pace of improvement with its intellect—to adapt Hawthorne's words about Ethan Brand—is a truism of our time. The sanctity of the human heart! Emerson and Whitman believed in this too, but they failed to recognize the forces which were inimical to the heart's sanctity.

The violation of personality—so often illustrated in Hawthorne's writings—does not necessarily involve the scientist or scientific experimentation. Its manifestations are many and various; it extends far beyond the scientific areas as such; it is subtle and often treacherous in its degrees and gradations; it may spring from the intrinsic inequality of human minds.

A frequently recurring situation in Hawthorne's stories shows the tyrannical domination of one mind by another. The stronger mind controls the weaker, casts, as it were, a hypnotic spell upon it. Ethan Brand obviously exercised a special power over Esther, an impressionable young girl. Chillingworth "could play upon the minister as he chose." In *The House of the Seven Gables* Matthew Maule became the complete master of Alice Pyncheon by means of hypnotism. In *The Blithedale Romance* Priscilla, another impressionable young girl, is the puppet in turn of three "stronger" characters—Westervelt, the hypnotist, Zenobia, the strong-minded feminist, and Hollingsworth, the iron-willed reformer. "What a gripe this man has laid upon her whole being!" Coverdale exclaimed in deprecation of Hollingsworth's influence over Priscilla. In *The Marble Faun* Miriam's model exercises over Miriam a mysterious, diabolical tyranny which can be broken only by his death.

Like Maule and Westervelt, Holgrave (in *The House of the Seven Gables*) possessed mesmeric power, but he refrained from using it to victimize Phoebe and thus saved himself from becoming a villain. "To a disposition like Holgrave's," the author says, "at once speculative and active, there is no temptation so great as the opportunity of acquiring empire over the human spirit. . . . Let us therefore concede to the daguerreotypist the rare and high quality of reverence for another's individuality."

Brand, we are told, lacked "the key of holy sympathy." Sympathy and reverence for one's fellow men, and the degree of their presence or absence, become a moral criterion in many of Hawthorne's stories. He apparently thought that a scientific obsession or the use of power over others was apt to destroy this faculty of the soul. Hawthorne's mesmerists might be taken as types of a large class of men who impose their wills upon weaker wills and inexorably, as if by natural law, draw disciples and converts into their strong orbits: the political demagogue, the leader of reform, even the philosopher who warps lesser minds to his system. Emerson spoke of "the magnetism which all original action exerts"; "every true man," he said, is followed by "a train of clients"; "the unstable estimates of men," he said again, "crowd to him whose mind is filled with a truth, as the heaped waves of the Atlantic follow the moon." Although he wished every man to be his own disciple, Emerson himself was followed by a great train of clients, and in praising the Transcendental truth which he invoked he sometimes described its possession in terms of a magnetic power over others. A keen observer of the life about him, Hawthorne appears not to have been unaware of this ironical aspect of Emerson's career, and indeed of the careers of many great doctrinaire teachers who, almost mesmerically, have damaged the integrity of their too pliable pupils. Seeing the eager, upturned faces at the Lyceum he may have been reminded, in one respect, of Alice Pyncheon before Maule, or the Veiled Lady yielding to the spell of Westervelt.

The two poles of human relations, to Hawthorne, were a cold aloofness and a warm sympathy. Not only those who studied human beings scientifically and those who exploited them but still another class—those who made an artistic portrayal—were in danger of being drawn too far away from the pole of sympathy. For the artist—whether painter, sculptor, or writer—must study his subject critically and dispassionately. The painter of "The Prophetic Pictures" "pried into the souls" of his subjects "with keenest insight." We are told that "he did not possess kindly feelings," that "his heart was cold." Coverdale, the poet, gave to his associates at Blithedale an intense scrutiny. Although his attitude toward them was not unkindly, he was motivated as much by philosophical curiosity as by human interest and a desire to help a fellow man or woman in distress. A saving grace, perhaps, is his awareness of the danger. "It is not," he says, "a healthy kind of mental occupation to devote ourselves too exclusively to the study of individual men and women. . . . I did Hollingsworth a great wrong by prying into his character. . . . But I could not help it. . . . He and Zenobia and Priscilla . . . stood forth as the indices of a problem which it was my business to solve. . . . That cold tendency, between instinct and intellect, which made me pry with a speculative interest into people's passions and impulses, appeared to have gone far towards unhumanizing my heart." But Coverdale is not as aloof as he seems, for at the end he confesses his love for Priscilla. Kenyon, the sculptor (in *The Marble Faun*), is aware of the same danger in the life of an artist. Miriam accuses him of being as cold and pitiless as his own marble, and the author speaks of "his cold artistic life." But Kenyon is human though an artist. He earnestly seeks to help Donatello, inviting the confidence of his troubled mind. He loves Hilda more than sculpture, and so, the author observes, "could hardly be reckoned a consummate artist, because there was something dearer to him than his art." Neither could Hawthorne himself be so reckoned by the same token, devoted artist though he was. If he felt an incompatibility between the affections and the austere devotion to his craft, he was able to put aside the craft long enough to warm his heart at the domestic fireside.

Hawthorne was an analyst of human relations, of the nice relationship of person to person, of the adjustment of the individual to society. The most tragic persons in the world are those who are divorced from the social scheme. "I want my place!" wails a pathetic, nameless figure in "The Intelligence Office," "my own place! my true place in the world! my proper sphere! my thing to do, which nature intended me to perform when she fashioned me thus awry, and which I have vainly sought all my lifetime!" In story after story Hawthorne shows the varieties of maladjustment, of estrangement. That which unites in "holy sympathy" is good; that which divorces and estranges is evil.

It may not be farfetched to discover in Hawthorne's fiction a significant criticism of nineteenth-century individualism. Many of the romantic poets in the early part of the century emphasized the idiosyncratic, glorified the lonely, exceptional individual. They enjoyed and celebrated—Byron, for example, the most influential of them all—their differentness from the mass of humanity. To such a view Hawthorne would say that the surest basis of happiness is found not in traits which make one exceptional but in those which one possesses in common with others. As the result of an intensive "education" imposed by her father, Beatrice Rappaccini at last stood above—or at least apart from—other women. But her triumph was an empty, tragic one. She wanted to share the common lot; she "would fain have been loved, not feared." The author describes her at the end of the story as "the poor victim of man's ingenuity and of thwarted nature." Hawthorne's idea clearly extends beyond the romantic individualism of a Byron. It is applicable to those who (like Margaret Fuller, Hawthorne thought) make a religion of self-cultivation.

Emerson, the leader of the New England Transcendentalists, may have seemed to Hawthorne to place a dangerous emphasis upon individualism—an emphasis which might jeopardize both the mental health of the individual person and the happy functioning of a democratic society. "Trust thyself," said Emerson. "No law can be sacred to me but that of my nature." He urged that "the single man plant himself indomitably on his instincts, and there abide." If his Transcendental perception of Truth should require it, Emerson's self-reliant individual would divorce himself from "father, mother, wife, brother and friend" because he "cannot sell his liberty and power to save their sensibility." He would do this "not selfishly but humbly," Emerson said, but the humility would be suspect to Hawthorne. Would not such conduct denote pride of the most insidious kind—a pride of intellect—even though it stemmed from the Transcendental premises of innate goodness and the intuitive perception of truth? Would not true humility be more likely to stem from an entirely different premise—such a premise as St. Paul's, for example, that "all have sinned and come short of the glory of God"? Would not a humility so derived restrain the individual from the breaking of ties? Would not such a humility, indeed, be a better cement for the democratic society than the Transcendentalist doctrine?

For an idealism, however noble its aims in the abstract, is a mistaken idealism if it destroys human ties, if it rends apart the social fabric. The examples in Hawthorne's stories are legion of those who, in their quest of some imagined good, violate human relationships, depart from the broad highway of mixed and varied humanity, and discover, sometimes too late, the error of their ways. Aylmer sacrificed married happiness for a chemical formula. Wakefield, who had written on the lintels of *his* doorpost "Whim," deserted his wife to live a free, solitary life in the great city of London, and saw too late that "it is perilous to make a chasm in human affections." Hollingsworth devoted himself intensely to humanitarian reform, but in so doing he hardened his own heart and marred the lives of those closest to him. The religious and social "communities" which sprang up over the country in the nineteenth century operated, Hawthorne thought, on the wrong principle—the principle of separation. As regarded society at large, he pointed out ironically, the knot of dreamers at Blithedale—his fictional Brook Farm—"stood in a position of new hostility, rather than new brotherhood." They were "inevitably estranged from the rest of mankind." The celibacy of the Shakers was another unnatural way of life. Martha Pierson, who loves Adam Colburn (in "The Shaker Bridal") but is restrained from marriage by the laws of the sect, dies of frustration and despair: "her heart could endure the weight of its desolate agony no longer." The rule of celibacy for Catholic priests, Hawthorne likewise feared, could produce no good result. As Kenyon saw the matter in *The Marble Faun,* the priests of Rome "were placed in an unnatural relation with woman, and thereby lost the healthy, human conscience that pertains to other human beings, who own the sweet household ties connecting them with wife and daughter." Happy are those who do not sever these ties, or having severed them, can knit them firmly together again. "The limits of ordinary nature," "The boundaries of ordinary life"—how often these words or their equivalents recur in Hawthorne's stories! Of all the seekers after the Great Carbuncle, only Matthew and Hannah saw the error of the quest and repented of it. "Never again," said Matthew, "will we desire more light than all the world may share with us." Much of the evil of the world seemed to Hawthorne to issue from the attempt to appropriate something for one's exclusive use, to elevate one's self above one's fellows, to attain a fancied peculiar excellence, or in some other way to violate the human ties, to transgress the social boundaries.

Pride, in Hawthorne's analysis, is the root evil, for pride is a voluntary separation. Aristocratic family pride is a common manifestation. The inordinate family pride of the Pyncheons has been a source of evil for many generations. Hawthorne can take an almost proletarian delight in the abasement of aristocratic pretensions. They have no place in the modern democratic world. He repeatedly records with approval in *The American Notebooks* the decay of proud old families and the neglected ruins of ancestral mansions. Although sympathetic in his treatment of Hepzibah Pyncheon, he scarcely conceals his satisfaction in her reduced circumstances and the consequent necessity of her becoming a tradeswoman and opening a cent shop.

Though contemptible, aristocratic family pride is less sinister than spiritual pride. The proud woman—the female incarnation of pride—is often made to suffer retributive justice. Lady Eleanore, whose intense pride is symbolized by a richly embroidered mantle, is humbled by the loathesome smallpox. The proud cruel lady in "The White Old Maid" is shown, at the end of the story, on her knees before the gentle Edith whom she had wronged—a tableau of pride abased. Zenobia, whose exotic flower is a symbol of hauteur, drowns herself.

But pride has many less obvious and more devious manifestations and effects, which perhaps only a learned casuist could disentangle. There is the pride of the religious zealot in Endicott and in Catherine, the Quakeress. There is pride of intellect as shown in characters like Aylmer, Brand, and Dr. Rappaccini. There is the moral pride of a ruthless reformer like Hollingsworth. There is even the pride of purity. Hilda is a spotless maiden who is too intent upon preserving her snow-white innocence. Though gentle and kind she is capable of a surprising hardness in her judgment of human frailty. She is so horrified at the discovery of evil that she coldly rejects the evildoer, Miriam, formerly her close friend. Hawthorne would have agreed with Miriam when she told Hilda, "You need a sin to soften you." Pride of whatever sort is evil, Hawthorne would say, because it draws one into aloofness.

Roderick Elliston (in "Egotism; or the Bosom Serpent") willfully destroyed his domestic happiness, and after his separation from his wife he was tortured by a serpent gnawing at his breast. He became "the snake-possessed." "All persons chronically diseased," the author declares,

are egotists, whether the disease be of the mind or body; whether it be sin, sorrow, or merely the more tolerable calamity of some endless pain, such individuals are made acutely conscious of self. . . . The snake in Roderick's bosom seemed the symbol of a monstrous egotism to which everything was referred, and which he pampered, night and day, with a continual and exclusive sacrifice of devil worship. . . . In some of his moods, strange to say, he prided and gloried himself on being marked out from the ordinary experience of mankind by the possession of a double nature and a life within a life.

Roderick was not unaware of the nature of his malady but he appeared unable to throw it off. "Could I for one instant forget myself," he declared with extraordinary insight, "the serpent might not abide within me. It is my diseased self-contemplation that has engendered and nourished him."

The theme of diseased self-contemplation runs through many stories. The Reverend Mr. Hooper (in "The Minister's Black Veil") concealed his face at all times by a piece of black crepe. The veil, he said, was the symbol of the concealment practised by everyone; no one shows his inmost heart. Hawthorne leaves undetermined the reason for the minister's strange act. But whatever the reason the wearing of the veil was an act of separation, estranging Mr. Hooper from the community at large, his parishoners, even the girl he was engaged to marry. Was it not a freak of conscience, a kind of spiritual pride, which impelled him to act thus?

Reuben Bourne (in "Roger Malvin's Burial") likewise felt himself guilty of the sin of concealment. His relationship to others suffered serious disturbance from his failure to tell his wife that after the battle with the Indians he had left her mortally wounded father to lie unburied in the wilderness. Reuben felt justified in what he had done, for Malvin was dying and Reuben, himself seriously wounded, had barely reached the settlement alive. "But concealment," the author points out, "had imparted to a justifiable act much of the secret effect of guilt. . . . His one secret thought became like a serpent gnawing into his heart; and he was transformed into a sad and downcast yet irritable man."

The classic example of the morbid mind is the Rev. Arthur Dimmesdale in *The Scarlet Letter*. Concealed guilt is again the initial cause. The minister has committed adultery with Hester Prynne, and his sense of guilt is aggravated and made almost intolerable by his hypersensitive conscience, the strict mores of Puritan Boston in the seventeenth century, and his constant hypocrisy before his congregation. He resorts to flagellation and other monkish tortures; he brands, the reader is led to suppose, the letter A on his breast. He lives in constant fear lest he betray the secret in an unguarded moment, or commit some wayward act which will reveal the evil in his life. While walking the village streets he is constantly tempted by the devil to do some overt wicked deed, which would be done "in spite of himself, yet growing out of a profounder self than that which opposed the impulse": to make a blasphemous remark respecting the communion supper to an excellent deacon, to whisper in a dear old lady's ear an argument against the soul's immortality, to teach profane language to a group of children, to suggest a carnal thought to a young virgin recently converted to the church. Truly the minister is "in a maze." "Am I mad?" he cries. "Am I given over utterly to the fiend?" Torn apart by conflict Dimmesdale is on the verge of a complete physical and nervous breakdown. He must re-establish free, unconstrained relations with others before he can enjoy peace of mind again.

In his portrayal of Elliston, Hooper, Bourne, Dimmesdale, and other cases of conscience, Hawthorne doubtless intended a criticism of the introspective habits of the New England mind. Minute self-examination was a fostered Puritan practice. The following entry in Cotton Mather's *Diary* suggests Dimmesdale himself: "Was ever man more tempted than the miserable Mather? Should I tell in how many forms the Devil has assaulted me, it would strike my friends with horror." Jonathan Edwards' *Diary* contains such entries as this: "To set apart days of meditation on particular subjects, as sometimes, to set apart a day for the consideration of the Greatness of my sins." If the Puritan examined his inner consciousness to assess his sinfulness, his proneness to sin, and so the better to guard against the assaults of the Evil One, the Transcendentalist looked inward to discover hints and intimations of the divine mind which is in all men. "A man should learn," Emerson said, "to detect and watch that gleam of light which flashes across his mind from within." "If one listens," Thoreau said, repeating and amplifying Emerson's thought, "to the faintest but constant suggestions of his genius, which are certainly true, he sees not to what extremes, or even insanity, it may lead him; and yet that way, as he grows more resolute and faithful, his road lies." While recognizing the danger Thoreau recommended introspection because the Transcendental doctrine of God within required it. He and Emerson were sufficiently active in the world about them to escape the morbid effects of the inward gaze, but Hawthorne could have pointed to the Transcendentalist Charles King Newcomb as an example of self-contemplation carried to dangerous excess. The New England mind, when Hawthorne wrote, had searched itself for more than two centuries—inexorably and often with fierce castigation in Puritan times, benignly and hopefully in the contemporary age of Transcendentalism. The practice in either case was motivated by the laudable desire for perfection, for Puritans and Transcendentalists alike took to heart the biblical text, "Be ye therefore perfect, even as your Father which is in heaven is perfect." But would not the constant inward-looker become morbid? Would not the assiduous self-improver become cold and aloof? Hawthorne's stories contain many instances of the sort.

What does Hawthorne oppose as a corrective to excessive self-examination? What therapy does he offer for morbidness? What cure for the sick soul? The answer is essentially the recognition of man's fallibility, the restoration of sympathy, the sharing of the common lot. Hawthorne's "moral" comprehends the Christian doctrine of charity, the psychological doctrine of participation, the social doctrine of the democratic way.

Hawthorne set great store by the normalizing, stabilizing power of the domestic affections. The experience of love, marriage, and children had such an effect upon his own life. "We are but shadows," he wrote to Sophia Peabody in 1840, "we are not endowed with real life, and all that seems most real about us is but the thinnest substance of a dream—till the heart be touched. That touch creates us, then we begin to be, thereby we are beings of reality and inheritors of eternity." In several pieces written during his bachelorhood (a bachelorhood abnormally prolonged, though not entirely from his own choice, one must believe) the author betrays his own sense of need. The wakeful sleeper would not have been plagued by specters of the mind (in "The Haunted Mind") if he had had a wife. "How pleasant in these night solitudes," the author observes, "would be the rise and fall of a softer breathing than your own, the slight pressure of a tenderer bosom, the quiet throb of a purer heart, imparting its peacefulness to your troubled one, as if the fond sleeper were involving you in her dream." The moral of "The Village Uncle," summed up at the end, points to a domestic and social therapy: "In chaste and warm affections, humble wishes, and honest toil for some useful end, there is health for the mind, and quiet for the heart, the prospect of a happy life, and the fairest hope of heaven." The same lesson was learned, the hard way, by the wanderer in "The Three-fold Destiny," who at last returned to his original home, married the sweetheart of his boyhood, and taught in the village school.

Roderick Elliston, the pathological individual who was tortured by a "bosom-serpent," was reconciled with his wife and their new love worked a cure. In the symbolical language of the story, Rosina's touch exorcised the serpent. Hepzibah's love for the unfortunate Clifford, and for Phoebe, was a saving grace in her life. Without these influences she would have been a completely crazed old woman. Kenyon's love for Hilda saved him from the coldness of his art. Inspired by love, Drowne, the wood-carver (in "Drowne's Wooden Image"), surpassed his usual self and created a statue worthy of Copley's praise. Even Feathertop— the "wretched simulacrum," the empty, foppish man of mode destitute of mind, heart, and soul—might have been changed from shadow to substance by the love of Polly Gookin—or he pathetically conjectured as much to Mother Rigby.

To private domestic love must be added a vital sense of one's connection with the larger world. The stories abound in illustrations. Hepzibah Pyncheon, we are told, "needed a walk along the noonday street to keep her sane." When a political procession, announced by banners and drums, marched by the house of the seven gables, Clifford Pyncheon—isolated from humanity by an overexquisite sensibility as Hepzibah was by an aristocratic pride —felt an impulse to jump from the balcony above into the passing throng. He felt, the author says, "a natural magnetism tending towards the great center of humanity," the need of "a deep, deep plunge into the ocean of human life," "a yearning to renew the broken links of brotherhood with his kind." The flight of Hepzibah and Clifford and their journey on the railroad are symbolical of an attempt to establish a connection with the world.

After prolonged, unremitting application to the writer's craft —of necessity a solitary occupation—Hawthorne himself often felt a similar social need; such application he thought was "unwholesome" in its personal effect. He enjoyed mingling in the life of a great city—in Boston, Liverpool, London. His employment in the various custom houses gave him a sense of social participation, as did his labor at Brook Farm. Coverdale spoke from the author's own experience when he said, "In the sweat of my brow I had earned bread and eaten it, and so established my claim to be on earth, and my fellowship with all the sons of labor." Repeatedly in his stories Hawthorne opposes "human sympathy" to "morbid sensibility." "I would make the wide world my cell," Kenyon declares when Donatello seems inclined to adopt the monastic life, "and good deeds to mankind my prayer."

Opening an intercourse with the world (the phrase is Hawthorne's own expression of his aim in publishing the *Twice-Told Tales*) is often difficult and seemingly impossible. Hawthorne's stories emphasize the obstacles to free, reciprocal relationships. Such an obstacle may be pride, or egoism, or solitary ambition, or secret sin. The harboring of secret sin, the practice of hypocrisy, estranges the soul from God and man. That full-blown hypocrite, Judge Pyncheon, was past redemption, past contrition and confession, but Hawthorne's prescription for salvation—had the Judge by a miracle of grace been capable of following it—is a good statement of the author's ethic: "Will he go forth a humbled and repentant man, sorrowful, gentle, seeking no profit, shrinking from worldly honor, hardly daring to love God, but bold to love his fellowman and to do him what good he may? Will he bear about with him . . . the tender sadness of a contrite heart, broken at last beneath its own weight of sin?" Judge Pyncheon was completely callous and suffered no remorse. Arthur Dimmesdale, on the other hand, was sensitive and was tortured by his conscience for seven years. When, upon the point of collapse and death, he summoned sufficient strength of will to make a public confession before the congregation and townspeople whom he had deceived, a magical change was at once made evident by his facial expression and his attitude toward Pearl: "There was a sweet and gentle smile over his face, as of a spirit sinking into deep repose; nay, now that the burden was removed, it seemed almost as if he would be sportive with the child."

Confession—whether viewed religiously or psychologically—is good for the soul. In *The Marble Faun* Hilda used the Roman confessional as a means of relieving her mind of a troublesome secret. The device proved effective, but Hilda herself had committed no sin. For sinners, Hawthorne must have regarded the public confession of the Puritans, by which the guilt was laid open before the congregation and community, as preferable to the private confessional of the Catholic Church, which did not sufficiently meet the social requirements. If sin is an estrangement, then the sinner must confess—as Dimmesdale did—before those from whom he has been estranged, for how otherwise can he be restored to free and full communion with them?

Though sin often estranges (the sin of pride, for example), it may be, paradoxically, a means of sympathy. Hawthorne often remarks on the sympathy between sinners. Goodman Brown's vision of evil admitted him to a sinful brotherhood. Elliston's "serpent" heard answering hisses (recalling a scene in *Paradise Lost*) from the bosoms of his fellow townsmen. Accomplices in murder, Miriam and Donatello were united in a bond of crime. Dimmesdale's experience of sin gave new meaning and power to his preaching. Indeed, since evil is an ever-present reality in human life, a knowledge of evil—of some sort and in some degree—would seem to be a necessary condition of sympathy.

The knowledge of evil may be good or bad, depending upon its effects. In Goodman Brown's case it led to sheer misanthropy. With Donatello and Miriam the bad effects greatly preponderated because their crime, while binding the two together, isolated them from the rest of the world. Dimmesdale's experience might have been entirely good in the end had it not been for the fatal flaw of hypocrisy. Hilda was "instructed by sorrow"; she became more tolerant, more sympathetic. But her knowledge was only vicarious and for that reason the sympathy thus acquired was comparatively shallow. In *The Marble Faun* the author speaks of "those dark caverns into which all men must descend if they would know anything beneath the surface and illusive pleasures of existence." "And when they emerge," he says, "they take truer and sadder views of life forever afterwards." Once again Hawthorne sets himself against the optimism of his age and the age's chief optimist in America, Emerson, who disarmingly declared on his fifty-eighth birthday, "I could never give much reality to evil and pain." Such an inability or lack of insight, to Hawthorne, is a mark of defective sympathy. The sympathy in any case is the important thing. A knowledge of both good and evil is essential to sympathy since the nature of man comprehends both. A knowledge of one only sets up barriers to sympathy.

The problem of evil is the greatest and most baffling of human problems. The Christian statement of the problem is: Why does God, who is all-good and all-powerful, permit evil in His world? In the tales and novels Hawthorne presented the problem in many of its protean forms. He presented it from the Puritan, which was also the Christian, standpoint (for the marks which distinguished Puritanism from the rest of Christendom were, in relation to the whole body of doctrine, few and unimportant). Toward the end of *The Marble Faun* he apparently attempted to formulate a more comprehensive and summary view of the matter than can be found in his previous works. Donatello, encouraged by Miriam, has committed murder. The deed has had a variety of important effects upon the characters in the story. To portray and evaluate these effects constitute the author's chief intention. The evil deed has humbled the proud Miriam. It has broadened and deepened the sympathies of Kenyon. It has enlightened and softened Hilda, making her less self-sufficient and more responsive to Kenyon's love. It has educated Donatello, who has lost his faunlike simplicity and innocence and has gained maturity and depth of character.

Hawthorne is particularly interested in Donatello's transformation and its implications. He presents the problem first in a dialogue between Miriam and Kenyon:

"Was the crime [Miriam asked] in which he and I were wedded—was it a blessing, in that strange disguise? Was it a means of education, bringing a simple and imperfect nature to a point of feeling and intelligence which it could have reached under no other discipline?"

"You stir up deep and perilous matter, Miriam," replied Kenyon. "I dare not follow you into the unfathomable abysses whither you are tending."

"Yet there is a pleasure in them! I delight to brood on the verge of this great mystery," returned she. "The story of the fall of man! Is it not repeated in our romance of Monte Beni? And may we follow the analogy yet further? Was that very sin,—into which Adam precipitated himself and all his race,—was it the destined means by which, over a long pathway of toil and sorrow, we are to attain a higher, brighter, and profounder happiness than our lost birthright gave? Will not this idea account for the permitted existence of sin, as no other theory can?"

In a later scene Kenyon restates Miriam's idea in a conversation with Hilda:

"Donatello perpetrated a great crime; and his remorse, gnawing into his soul, has awakened it; developing a thousand high capabilities, moral and intellectual, which we never should have dreamed of asking for, within the scanty compass of the Donatello whom we knew. . . . Sin has educated Donatello, and elevated him. Is sin, then—which we deem such a dreadful blackness in the Universe—is it, like sorrow, merely an element of human education, through which we struggle to a higher and purer state than we could otherwise have attained? Did Adam fall, that we might ultimately rise to a far loftier paradise than his?"

Although Hilda strongly dissents, the view twice stated would seem to be the author's theme.

"I first look at matters," Hawthorne once wrote to his wife, "in their darkest aspect, and having satisfied myself with that, I begin gradually to be consoled, to take into account the advantages of the case, and thus trudge on, with the light brightening around me." Readers of his stories are likely to complain of the prevalence of gloom, the comparative absence of light, and the complaint is not without some justification. And yet the light, though never garish, does brighten around a score of characters, and more, as the trials of the narrative draw to a close: around the Lord and Lady of the May, the young married pair of "The Great Carbuncle," the returned wanderer and his village sweetheart in "The Three-fold Destiny," Roderick and Rosina in "The Bosom Serpent," Holgrave and Phoebe, Kenyon and Hilda—around even Dimmesdale and Hester, though in the last instance the light only prefigures a possible happiness beyond this life. It should be observed, too, that the trials through which these and other characters have passed have enriched their lives and increased their capacities for happiness.

If, nevertheless, the emphasis of *The Collected Works*, the sum and synthesis of Hawthorne's knowledge and understanding of the world, seems to fall on the somber side, the explanation may be found in his sense of the stark realities, which he was unwilling to falsify or gloss over, and his critical reaction against an age which seemed to him to brush the human difficulties aside with too easy an optimism, and to put an extravagant and unrealistic faith both in man's abilities and in the new scientific and social machinery. From the perspective of today we can see that Hawthorne touched his times at point after point with admonitory finger, giving to his age the more earnest purpose, the deeper moral, and the closer and homelier truth which it seemed to him to require. It is an admonition and a gift which are timeless. In the light of the world today (which is the heir of the nineteenth century) no one is likely to impugn Hawthorne's central moral—the importance of understanding mankind in whole, and the need of man's sympathy with man based upon the honest recognition of the good and evil in our common nature.

CHIEF BIOGRAPHICAL SOURCES

Manuscripts

The principal collections of Hawthorne manuscripts (chiefly journals and letters) are found in the Pierpont Morgan Library, the Henry E. Huntington Library, the New York Public Library, the Library of the Essex Institute, the Houghton Library of Harvard University, and the Boston Public Library. Miscellaneous manuscripts relating to Hawthorne are in these libraries and in many others, notably that of the Massachusetts Historical Society.

Printed Materials and Other Sources

N. F. ADKINS, "The Early Projected Works of Nathaniel Hawthorne," *Papers of the Bibliographical Society of America*, Second Quarter, 1945.

HAROLD BLODGETT, "Hawthorne as Poetry Critic: Six Unpublished Letters to Lewis Mansfield," *American Literature*, May, 1940.

HORATIO BRIDGE, *Personal Recollections of Nathaniel Hawthorne*, New York, 1893.

E. L. CHANDLER, "Hawthorne's *Spectator*," *New England Quarterly*, April, 1931.

WILLIAM CHARVAT, "James T. Fields and the Beginnings of Book Promotion," *Huntington Library Quarterly*, November, 1944.

J. T. FIELDS, *Yesterdays with Authors*, Boston, 1871.

BERTHA FAUST, *Hawthorne's Contemporaneous Reputation*, Philadelphia, 1939.

JULIAN HAWTHORNE, *Nathaniel Hawthorne and His Wife*, Boston, 1884, 2 vols.

Hawthorne and His Circle, New York, 1903.

MANNING HAWTHORNE, "Parental and Family Influences on Hawthorne," *Essex Institute Historical Collections*, January, 1940.

"Hawthorne's Early Years," *ibid.*, January, 1938.

"Maria Louisa Hawthorne," *ibid.*, April, 1939.

"Hawthorne Prepares for College," *New England Quarterly*, March, 1938.

"Nathaniel Hawthorne at Bowdoin," *ibid.*, June, 1940.

"Hawthorne and 'The Man of God,'" *Colophon*, Winter, 1937.

"Nathaniel and Elizabeth Hawthorne, Editors," *ibid.*, September, 1939.

NATHANIEL HAWTHORNE, *Complete Works*, ed. George Parsons Lathrop, Boston, 1885, 13 vols.

SOPHIA PEABODY HAWTHORNE, *Notes in England and Italy*, New York, 1869.

HARRISON HAYFORD, "The Significance of Melville's 'Agatha' Letters," *Journal of English Literary History*, December, 1946.

W. D. HOWELLS, *Literary Friends and Acquaintance*, New York, 1900.

E. B. HUNGERFORD, "Hawthorne Gossips about Salem," *New England Quarterly*, September, 1933.

MARION L. KESSELRING, "Hawthorne's Reading 1828–1850: An Identification and Analysis of Titles Recorded in the Charge-Books of the Salem Athenaeum," unpublished Master's thesis at Brown University, 1943.

ROSE HAWTHORNE LATHROP, *Memories of Hawthorne*, Boston, 1897.

MARGARET M. LOTHROP, *The Wayside*, New York, 1940.

ELIZABETH MANNING, "The Boyhood of Hawthorne," *Wide Awake*, November, 1891.

S. E. MORISON, "Melville's 'Agatha' Letter to Hawthorne," *New England Quarterly*, April, 1929.

W. S. NEVINS, "Hawthorne's Removal from the Salem Custom House," *Essex Institute Historical Collections*, April, 1917.

R. F. NICHOLS, *Franklin Pierce*, Philadelphia, 1931.

NORMAN HOLMES PEARSON, "The College Years of Nathaniel Hawthorne," an unpublished monograph which won the Henry H. Strong Prize in American Literature at Yale University in 1932.

"The Italian Notebooks by Nathaniel Hawthorne," an unpublished doctoral dissertation at Yale University, 1942.

S. T. PICKARD, *Hawthorne's First Diary*, Boston, 1897.

RANDALL STEWART, *The American Notebooks by Nathaniel Hawthorne*, New Haven, 1932.

The English Notebooks by Nathaniel Hawthorne, New York, 1941.

"Ethan Brand," *Saturday Review of Literature*, April 27, 1929.

"Hawthorne and Politics," *New England Quarterly*, April, 1932.

"Hawthorne's Contributions to the Salem *Advertiser*," *American Literature*, January, 1934.

"Hawthorne's Speeches at Civic Banquets," *ibid.*, January, 1936.

"Recollections of Hawthorne by His Sister Elizabeth," *ibid.*, January, 1945.

"Hawthorne and the Civil War," *Studies in Philology*, January, 1937.

"Letters to Sophia," *Huntington Library Quarterly*, August, 1944.

"The Hawthornes at the Wayside," *More Books*, September, 1944.

"Hawthorne's Last Illness and Death," *ibid.*, October, 1944.

"Editing Hawthorne's Notebooks," *ibid.*, September, 1945.

"Mrs. Hawthorne's Financial Difficulties," *ibid.*, February, 1946.

"Mrs. Hawthorne's Quarrel with James T. Fields," *ibid.*, September, 1946.

LAWRANCE THOMPSON, *Young Longfellow*, New York, 1938.

WILLARD THORP, *Herman Melville*, New York, 1938.

CAROLINE TICKNOR, *Hawthorne and His Publisher*, Boston, 1913.

ARLIN TURNER, "Hawthorne and Martha's Vineyard," *New England Quarterly*, June, 1938.

Hawthorne as Editor, University, Louisiana, 1941.

INDEX

Abbot, John, 15
Abbotsford, 177
Adams, John Quincy, 20
Addison, Joseph, 9
Adkins, N. F., 29
Agassiz, Louis J. R., 218
"Agatha story," 134–136
Ainsworth, Miss C. C., 51
Ainsworth, Mrs. Peter, 162
Albany, N. Y., 42, 61
Albert, Consort of Queen Victoria, 164
Albury, 166
Alcott, Amos Bronson, 65, 70, 73, 80, 84, 123, 124, 214, 222, 223, 235, 238
Alcott, Mrs. Amos Bronson, 235
Alcott, Louisa, 217
Aldershot Camp, 166
Allen, Rev. William, 15, 18, 21, 23
American Magazine of Useful and Entertaining Knowledge, 32, 39, 42
American Monthly Magazine, 34, 47
American Revolution, 243
American Whig Review, 69
Amiens, 183
Androscoggin River, 23
Anne, Queen, 175
Antioch College, 49, 172, 183
Apollo Belvedere, 197
Appian Way, 203
Appledore Island, 130, 131
Arabian Nights, 8
Arch of Titus, 187
Archer, Samuel H., 6
Arcturus, 69
Arezzo, 200
Arnold, Matthew, 162
Assabeth River, 80
Athenean Society, 19, 20, 25, 38, 39, 242
Atherton, Charles Gordon, 77, 122, 127
Atlantic Monthly, 211, 217, 221, 224, 226, 228, 229, 239, 240
Augusta, Maine, 45, 46, 73, 130
Aurelius, Marcus, 187
Avignon, 206

Bacci, Constantino, 203
Bacon, Delia, 168, 224
Bacon, Francis, 28, 73
Badger, Clay, 183, 184, 186, 190–191, 204, 207
Baltimore, Md., 127, 144
Bancroft, George, 53, 58, 64, 75–76, 77, 78, 124, 162
Bancroft, Mrs. George, 77, 162
Barlow, Francis C., 222
Bartholomew, E. S., 197
Batavia, 2
Bath, 212–213
Beattie, James, 19
Bebbington, 173
Bellingham, Richard, 2
Benjamin, Park, 32, 34
Bennoch, Francis, 166, 168, 169, 172, 207, 224
Beverly, Mass., 79, 140, 219
Bible, 14, 16, 17, 126, 167, 181, 190, 254, 259
Black Heath, 168, 173
Blagden, Isabella, 201
Blodgett, Mrs., 163, 164, 213
Bolton le Moors, 162
Borghese Grounds, 206
Borghetto, 200
Borrow, George, 105
Boston, England, 177
Boston, Mass., 3, 32, 33, 35, 38, 39, 40, 47, 49, 51, 58, 62, 68, 76, 77, 79, 83, 85, 86, 99, 118, 119, 126, 136, 146, 154, 161, 198, 211, 212, 214, 233
Boston Athenaeum, 99
Boston Custom House, 49, 53, 57, 58, 60, 64, 67, 68, 73, 75, 137
Boston *Daily Advertiser*, 87
Boston Miscellany, 47
Boston Museum, 93
Boston Quarterly, 69
Boston *Times*, 127
Boswell, James, 235
Boulogne, 182, 183

Bowdoin College, 10, 13, 14, 15, 20, 21, 22, 23–24, 25, 27, 28, 35, 129, 130, 235, 242
Bradford, Alden, 28
Bradford, George, 216
Bramley-Moore, John, 162
Bremer, Fredrika, 107
Bridge, Horatio, 19–20, 23, 29, 32, 33, 35, 38, 39–40, 43, 45, 53, 64, 67, 68–69, 76–77, 78, 79, 84, 85, 94, 95, 97, 98, 99, 106, 107, 112, 115, 118, 120, 122, 126, 133, 134, 142, 155, 181, 188, 216, 226, 231, 239
Bridge, Mrs. Horatio, 122
Bright, Henry, 160, 161, 168, 170, 209, 211, 213, 231, 239
British Museum, 176
Brontë, Charlotte, 114
Brook Farm, 49, 58, 59, 60, 64, 73, 77, 80–81, 122, 216
Brooks, Preston, 152
Brown, John, 244
Brown, Nehemiah, 87
Browne, Benjamin F., 76, 86, 92, 120, 137
Browning, Elizabeth Barrett, 168, 200, 201, 202, 205
Browning, Pennini, 200–201
Browning, Robert, 168, 202, 241
Brownson, Orestes A., 69, 97
Brownson's Review, 97
Brunswick, Maine, 10, 13, 14, 17, 22, 129, 130
Brunswick Terrace, 169
Bryant, William Cullen, 69
Buchanan, James, 181
Bull, Ephraim, 126, 216
Bunyan, John, 4, 5, 57, 60, 242, 245
Burchmore, Zachariah, 79, 80, 99, 100, 109, 119, 122, 137–138, 222
Burley, Miss S., 51
Burlington, Vt., 42
Burns, James G., 162
Burns, Robert, 162, 167, 177
Burns, William Nicol, 162
Burritt, Elihu, 72
Butler, Joseph, 17
Byron, Lord, 25, 187, 253

Cambridge University, 160, 213
Canterbury, N. H., 41

Casa del Bello, 200
Cass, Lewis, 134, 150, 152–153
Castle of Chillon, 206
Cervantes, 158
Channing, Ellery, 64, 65, 66, 73, 80, 145, 214
Channing, William Ellery, 244
Chapman and Hall, 123, 143
Charlecote Park, 173
Charles I, 243
Charles II, 1
Charlestown Navy Yard, 76
Chase, Lydia, 91
Chase, Maria, 91
Chelsea Hospital, 76
Chester, 170, 173
Chorley, Henry, 34, 69, 96, 113, 207, 211
Church Review, 97
Cicero, 13, 18
Cilley, Jonathan, 19–20, 22, 46, 53, 75
Civitavecchia, 185, 186, 206
Clarendon, Edward Hyde, first Earl of, 28
Clarke, Rev. James Freeman, 61, 238
Cleaveland, Parker, 15, 17
Clough, Arthur Hugh, 146
Clough, Benjamin C., 43
Coliseum, 187, 204
Concord, Mass., 61, 62, 65, 71, 73, 123, 125, 126, 204, 214, 215, 216, 219, 220, 233, 234
Concord, N. H., 230, 235, 238
Concord River, 64
Confucius, 246
Conolly, Horace L., 37, 41, 64, 85, 100, 119, 120
Cooper, James Fenimore, 19, 242
Cornwall, Barry, 141
Correggio, 101
Coxe, A. C., 97
Coryate, Thomas, 28
Crabbe, George, 28
Crawford's Inn, 42
Crawford, Thomas, 192
Crimean War, 163–164, 178
Crosland, Mrs. Newton, 166
Crystal Palace, 176
Cumberland, 226
Curtis, Burrill, 107
Curtis, George W., 64, 105, 109, 122, 225, 233, 239

Dallas, Eneas Sweetland, 167
Dallas, George M., 182
Dante, 210
Danvers, Mass., 40
Dartmouth College, 13
Davis, Jefferson, 231
Davis, Rebecca Harding, 223–224
Defoe, Daniel, 118, 158, 175
Democratic Review, 46–47, 53, 61, 71, 86, 92
DeQuincey, Thomas, 105, 141
Detroit, Mich., 42, 43
De Vere, Aubrey, 205
Dial, 58, 70
Dickens, Charles, 105, 168, 233
Dike, John S., 37, 38, 43, 128
Disraeli, 167
Douglas, Stephen A., 154
Dresden, Germany, 240
Dryden, John, 89, 167
Dufferin, Lord, 213
Dumas, Alexandre, 96
Dumfries, 177
Dummer, Jeremiah, 22
Dutch East Indies, 2
Dutch Guiana, 2
Duyckinck, E. A., 68, 69, 70, 77, 96, 104, 105, 107, 108, 109, 112, 119, 123

Eastham, 173
Edgeworth, Maria, 8
Edinburgh, 177
Edinburgh Review, 28
Edwards, Jonathan, 247, 258
Emerson, Edith, 215
Emerson, Edward, 126, 215
Emerson, Ralph Waldo, 58, 62, 64, 65, 66, 73, 80, 84, 86, 124, 126, 141, 145, 146, 168, 171, 176, 197, 214, 215, 218, 220, 221, 222, 236, 238, 239, 244, 249, 251, 253, 258, 263
Emerson, Mrs. Ralph Waldo, 215, 216
Essex County, 78
Essex Institute, 22, 27
Euclid, 16

Farley, Frank, 64
Farquhar, George, 175
Faust, Bertha, 34
Fernando, Regent of Portugal, 164

Field, Dudley, 106
Fielding, Henry, 8
Fields, Annie, 207, 213, 214, 216, 217, 218, 223, 233, 235, 236–237, 238, 239, 240
Fields, James T., 94–95, 97, 99, 104, 105, 107, 112–113, 114, 115, 116, 117, 121, 122–123, 126, 134, 135, 140, 141, 143, 146, 167, 179, 202, 207, 210, 211, 212, 213, 214, 215, 217, 218, 221, 223, 224–225, 226, 228–230, 233, 234, 235, 238, 240
Flint Pond, 216
Florence, 199, 200, 202–203, 208
Foligno, 200
Fortress Monroe, 226
Forum, 187
Fourier, Charles, 122
Franco, Dr., 204, 205, 206, 207
Franklin, Benjamin, 167
Frost, Rev. Barzillai, 64
Furness Abbey, 174

Geneva, 206
Genoa, 186, 206
Gibbs, Eliza, 43–44
Gibson, John, 192
Gibson, Walter M., 154
Glyn, Isabella Dallas, 167
Godey's Lady's Book, 47, 67, 70
Godwin, William, 8
Goldsmith, Oliver, 175–176, 239
Goodrich, Samuel G., 30, 31, 32–33, 35
Gosport, N. H., 131
Graham's Magazine, 47, 69, 96, 113
Grasmere, 174
Graves, William J., 75
Greenwich Fair, 189
Greenwich Hospital, 176
Griswold, Rufus W., 115
Guido Reni, 196, 245

Hail Columbia, 155
Hale, Benjamin, 15
Hall, Samuel Carter, 155, 167, 168
Hamilton, Gail, 221, 223–224
Harper's Ferry, 226
Harvard College, 13, 216, 240
Harvard, Mass., 66
Hathorne, Daniel, 2, 3

Hathorne, Elizabeth Clarke Manning, 2, 3, 4, 5, 6, 7, 10, 14, 21, 27, 50, 61, 90, 91

Hathorne, John, 2

Hathorne, Joseph, 2

Hathorne, Nathaniel, 2, 3, 4

Hathorne, William, 1–2

Havana, 52, 235

Havre, 206

Hawthorne, Elizabeth Manning 2, 4, 5, 7, 10, 18, 20, 21, 23–24, 27, 28, 29, 30, 32–33, 34, 38, 43, 50, 61, 70, 90, 91, 112, 140, 219

Hawthorne, Julian, 49, 62, 81, 82, 89, 91, 94, 102–104, 106, 114, 119, 124–125, 126, 143, 144, 145, 148, 158, 163, 164, 170, 176, 188–189, 200, 203, 206, 212, 215, 216, 217, 219, 220, 223, 234, 240, 241

Hawthorne, Manning, 3, 52

Hawthorne, Maria Louisa, 2, 6, 7, 9, 12, 27, 33, 37, 41, 50, 51, 61, 64, 90, 91, 106, 117, 118, 127–128

Hawthorne, Nathaniel, ancestry, 1–4; boyhood in Salem, 4–5, 6–12; boyhood in Maine, 5; early reading, 4–5, 8; schooling in Salem, 4, 6–7; choice of profession, 11; at Bowdoin, teachers, 15; curriculum, 16–17; academic standing, 18; extracurricular activities, 18–26; breaches of academic discipline, 21–22; early reading after college, 28; writing and publication of early tales, 28–35; friendships and recreations in the "solitary years," 37–44; early travels in New England, 40–43; interest in women, 43–44; visit to Bridge at Augusta, 45–46; visit to North Adams, 47–49; meets and falls in love with Sophia Peabody, 50–52; dedicates "The Gentle Boy" to Sophia Peabody, 52; measurer at the Boston Custom House, 52–58; at Brook Farm, 58–60; letters to Sophia Peabody during their betrothal, 53–62; marriage, 62; reading at the Old Manse, 64; visitors at the Old Manse, 64–65; relations with the Concord Transcendentalists, 65–66; financial difficulties at the Old Manse, 66–67; writing and publication while at the Old Manse, 68–73; widening social outlook in Old Manse writings, 71–72; skepticism of reform and of Platonism, 72–73; political activities leading to appointment as surveyor in the Salem Custom House, 75–79; employment at the Salem Custom House, 79–80; descriptions of his children, 81–83; devotion to wife and children, 83–84; secretary of the Salem Lyceum, 84–85; friendships, 85–86; dismissal from the Salem Custom House, 86–89; grief at his dying mother's bedside, 90; religious faith, 90; writings at Salem, 1846–49, 92–93; magazine writing poorly paid, 93; writing, publication, and reception of *The Scarlet Letter*, 93–99; recuperation in the Berkshires, 102–104; playmate to his children, 102–104; reading at the Little Red House, 105; social activities in the Berkshires, 105–107; friendship with Melville, 107–112; high opinion of Melville's books, 107; writing, publication, and reception of *The House of the Seven Gables*, 112–114; other writing and publication in the Berkshires, 114–116; financial improvement, 117; growing discontent in the Berkshires, 118–120; removal to West Newton, 120–121; writing, publication, and reception of *The Blithedale Romance*, 122–123; purchase of and removal to the Wayside, 123–124; recreations at the Wayside, 124–126; death of Louisa Hawthorne, 127–128; *Life of Pierce*, 127, 128–129, 132–133; attitude toward Pierce, 133–134; attendance at Bowdoin semicentennial, 129–130; visit to the Isles of Shoals, 130–131; the "Agatha story," 134–136; Melville at the Wayside, 135–136; political influence after Pierce's election, 136–140; appointment as consul to Liverpool, 140; reasons for accepting consulship, 140–142; income from his books, 140–141;

Tanglewood Tales, 142–143; visit to Washington, 1853, 143–145; departure for Liverpool, 145–147; duties of the consulship, 149–157; efforts for maritime reform, 151–153; speeches at civic banquets, 155–157; reading in England, 158, 168, 218–219; aversion to new fashions, 161–162; social activities in England, 160–162; at Mrs. Blodgett's boardinghouse, 164; low spirits during his wife's absence in Portugal, 164–165; London excursion with Bennoch, 166–168; summer at Black Heath, 168–169; winter at Southport, 169–170; Melville's visit, 169–170; visits to the Manchester Exhibition, 170–172; travels in England and Scotland, 173–177; attitudes toward England, 177–178; writing in England, 180–181; financial improvement, 181; departure from England for the continent, 182; travels in France, 183–185; admiration for his wife's travel sketches, 189–190; association with artists in Rome, 191–194; study of sculpture and painting in Rome, 196–197; view of Roman Catholicism, 198–199; summer in Florence, 199–203; association with the Brownings, 200–202; Una's illness, 204; friendship with Pierce, 205; return to England via France and Switzerland, 205–207; financial condition reviewed, 207–208; composition, publication, and reception of *The Marble Faun*, 208–211; homesickness, 212; return to America, 213–214; rebuilding and redecorating the Wayside, 215–216; social activities at the Wayside, 216–217; friendship with the James T. Fields, 217–218; attendance at Saturday Club, 218; summer excursions to New England beaches, 219–221; description of, by Gail Hamilton, 221; guests at the Wayside, 221–222; reading at the Wayside, 223–224; writing and reception of the English sketches, 224–225; gratitude to Fields, 225–226; visit to Washington, 1862, 226–228; last

fiction, 228–229; reception of *Our Old Home*, 230–231, 233; loyalty to Pierce, 232; growing anxiety and ill-health, 234–238; death and burial, 238; tributes of friends, 239.

WORKS: "Alice Doane's Appeal," 30; "Ambitious Guest," 32, 42, 68; *American Notebooks*, 40, 45–46, 47–49, 63–64, 65, 66, 90, 103–104, 106, 109, 110, 118, 146, 220, 240, 255; *Ancestral Footstep*, 208, 229; "Birthmark," 249, 254, 256; *Blithedale Romance*, 60, 122–123, 134, 135, 141, 195–196, 245, 246, 250, 251–252, 254, 255, 256, 261; "Canterbury Pilgrims," 116; "Celestial Railroad," 69, 84, 111, 245–246; "Chiefly About War Matters," 226–227; "Christmas Banquet," 71; "Custom House," 1, 2, 79, 80, 94, 96, 98; "Devil in Manuscript," 29–30, 31, 116; *Dr. Grimshawe's Secret*, 174, 177, 229, 241; *Dolliver Romance*, 229, 238; "Drowne's Wooden Image," 67, 260; "Earth's Holocaust," 71, 72, 246–247; "Egotism or the Bosom Serpent," 256, 257, 260, 262, 265; "Endicott and the Red Cross," 68, 243, 256; *English Notebooks*, 148–149, 150, 151, 153, 154, 155–156, 157, 160, 162, 163, 164, 165, 169–170, 175, 176, 177, 178, 179–180, 180–181, 240; "Ethan Brand," 48, 92, 111, 115, 248, 249, 250, 256; *Fanshawe*, 14–15, 23, 24, 28–29, 31; "Feathertop," 114–115, 260; *First Diary*, 5; "Gentle Boy," 30, 31, 32, 34, 52, 70, 243, 256; *Grandfather's Chair*, 68, 143; "Gray Champion," 31, 32, 243; "Great Carbuncle," 248, 255, 265; "Great Stone Face," 92, 93, 115; "Hall of Fantasy," 71, 72, 73; "Haunted Mind," 259; "Hollow of the Three Hills," 30; *House of the Seven Gables*, 47, 89, 112–114, 115, 119, 121, 122, 244, 250, 251, 255, 260, 261, 265; "Intelligence Office," 252; *Italian Notebooks*, 188, 189, 196, 197, 198, 240; *Journal of an African Cruiser*, 68, 69, 77; "Lady Eleanore's Mantle," 255; *Life of Franklin Pierce*, 124; "Main Street," 92, 115;

Hawthorne, Nathaniel (*continued*)
  Marble Faun, 167, 188, 192, 193, 194, 196, 198–199, 202, 208–211, 212, 213, 215, 245, 250, 252, 254, 256, 260, 261, 262, 263–264, 265; "Maypole of Merry Mount," 34, 243, 265; "Minister's Black Veil," 34, 149, 256–257, 258; *Mosses from an Old Manse,* 68, 69, 70, 80, 92, 108, 112, 115, 116, 141; "Mr. Higginbotham's Catastrophe," 32; "My Kinsman, Major Molineux," 30; "New Adam and Eve," 71; "Old Manse," 67, 96; *Our Old Home,* 153, 160, 166, 174, 224–225, 229–231, 232, 233; *Papers of an Old Dartmoor Prisoner,* 86, 92; *Peter Parley's Universal History,* 33; *Pocket Diary, 1856,* 169; *Pocket Diary, 1859,* 207–208, 209–210; "Procession of Life," 72, 154; "Prophetic Pictures," 251; "Rappaccini's Daughter," 70, 71, 248–249, 253, 256; reviews of Melville's *Typee* and Longfellow's *Evangeline,* 92; "Roger Malvin's Burial," 30, 69, 257, 258; *Scarlet Letter,* 92, 93–99, 100, 105, 107, 112, 113, 114, 115, 121, 122, 131, 134, 135, 141, 149, 166, 198, 199, 243, 249, 250, 257–258, 261–262, 265; *Septimius Felton,* 229, 241; "Seven Tales of My Native Land," 24, 29; "Shaker Bridal," 254; "Snow Image," 115; *Snow Image and Other Twice-Told Tales,* 23, 94, 114, 115, 116; "Spectator," 8–9; "Story Teller," 31; *Tanglewood Tales,* 124, 142–143, 148; "Three-Fold Destiny," 260, 265; *Twice-Told Tales,* 27, 31, 33, 34, 35, 44, 45, 46, 50, 68, 69, 70, 80, 114, 115, 116, 261; "Village Uncle," 259–260; "Wakefield," 135, 254; "Wedding Knell," 34; "White Old Maid," 255; "Wives of the Dead," 30; *Wonder Book,* 114, 116, 143; "Young Goodman Brown," 32, 69, 71, 262
Hawthorne, Rose, 117, 124–125, 144, 163, 183, 188–189, 199, 216, 217, 219, 220, 222, 240, 241
Hawthorne, Sophia A. Peabody, early life, personality, illness, 49–50; meets and falls in love with Hawthorne, 50–51; sketch of Ilbrahim, 52; Cuban journal, 52; marriage, 62; Old Manse journal, 63; conversion to her husband's view of the Concord Transcendentalists, 65–66; birth of first child, Una, 67; opinion of Bancroft, 76; resignation to poverty, 78; birth of Julian, 81; devotion to husband and children, 81, 84; account of Thoreau's lectures, 85; makes articles for sale, 91; emotional reaction to *The Scarlet Letter,* 95; interior decoration of the Little Red House, 101–102; enjoyment of her husband's reading aloud, 105; reaction to Melville, 108–109, 136; aversion to tobacco, 109; praise of *The House of the Seven Gables,* 113; birth of Rose, 117; living costs in the Berkshires in 1851, 117; decoration of the Wayside, 124; description of Rose, 125; instruction of children, 126; religious faith, 128; trials during husband's absence, 131–132; defense of *The Life of Pierce,* 134; attachment to the Wayside, 145; burning of her "maiden letters," 146; first Christmas in England, 156–160; party dress, 161; winter in Portugal, 163–164; return from Portugal, 168; defense of her husband's views of abolitionism, 179; interest in Italy, 186–187; tirelessness in sightseeing, keeping a journal, and sketching, 189–190; personality and character as seen by Ada Shepard, 191; fortitude during Una's illness, 204; serious illness in winter, 1859–60, 212–213; visits to the Fields' home, 217–218; distress over her husband's illness, 236–237; mystic faith upon her husband's death, 238–239; editing of husband's notebooks, 240; removal abroad and death, 240
Hawthorne, Una, 67, 81, 82–83, 90, 102–103, 114, 124–125, 126, 144, 146, 148, 163, 170, 188–189, 202, 204–205, 206, 207, 215, 216, 217, 234, 240, 241

Heenan, John, 212
Heywood, Mrs. John P., 161
Hillard, George, 64, 77, 80, 85, 87, 88, 91, 93, 122, 181, 209, 212, 238, 239
Hillard, Mrs. George, 64
Hoar, Elizabeth, 64
Hoar, Judge Rockwood, 145, 217
Hogarth, William, 171
Hogg, James, 8
Holmes, Oliver Wendell, 107, 122, 130, 218, 225, 237–238, 239
Homer, 16
Hood, George, 78
Horace, 16
Hosmer, Harriet, 192–193
Hotel du Louvre, 184, 185
Houghton Library of Harvard, 108
House of Commons, 167
Howard, John D., 78
Howe, Julia Ward, 64, 222
Howe, Samuel Gridley, 64, 218
Howell, Thomas Bayly, 28
Howells, William Dean, 123, 221
Hull, Isaac, 42
Hunt, W. M., 214
Hutchinson, Thomas, 28

Inchbald, Elizabeth, 8
Incisa, 200
International Magazine, 114
Ipswich, Mass., 40
Ireland, Alexander, 171
Irving, Washington, 19, 25, 34, 108, 122, 141, 211, 223, 242
Isle of Man, 173
Isles of Shoals, 129, 130, 135

Jackson, Andrew, 20, 38, 86
James, G. P. R., 107, 122
James, Henry, Jr., 192
Jameson, Anna B., 197
Jefferson, Thomas, 86
Jerrold, Douglas, 167
Johnson, Samuel, 19, 167, 174, 175, 242

Kean, Edmund, 8
Kemble, Fanny, 106, 114
Kennebec River, 45
Keswick, 175

Kittery Point, 120
Knight, Sarah Kemble, 28

Laighton's Hotel, 130
Lake Geneva, 206
Lake Windermere, 174
Lander, Maria Louisa, 192–193
Lansdowne Circus, 172
Las Cases, de, Emmanuel Augustin, 19
Lathrop, George Parsons, 116, 240
Leamington, 172, 174
Leghorn, 186, 206
Leicester's Hospital, 173, 177
Leitch, Captain, 146, 148, 213
Lenox, Mass., 99, 100, 104
Leonardo da Vinci, 101
Leutze, Emanuel, 226
Lewis, Matthew Gregory, 8
Lilley, William, 154
Lincoln, Abraham, 227–228
Lincoln, England, 177
Lind, Jenny, 168
Lisbon, 164
Litchfield, 174
Literary World, 96, 108
Little Red House, 100, 101–102, 109, 118, 120, 121
Liverpool, 140, 142, 145, 146, 148, 149, 150, 153, 155, 158, 159, 161, 163, 164, 168, 169, 170, 173, 178, 213
Livy, 16
Lloyd, Elizabeth, 106
Locke, John, 16
Lockhart, John G., 223
London, 163, 166, 167, 168, 172, 175–176, 177, 182, 184, 185, 204, 207, 210, 240
London Athenaeum, 34, 69, 96, 113, 211
London Examiner, 157, 211, 239
London Times, 167, 211
London Tower, 176
Longfellow, Henry W., 20, 22, 25, 34–35, 43–44, 45, 53, 58, 68, 69, 72, 80, 85, 89, 91, 92, 122, 130, 135, 141, 146, 160, 179, 180, 215, 218, 223–224, 225, 226, 233, 235, 238, 239
Longfellow, Samuel, 146
Longfellow, Stephen, 64
Lord Mayor of Liverpool, 155, 156
Lord Mayor of London, 156

Lothrop, Margaret M., 123
Louvre, 184
Lowell, James Russell, 107, 114, 130, 146, 198, 211, 215, 218, 225, 233, 238, 239
Luther, Martin, 124
Lynch, Anne Charlotte, 144
Lynn, Mass., 78

Macaulay, Thomas Babington, 168
Mackay, Charles, 167
Maine Liquor Law, 126, 246
Manassas, 226
Manchester, 145, 170, 179
Manchester Cathedral, 178
Manchester *Examiner*, 171
Mann, Horace, 49, 83, 84, 88, 103, 120, 123, 172, 191, 214
Mann, Mary Peabody, 49, 58, 83, 103, 120, 191, 214, 233
Manning, Mary, 9, 10, 28
Manning, Richard, 5
Manning, Robert, 3, 4, 5, 6, 7, 10, 11, 13, 14, 24
Manning, Samuel, 41
Mansfield, L. W., 106, 109, 122
Marblehead, Mass., 3
Marlborough House, 172
Marseilles, 184, 185, 206
Martha's Vineyard, 42, 43
Mason, Alfred, 22
Mather, Cotton, 96, 131, 177, 258
Maturin, Charles Robert, 8
Melville, Herman, 70, 92, 107–112, 119, 121, 122, 134–136, 138, 139–140, 142, 154, 169–170
Merrimac, 226
Mersey River, 148
Mexican War, 127, 129
Miller, Ephraim, 119–120
Miller, General James, 80, 138
Millot, C. F. X., 28
Milnes, Richard Monkton, 168, 201
Milton Club, 167
Milton, John, 26, 64, 105, 160, 169, 207, 232, 242, 262
Mitchell, Donald Grant, 223–224
Mitchell, Maria, 185, 188–189, 191
Mitford, Mary Russell, 104, 123, 134, 141

Monitor, 226
Monroe, James, 68, 115
Montaigne, 28
Mont Blanc, 206
Montreal, 42
Monument Mountain, 107, 113
Moon, Sir Francis, 207
Morton, Marcus, 78
Motley, John Lothrop, 211, 213, 218
Mount Vernon, 145
Mount Washington, 42
Mozier, Joseph, 194
Mumford, Lewis, 111
Murillo, Bartholomé Esteban, 171

Nahant, Mass., 40
Nantucket, 185
Napoleon, Louis, 164, 206
National Era, 93
National Gallery, London, 172
Nelson, Horatio, 176
Newburyport, Mass., 3
Newby Bridge, 174
Newcomb, Charles King, 66, 258
New England Magazine, 31, 32, 34, 42
New Haven, Conn., 41
Newman, Samuel P., 14, 15
New Orleans, 151, 154
Newstead Abbey, 177
Newton, Isaac, 4
New York City, 79, 82, 105, 106, 119, 128, 132, 144, 207, 235, 241
New York City Custom House, 139
New York *Evening Post*, 230–231
New York *Tribune*, 157
Niagara, N.Y., 42
Nightingale, Florence, 168
Norris Green, 160–161
North Adams, Mass., 48, 49, 73, 130
North American Review, 69, 70, 239
Northampton, Mass., 47
Norton, Hon. Caroline, 213
Norton, Charles Eliot, 146, 218, 233
Notre Dame, 184

Old Manse, 61, 62, 63, 64–65, 66, 67, 70, 71, 73, 76, 92, 123, 124, 217
Old Trafford, 170, 172
Oliver, Benjamin L., 7, 13

Ossoli, Marchese Giovanni Angelo, 194
Ossoli, Margaret Fuller, 58, 60, 61, 64, 65, 66, 194–196, 253
O'Sullivan, J. L., 46–47, 61, 66, 75–76, 78, 106, 137, 144, 163, 164, 181, 208
Oxford University, 169

Packard, Alpheus S., 15, 129
Paley, William, 16, 17
Pantheon, 187
Paris, 182, 183, 184, 185, 188, 206
Parker House, 99, 136, 218
Parliament, Houses of, 176
Passignano, 200
Patmore, Coventry, 168, 172
Paulding, James Kirke, 19
Peabody, Elizabeth, 49, 50–51, 53, 58, 83, 92–93, 101, 117, 171, 174, 179, 187, 205, 208, 210, 231, 233
Peabody, Nathaniel, 145, 214
Peabody, Dr. Nathaniel, 49, 83, 99, 106, 122, 146
Peabody, Mrs. Nathaniel, 83, 99, 106, 124, 125, 128, 132, 134
Pearson, Norman Holmes, 13, 183, 193
Pedro V, King of Portugal, 164
Percy, Thomas, 19
Perry, Bliss, 48
Perugia, 200
Peterborough, 177
Peucinian Society, 20
Philadelphia, 144, 154, 236
Pierce, Franklin, 19–20, 22, 38, 39, 53, 64–65, 67, 76–77, 122, 127, 129, 130, 132–133, 134, 136–138, 139, 140, 142, 143, 144–145, 149, 155, 179, 181, 205, 215, 221–222, 230–231, 232, 233, 237–238, 239
Pierce, Mrs. Franklin, 235
Pierce, George W., 22
Pike, William B., 53, 86, 99, 109, 118, 119–120, 126, 128, 137, 179, 222
Pincian Hill, 206
Pioneer, 47
Pittsfield, Mass., 107, 121
Plato, 16, 73, 246
Plymouth, N. H., 238
Poe, Edgar Allan, 69, 70, 71
Polk, James K., 67, 75, 77, 79

Pope, Alexander, 105, 175
Pope Pius IX, 198
Portsmouth, N. H., 76, 77, 85, 99, 129, 130, 131
Pot-8-o Club, 22, 25
Powers, Hiram, 200
Prescott, William Hickling, 218
Punch, 167

Quebec, 42

Raleigh, Sir Walter, 176
Raphael, 101
Reade, Charles, 167
Redcar, 209
Rees, Abraham, 19
Reform Club, 167
Richardson, Philip, 154
Ripley, Ezra, 61
Ripley, George, 58, 59, 77
Ripley, Samuel, 67, 86
Roberts, David, 37, 53, 64, 86, 120
Rock Ferry Hotel, 148
Rock Park, 148, 158, 160, 162
Roman Carnival, 188–189, 204, 211
Rome, 185, 186, 187, 188, 189, 192, 193, 196, 203, 204, 205–206, 208
Rotherhithe, 176
Rousseau, Jean Jacques, 8
Ruskin, John, 214
Rydal Lake, 174

Sacra Via, 187
Salem, Mass., 1, 2, 3, 6, 39, 40, 67, 78, 79, 84, 85, 92, 98–99, 102, 105, 119, 126, 137–138, 204
Salem Advertiser, 79, 87–88, 92, 107
Salem Athenaeum, 27, 28
Salem Custom House, 79, 80, 82, 84, 87, 92, 119, 136, 137, 181
Salem Gazette, 2, 3, 6, 7, 30, 34
Salem Register, 98
Salisbury, 176
Salisbury Close, 176–177
Sallust, 14
Sanborn, Frank, 214–215, 216
Sand, George, 96
Sandheys, 160
San Lorenzo Cathedral, 186
Santa Rosa Island, 76

Saratoga Springs, 128
Sargeant's Magazine, 47
Sarpi, Paolo, 28
Saturday Club, 218, 236
Scott, Sir Walter, 8, 25, 158, 176, 177, 223, 242
Sebago Lake, 5, 10
Sedgwick, Henry, 106
Sewall, Samuel, 2, 161
Shakers, 41, 43, 66, 72
Shakespeare, William, 5, 8, 64, 108, 113, 167, 168, 173–174, 175, 236, 239
Shaw, Anna, 64
Shaw, Sarah, 64
Shepard, Ada, 172, 182, 183, 184, 186, 188–189, 190–191, 200, 201, 202, 204, 206–207, 212
Shepard, Thomas, 245
Shipley, David, 22
Shrewsbury, 175
Siena, 203
Sleepy Hollow, 124, 238
Smith and Elder, 207, 210
Smith, Capt. John, 131
Smith, Nathan, 15
Smithell's Hall, 162
Smollett, Tobias George, 8, 186
Southampton, 163, 207
Southern Literary Messenger, 113
Southern Rose, 47
Southey, Robert, 105, 175
Southport, 169, 173
Spectator Papers, 175
Spenser, Edmund, 4, 67, 76, 242
Spillman's Hotel, 186
Spofford, Harriet Prescott, 223–224
Steele, Richard, 9
Stevens, Henry, 167
Stewart, Dugald, 17
Stoddard, Elizabeth Drew, 223
Stoddard, Richard Henry, 137, 138–139, 143
Story, William Wetmore, 192
Story, Mrs. William Wetmore, 205
Stoughton, William, 2
Stowe, Harriet Beecher, 222, 233
St. Paul's, 176
St. Peter's, 187, 188, 198, 199, 206
Stratford, 174
Stylus, 69

Sue, Eugène, 96
Sumner, Charles, 77, 84, 89, 140, 152
Swampscott, Mass., 43
Swan Inn, 174
Swift, Jonathan, 19, 176, 242

Talfourd, Field, 148
Tanglewood, 107
Tappan, Mrs. W. A., 120, 121
Taylor, Bayard, 226
Taylor, Jeremy, 28
Taylor, Zachary, 86, 88, 119, 149
Tennyson, Alfred, 171–172, 217
Terni, 200
Thackeray, William Makepeace, 236
Thaxter, Celia, 131
Thaxter, Levi, 131
Thomas, Seth, 75
Thomaston, Maine, 46
Thompson, Cephas G., 99, 192
Thomson, James, 4
Thoreau, Henry David, 40, 64, 65, 66, 73, 80, 84–85, 92, 141, 142, 167, 214, 229, 258
Ticknor, George, 99
Ticknor, Howard, 236
Ticknor, W. D., 94, 114, 117, 121, 122, 126, 129, 132, 143, 144, 146, 150, 152, 153, 155, 160, 178, 179, 181, 189–190, 210, 212, 215–216, 222, 223, 224, 226, 229–230, 235, 236, 237
Titian, 197
Token, 30, 31, 32, 34, 39, 46
Trollope, Anthony, 218–219
Tucker, Beverly, 181
Tuckerman, F. G., 223–224
Tuckerman, H. T., 113, 122
Tupper, Martin Farquhar, 166
Tyler, John, 75, 76

Upham, Charles W., 87, 88, 89, 100
Uttoxeter, 174

Victoria, Queen, 163
Villa Montauto, 202, 203
Virgil, 14, 167

Walden, 80, 85, 124, 145
Ward, Samuel G., 64, 149
Ward, Mrs. Samuel G., 145, 205

Warren, Samuel, 162
Warwick, 173, 177
Washington, D. C., 76, 78, 88, 120, 138, 139, 143, 144–145, 226
Watertown Arsenal, 76
Wayside, 123, 124, 125, 126, 127, 135–136, 144, 145, 146, 157, 170, 179, 203, 207, 208, 214, 215–216, 217, 219, 221, 229, 236, 240
Webber, C. W., 69, 93
Webster, Daniel, 84, 104
Weiss, John, 131
Wells, John D., 15
West Goldsborough, Maine, 220
Westminster Abbey, 176
West Newton, Mass., 83, 84, 103–104, 109, 120, 122, 123
West Roxbury, 59
West, Thomas, 174
Whipple, E. P., 96, 97, 107, 113, 122, 211, 218, 238
White, Thomas, 174
Whitman, Walt, 249

Whittier, John Greenleaf, 93, 106, 218, 246
Wilding, Henry, 150, 151, 181
Wiley and Putnam, 68, 141
Wilkes, Charles, 53
Wilkinson, James John Garth, 172
Williams College, 48
Williamstown, Mass., 48
Winthrop, John, 1
Wise, Henry A., 75
Woking, 167
Woodman, Horatio, 218
Worcester, Mass., 47, 88
Worcester, J. E., 4
Wordsworth, William, 174–175
Wrigley, Fanny, 163, 169, 174

Xenophon, 16

Yale College, 41
Yankee Doodle, 155
York, 178